THE JOURNAL OF
HÉLÈNE BERR

THE JOURNAL OF
HÉLÈNE BERR

Translated from the French by David Bellos,
with an introduction and
an essay by David Bellos,
and an afterword by Mariette Job

McClelland & Stewart

First published in Canada in 2008 by McClelland & Stewart

First published in Great Britain in 2008 by MacLehose Press, an imprint of Quercus

Journal d'Hélène Berr © Editions Tallandier, 2008

English translation of *Journal* by Hélène Berr and of "A Stolen Life" by Mariette Job
copyright © David Bellos 2008

Introduction, "France and the Jews," and glossaries copyright © David Bellos 2008

Quotations on pp. 167–8, 178–82, 191–2 from Roger Martin du Gard's *Les Thibault* are taken
from Stuart Gilbert's translation entitled *Summer 1914* (New York, 1941). This contains
Parts 6–8 of the cycle, which are theparts Hélène Berr quotes from. The earlier sections
were published in English under the title *The World of the Thibaults*.

Photographs and facsimiles on pp. 14, 23, 53, 119, 206, 265
copyright © Mémorial de la Shoah, Paris, Collection Job
Photograph of Raymond Berr, all rights reserved

Library and Archives Canada Cataloguing in Publication

Berr, Hélène, 1921–1945.
The journal of Hélène Berr / translated by David Bellos.

Translation of: Journal, 1942-1944.
ISBN 978-0-7710-1313-3

1. Berr, Hélène, 1921–1945–Diaries. 2. Jews–Persecution–
France–Paris. 3. Jews–France–Paris–Diaries. 4. Holocaust, Jewish
(1939–1945)–France–Paris. 5. College students–France–Paris–Diaries.
6. Holocaust victims–France–Diaries. 7. Holocaust, Jewish (1939-1945)–
France–Personal narratives. I. Bellos, David II. Title.
DS135.F9B4713 2008   940.53'18092   C2008-901951-2

We acknowledge the financial support of the Government of Canada through the Book
Publishing Industry Development Program and that of the Government of Ontario
through the Ontario Media Development Corporation's Ontario Book Initiative.
We further acknowledge the support of the Canada Council for the Arts and
the Ontario Arts Council for our publishing program.

Printed and bound in the United States of America

McClelland & Stewart Ltd.
75 Sherbourne Street
Toronto, Ontario
M5A 2P9
www.mcclelland.com

1   2   3   4   5   12   11   10   09   08

Contents

Introduction

D A V I D   B E L L O S

This remarkable book is not a novel. It is a personal diary, not intended for publication, and, like any private document, it is occasionally enigmatic. Written by a passionate, intelligent and musically gifted woman of twenty-one from a cultivated and prominent French family, it is, to begin with, just a diary. Hélène tries to analyze her feelings for one young man, Gérard, whose background is similar to her own, then slowly realizes that she has fallen in love with another, the handsome Jean Morawiecki.

Hélène began her *Journal* in the spring of 1942. Despite nearly two years of German occupation, life among the élite of French youth seemed almost unchanged, at least on the surface. Up to that time Hélène had not wanted to admit even to herself that the persecution of Jews was affecting her. As spring turned to summer, however, increasingly flagrant acts of oppression opened her eyes to reality. Her personal diary becomes a precious, horrified and horrifying eyewitness account of the means by which the Nazis' "Final Solution to the Jewish Question" was implemented in France.

Hélène's rich and busy life moved between four overlapping sets of people. She had a crowd of student friends in the English Studies Department at the Sorbonne (some of them went by nicknames borrowed from their favourite books or authors: "Sparkenbroke", "Charlotte Brontë", "Lancelot of the Lake"). Secondly, she played the violin in a group of gifted amateur musicians, one of whom was Gérard's father, a high-court judge. In her own comfortable home in avenue Elisée-Reclus, Hélène lived with her older sister Denise and their two parents (as well as the domestic staff). During the summer months they often took the half-hour train ride from Gare Saint-Lazare to the family's country seat at Aubergenville, usually with friends and relatives in tow. Hélène's fourth circle centred on her maternal grandmother's apartment in rue Raynouard and the family of her beloved cousin Nicole S.

France was at the time divided in two, and some people in Hélène's circles had fled the Occupied Zone to seek refuge in the south. Her own sister and brother had crossed the line already, while Gérard was on his way to join the Free French. Over the following months Hélène came under strong pressure to follow suit. But because she made the firm and conscious decision to stay in Paris with her parents and older relatives, she entered a fifth and entirely new circle – that of the Jewish support and relief agencies, in which she forged strong friendships, notably with Françoise Bernheim, an acquaintance of Sylvia Beach, the famous bookseller.

Even in wartime, the Berrs led an extremely sociable life. People were invited to lunch, tea and dinner quite frequently, and hospitality was extended to those who just happened to call. Face-to-face conversation was the main source of information, as newspapers were just propaganda, telephones were few and far between, television service did not exist, and people of Hélène's standing and class did not frequent bars or cafés. (By the evidence of her *Journal*, she did not go the cinema either.) Her intense and varied social life took place in the library and courtyard of the Sorbonne, in the Luxembourg Gardens, but mostly in her own or her friends' families' homes.

One feature of Hélène Berr's writing that is hidden from readers of this translation is that it is to a surprising degree in English in the original. Like many European families of their class and period, the Berrs were keen Anglophiles. English was the language of good taste and the social graces, and they gave their daughters, among other things, an English nanny and a taste for Dundee marmalade. As a student, Hélène specialized in English language and literature, and she could well have become a professor of English. She was well read in British literature, especially the Romantic poets, and was familiar with many English and American writers of her own day (Walter de la Mare, Aldous Huxley, Louis Bromfield, Maurice Baring). Literature in English came to her mind more often than French as she wrote her first-hand account of France's dark years, and English words and expressions crop up on every page. The significance of using English in French is hard to represent *in English*. Hélène has constant recourse to the language, whether for single words (she uses "maid" for *bonne*, "potatoes" for *pommes de terre*, "blight", "exhilaration", "damn it!" and so on), or for expressions that cannot be put succinctly in French, such as "singleness of mind", "self-pity", "glorious muddle" and "better self". Sometimes she uses whole expressions, such as "there's no-one to blame but yourself", as well as literary allusions and quotations: "The pity of it, Iago", "naked to the awaited stroke", "captain of my soul". When Françoise Bernheim was arrested together with a whole group of friends and co-workers, what comes to Hélène's tortured mind are words *in English* from the Book of Job, as quoted by Hermann Melville in *Moby Dick*: "And I alone am escaped to tell thee." The last words Hélène was able to write in her journal are also in English; they come from Shakespeare's *Macbeth*.

I have not sought to indicate which of Hélène Berr's words were written in English in this translation so as not to introduce distracting or misleading emphases. This produces an unusual, somewhat paradoxical effect: the translation contains fewer foreign words and expressions than the original, and is therefore a *plainer* text. Another unintended consequence of a linguistic transposition that is also, unavoidably, a change of cultural frame, is to allow Hélène's literary allusions to echo more fully in English readers' minds. It is not the translator, but the simple fact of translation that has made the *Journal* in English more straight-forward, and if that were conceivable, even more moving than it is in French.

Hélène wrote her diary straight off and never had the opportu-nity to correct it. At times she thought it would serve as a basis for a book about the persecution of French Jews to be written after the war; at other times, she wanted it to serve most of all as a message to her fiancé, Jean, perhaps from beyond her own grave. To give her writing a better chance of surviving than she herself could have, she gave the sheets in small batches to the family cook, Andrée Bardiau, who was not Jewish. This means that when she sat down to write an entry, Hélène did not always have access to what she had written the day or the week before. Despite these difficulties, her writing is strong and clear. (One sentence that remains obscure, possibly because it has a coded meaning now lost, has been left in French (p. 48); Hélène also mistakes the date, usually by one day, on pp. 90, 92, 152, 153, 154, 237 and 246. Struggling to come to terms with the horrors before her eyes, to separate rumour from historical fact, and to give an honest account of her city, her people, her heart and her soul, she never slips into telegraphese, vulgarity or vagueness. Translation tends to shift the tone of the original by a notch, and something of the informal, chatty or girlish nature of parts of the *Journal* has been lost. But I do not think that the slightly greater polish of the English version seriously misrepresents Hélène Berr's unique achievement. What she wrote was a clear-headed, elegant and heartrendingly beautiful account of a descent to hell.

In the manuscript, many initials are used in place of personal names. Wherever possible these have been expanded into full names. But with the passage of so many years and the disappearance of all but a tiny handful of the people who appear in the diary, it has not been possible to recover the identities of them all. Readers interested in knowing more about the people who crossed Hélène Berr's path should consult the Index of Personal Names on pp. 302–306, where I have given as much of the key information as is possible at the present time.

Readers of the French text may detect a small number of changes. Save for any inadvertent slips on my part, the differences in meaning, names and spellings bear witness to continuing research into the text by the French editors.

One sentence whose meaning is not in doubt I have left in French. In February 1944, Hélène realized that she probably had little time left, knowing that deportation meant certain death, but she did not know *how* the Germans were disposing of the trainloads of Jews deported from Drancy. She turned to an older friend, Mme Loewe, for moral support. "Don't let things get you down", Mme Loewe said. "We'll be together in the same batch, we'll be in the same cattle-truck." Her intention was to boost Hélène's morale by saying they would be picked up in the same raid and stay together through the ensuing ordeal. The word Mme Loewe used for "same batch" is the ordinary one for a baker's tray of loaves: "*la même fournée*" – made out of the suffix "*–née*" attached to a stem, "*four*", whose literal meaning is "oven". The French makes your heart miss a beat. The language itself seems to know what the speaker did not. I cannot reproduce in English the hideous lurch into prophecy made by this phrase in French, and so I have left it alone.

I would like to express my gratitude to Mariette Job, the niece of Hélène Berr and the person responsible – along with Henri Bovet and Antoine Sabbagh, the publisher and editor of the French edition – for making this extraordinary document available to the public. She made generous efforts to answer my unending questions about the text of the *Journal* and its background, and also enriched and revised her invaluable afterword specifically for this English-language edition. My thanks also go to the many people who contributed knowledge and expertise to make this edition what it is, among them Annette Becker, Andrea Belloli, Jean-Marc Dreyfus, and especially Christopher MacLehose, who is both a publisher and still a friend.

Princeton, N.J.
14.vii.2008

1. Hélène Berr's Paris

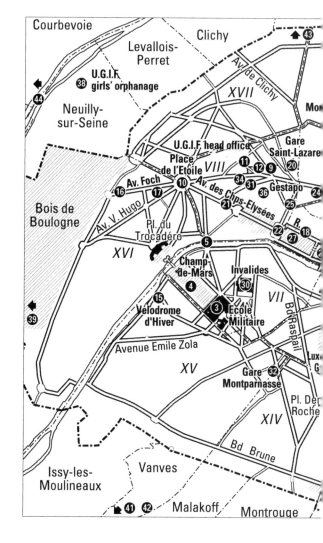

1. Préfecture de Police
2. Hôpital Rothschild
   (11, rue Santerre)
3. Ecole Militaire
4. Champ-de-Mars
5. Pont de l'Alma
6. Luxembourg Gardens,
   Sénat
7. Sorbonne
   (English Department)
8. Synagogue
   (44, rue de la Victoire)
9. Eglise Saint-Augustin
10. Place de l'Etoile
11. U.G.I.F. head office
    (19, rue de Téhéran)
12. U.G.I.F. offices (29, rue
    de la Bienfaisance)
13. Faubourg Saint-Denis
14. Montmartre
15. Vélodrome d'Hiver
16. Avenue Foch
17. Home of Paul Valéry
    (40, rue de Villejust)
18. Galignani bookshop
    (224, rue de Rivoli)
19. Notre-Dame
20. Gare Saint-Lazare
    (station serving
    Aubergenville)
21. Champs-Elysées
22. Place de la Concorde
23. Palais Royal
24. Opéra
25. Eglise de la Madeleine
26. Pont des Arts

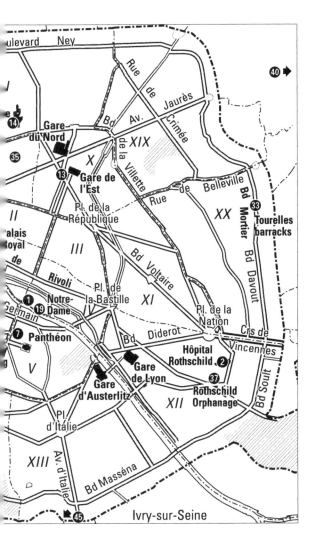

2. The Latin Quarter in 1942

1. Gilbert bookshop (30, boulevard Saint-Michel)
2. Boulevard Saint-Germain
3. Klincksieck bookshop (6, rue de la Sorbonne)
4. U.G.I.F. girls' hostel (9, rue Vauquelin)
5. U.G.I.F. boys' hostel (60, rue Claude Bernard)
6. Rue Gay Lussac
7. Faculté de Droit (12, place du Panthéon)
8. Ecole Normale Supérieure (45, rue d'Ulm)
9. Rue de l'Odéon
10. Rue de l'Ecole-de-Médecine
11. Lycée Henri IV
12. Rue de Médicis
13. Student centre; Didier bookshop (15, rue Soufflot)
14. Budé bookshop (place de la Sorbonne)

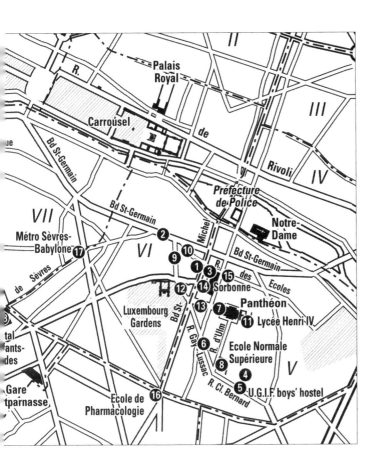

This is my journal.
The rest is at Aubergenville.

Mardi 7 Avril   1

4h

Je reviens .... de chez la concierge de Paul Valéry — Je me suis enfin décidée à aller chercher mon livre — Après le déjeuner, le soleil brillait ; il n'y avait pas de menace de giboulée — J'ai pris le 92 jusqu'à l'Étoile. En descendant l'avenue Victor-Hugo, mes appréhensions ont commencé — Au coin de la Rue de Villejust, j'ai eu un moment de panique . Et tout de suite la réaction : il faut que je prenne les responsabilités de mes actes. there's no one to blame but you —, Et toute ma confiance est revenue. Je me suis demandée comment j'avais pu avoir peur. La semaine dernière, même jusqu'à ce moment, je trouvais cela tout naturel — c'est maman qui m'a rendue intimidée , en me montrant qu'elle était très étonnée de mon audace . Autrement je trouvais cela tout simple — toujours mon état de demi-rêve, —   J'ai sonné au 40 — un fox-terrier s'est précipité sur moi en aboyant. La concierge l'a appelé . Elle m'a demandé d'un air méfiant ; qu'est-ce que c'est — J'ai répondu de mon ton le plus naturel : est-ce que Mr. Valéry n'a pas laissé un petit paquet pour moi " (tout de même, de loin, je m'étonnais de mon aplomb, mais de très loin) La concierge est entrée dans sa loge " à quel nom ? " — " Mademoiselle B***. " Elle s'est dirigée vers la table — Je savais d'avance qu'il était là — Elle a fouillé , et m'a tendu mon paquet ; dans le même papier blanc — J'ai dit " merci beaucoup ! " — très aimablement, elle a répondu " à votre service ". Et je suis repartie, ayant juste eu le temps de voir que mon nom était inscrit d'une écriture très nette, à l'encre noire sur le paquet. Une fois de l'autre côté de la porte je l'ai défait — sur la page de garde, il y avait écrit

1942

Tuesday, 7 April, 4.00 p.m.

I'm just back from . . . Paul Valéry's concierge. I finally decided to go and fetch my book. After lunch the sun was out and there was no threat of a squall. I took the 92 to place de l'Etoile. As I walked down avenue Victor Hugo, I began to feel nervous. When I got to the corner of rue de Villejust, I panicked. Immediately a reaction set in: "I must take responsibility for my own actions. You've no-one to blame but yourself." All my self-confidence flooded back. I wondered how I could have felt frightened. All last week, up to that very moment, I thought it all perfectly natural. It was Maman who had frightened me by showing how amazed she was by my daring. Otherwise I found it quite ordinary. My usual sleepwalking state! I rang the bell at number 40. A yapping fox terrier rushed at me and the concierge called it to order. She asked me suspiciously: "What is it?" I replied in my most natural tone of voice: "Did M. Valéry not leave a packet for me?" (I was nonetheless amazed at my aplomb but from afar, so to speak, from far away.) The concierge retreated into her office.

"Name?"

"Mlle Berr."

She went over to the table; I already knew that the book was there. She rummaged through the pile and handed me a packet wrapped in white paper like the others. I said: "Thank you very much indeed"; she responded amiably: "Happy to oblige!" and off I went, having had time only to glimpse my name written very neatly, in black ink, on the outside. I opened the packet as soon as I was out on the street. On the half-title page, in the same hand-writing, was written: "Copy for Mademoiselle Hélène Berr" and, above that: "*On waking, so soft is the light and so fine this living blue.* Paul Valéry".

And joy swept over me, a joy that confirmed my self-confidence, in complete harmony with the joyful sunlight and the pastel blue of the sky above the puffball clouds. I walked home feeling gently triumphant about what my parents would say and with the impression that what is extraordinary is real, and that the real is the extraordinary.

———

Now I am waiting for Miss Day to arrive for tea. The sky has suddenly become overcast and rain is rattling the windowpanes. It looks bad – there was thunder and lightning just now. Tomorrow we are supposed to have a picnic at Aubergenville with François and Nicole Job, Françoise and Jean Pineau, and Jacques Clère. As I came down the steps of the Trocadéro I thought about tomorrow with pleasure; there are bound to be bright spells one way or another. Now my joy has clouded over. But the sun will be back soon, the squall is nearly past. Why is the weather so changeable? It's like a child crying and laughing at the same time.

Last night I went to sleep after reading Part Two of *The Rains Came*. It's magnificent. The more I read, the more I find beauty in this book. The day before yesterday it was the scene between Fern and her mother, the two spinsters. Yesterday evening it was the flood, the Bannerjees' house and the Smileys. I feel like I am living among these people. Ransome is now an old friend; he's very endearing.

———

The evening has been full of excitement about tomorrow. Not an outpouring but a kind of underlying joy that got forgotten now and again and then gently resurfaced. Everything had to be got ready as if we were going on a journey. The train is at 8.33. We'll have to be up at 6.45.

———

Wednesday, 8 April

I'm just back from Aubergenville. I'm so sated with fresh air, bright sunshine, wind, showers, fatigue and pleasure that I'm not sure where I am. All I know is that I felt depressed before dinner, in Maman's bedroom, for no straightforward or obvious reason; the cause was sorrow to see such a marvellous day end, to be suddenly deprived of its atmosphere. I've never been able to get used to the fact that nice things end. I wasn't expecting to feel despair. I thought I had left such childish things behind, but it came on without my being aware of it, and without my trying to stop it either. Then when I got home I found a postcard from Odile and one from Gérard, and his was hurtful and nasty. He's making fun of me and the card I sent him. I can't remember what it was about, but I thought he would understand. I'm going to reply in the same vein.

———

I can't keep my eyes open. The day's events pass through my groggy mind in fits and starts: setting off from the station beneath grey skies and in pounding rain; the train journey with its jokes and high spirits, the feeling that the whole day would be good, the first walk through the wet grass in the garden, in the rain, and the sudden appearance of a sunny blue sky over the little meadow, the game of deck tennis before lunch, the kitchen table and the lively, jolly meal, everyone helping with the washing up, Françoise Pineau methodically doing the drying and Job the putting away, with his pipe in his mouth. Jean Pineau putting away a fork and a plate simultaneously and laughing every time he was caught, throwing up his hands in a gesture of evasiveness. The walk along the plateau road, in full sun, the short, sharp shower, my conversation with Jean Pineau, then coming back down to the village, where we met Jacques Clère, then the walk to Nezel under a scoured sky and an ever wider and brighter horizon, then the lovely tea with unsweetened and tasteless hot chocolate, bread and jam; the feeling that everyone was happy, then coming back with Denise and the two Nicoles[1] squeezing together on a single seat so that Job could get in beside us, and my burning cheeks; the fine face of Jean Pineau opposite me, with his pale eyes and strong features, saying goodbye in the métro, and smiles expressing genuine and honest enjoyment of the day. All that now seems strangely close and strangely distant. I know it's over, that I'm here in my bedroom, and at the same time I can hear the voices, see the faces and the shapes, as if I were surrounded by living ghosts. It's because the day is no longer entirely Present but not yet quite Past. The silence rustles with memories and images.

---

1   Nicole S. and Nicole Job.

Thursday, 9 April, morning

I awoke at 7.00. My mind was a muddle. Yesterday's joyfulness, the evening's disappointment, the state of unpreparedness in which I find myself today, since I have had nothing in mind for the day after yesterday, my irritation with Gérard, which dissolves if I think about it, because basically he is right to make fun of me; the serious and also passionate face of Jean Pineau on the train; the thought that Odile really is gone for good, just when our friendship was about to blossom and mature. How am I going to cope without her?

———

Saturday, 11 April

This evening I've a mad desire to throw it all over. I am *fed up* with not being normal. I am fed up with no longer feeling as free as air, as I did last year. I am fed up with feeling I do not have the right to be as I was. It seems that I have become attached to some-thing invisible and that I cannot move away from it as I wish to, and it makes me hate this thing, and deform it.

The worst of it is that for myself I feel unchanged and entirely free, but that for others, for my parents, for Nicole and for Gérard himself, I am *obliged* to act a part. Because whatever I might say to them, they will remain certain that my life has changed. As time passes, the gulf between inside and outside grows ever deeper. There's the me who now aspires with all my strength to revert to what it was before and what it would be now if nothing had happened, and the me whom others necessarily believe has taken its place. Maybe that second self is a figment of my imagination. But I don't think so.

The more time goes by, the more my situation becomes distorted. Why do I now think of it as a malaise I'm fleeing from almost as fast as I can run?

That's why, when I came home this evening and found the postcard from Gérard telling me he would not see me again until the autumn, I wept, and those were my first tears in months. Not because I am upset, but because I am so fed up with this unspoken malaise. I am fed up to the gills with this false position; it is false to him, false to my parents, false to Denise, Nicole and Yvonne. I was hoping that a visit from him would at least clear the air. But now I've got all spring and summer to live like this . . . And I can't explain it to anyone. As I raised my head, I wanted to challenge something or somebody; I told myself I will get my own back: I would give myself entirely, without reservation, since things are the way they are; then I buried the whole story under the clutter of daily life, I put it away to "think about it tomorrow", because I knew it was a rotten story.

I am perfectly aware that I am making a travesty of everything, but where does that come from?

In essence: thinking it through always leads me back to the same conclusion: that I can decide *nothing* until I have seen him again and learned to know him better.

Everyone agrees that is right; the reason I don't believe my parents understand is because this conclusion has become absolute and unreserved: that I know *absolutely* nothing about what will come of it; that I have absolutely no wish for any particular solution, that I must wait for the result as if it were the outcome of a match I am not involved in.

All this presumably comes from my inability to accept an unclear situation. I like to have things cut and dried, maybe so I can get rid of them and return to normal. It's much the same as the bother I feel at any disruption of my routines. Denise would call me a "homebody".

So, ever since I reached my conclusion, I have been waiting for a match that has become totally indifferent and external to me. It is the only thing I am waiting for.

Only, in the long run, the tension becomes unbearable. That's why I couldn't bear the idea that it had to continue.

That's why the whole affair has become a horror and why I joke about it, almost intentionally. Basically I do not want to change; but with things like this a change is inevitable. The change has to be sharp, and it has especially to be flooded with joy, as it should be when things are right.

This evening, if I wanted to, I could throw myself on to my bed, burst into tears and tell Maman that I want to hang on as hard as I can to what I was before. And Maman would surely console me, and I would fall asleep with the taste of tears on my lips and a feeling of peace. But next door Maman would be making herself a little more ill with worry.

And I don't even know if I could do that. It would be self-pity, and I have become hard on myself because nothing seems more essential at the moment. That's the only reason why: I am not constrained by a sense of dignity. With Maman dignity would be a crime. Nor is it because I would exhibit and exploit an emotion or feeling that I don't really feel, and end up cheapening it. For all that I would tell her would be perfectly sincere and true. But

I don't want to hurt Maman. Already this evening Papa got an expropriation notice, and Maman is taking everything on herself and keeping it all under wraps.

It sufficeth that I have told thee, dear little writing paper; I'm feeling better already.

———

Let's think about something else. About the unreal beauty of this summer's day at Aubergenville. A day that unfolded in perfection, from the rising of a cool and luminous sun full of promise to the soft, calm dusk so rich with sweet feeling that bathed me as I closed the shutters just now.

This morning, when I got there, I peeled some potatoes and then ran into the garden, confident of the joy that awaited me. Last summer's sensations came back to me, fresh and new, as if they had been waiting there like old friends. Light pouring from the kitchen garden like an explosion, light-heartedness emanating from the morning sun's triumphant progress across the sky, the endless succession of joyful discoveries, the subtle odour of flowering box, the buzzing of the bees and the abrupt appearance of a butterfly hovering unsteadily in the air, as if it were slightly drunk: I *recognized* all those things with a unique joy. I sat dreaming on the bench and gave myself over to the caresses of an atmosphere so sweet that it made my heart melt like wax; and at every instant I became aware of some new splendour – an apprentice bird in a still leafless tree I hadn't noticed before that suddenly filled the silence with its song, the distant cooing of pigeons and the twittering of more birds; I played a game, looking at dewdrops on blades of grass – by tilting my head I could make their colour change from

Hélène Berr, 1942

diamantine to emerald to vermilion. One of them even turned ruby-red, a tiny lighthouse. I tipped my head right over to see the world upside down, and I suddenly became aware of the magical harmony of the colours of the landscape around me, from the blue of the sky to the soft blue contours of the hills, the pink and dark and misty greens of the fields, the calm browns and ochres of the rooftops, the peaceful grey of the belltower, all of them steeped in luminous tranquillity. The only harsher tone came from the cool green grass at my feet, as if it alone was alive in this dreamscape. I thought: "In a painting, among all these pastel shades, this green would look unreal." But it was real.

Wednesday, 15 April

I am writing this down because I do not know who to talk to. I've just received a postcard full of bitterness and disappointment and from the brink of despair. When I read it my first reaction was almost a feeling of triumph, to see that he was like me. My second reaction was terror, to see that I could not turn my own feelings on and off just like that without causing pain to another.

Some sentences made me shudder – you are following a different path . . . we are headed towards a dead end . . . – because it suddenly seemed to me that they confirmed the vague, unspoken intuitions I had always had. And now I am frightened.

What's to be done? We are both in pain. But we cannot share the pain as another couple might. For if I tried to console him, I would only say that I am feeling the same way and wouldn't that be even more painful for him? If I respond affectionately, I will be lying, or merely being sentimental.

At the same time I feel that I am up against something I do not know about and have no experience of – a man. I do not know how to behave towards him.

Maman is the only person who could help me. But I know she would think of Papa, that she would make comparisons with Papa, and she won't understand when I cringe at her putting Gérard in Papa's place. I cannot conceive of them as being similar.

He mentions how lyrical my postcards are. That's why his path is diverging from mine. But doesn't he understand that if I send him "landscape portraits" it's because I can't write about anything else, about my feelings, which are not certain, as his are? But I can't explain that to him either.

At times I am overcome by silent desperation. I think: I have always known we weren't made for each other. I felt it, and it frightened me when I saw other people imagining a different outcome. There's something of the Hindu in my personality.

Good God! What is to be done? How will I reply?

The end of his message is cynical. But it doesn't hurt me. If only he knew!

Why has life become so complicated?

Wednesday, 15 April

I worked all day, to escape. I managed to forget. Three hours later, I returned from a distant land, and once again I felt that all of this lacks substance.

I also worked all afternoon typing my chapter on Brutus. The sun was so strong that I had to close the shutters. Outside it was high summer.

At 4.00 I went out in the full summer heat – a strange feeling – to the Sorbonne, to Escarpit's seminar. It reminded me of last year's exams, but all the same I feel freer, more mobile, less oppressed.

I finished *The Rains Came* before going to bed. But I slept very badly.

Thursday, 16 April

I went to the Sorbonne this morning for a change of scene. I was disappointed because I was hoping to see Sparkenbroke.[2] But I caught up with him this afternoon. I got there too early, of course. I went up to the library for a few minutes, and as I was coming down I heard someone singing his head off in the stairwell. It was Escarpit, on the ground floor, with his fiancée. He was probably singing because he was happy – happy with happiness, with his work. He's a wonderfully well-balanced young man. Despite not being terribly cultivated, he's brimming with intellectual and moral health. I stopped in my tracks at the foot of the stairs when I recognized him. He laughed without the slightest embarrassment; I laughed; his girlfriend laughed. A wave of fellow feeling swept over me.

I waited in the courtyard, chatting with Charlotte Brontë, the girl who did her thesis on Charlotte Brontë. She's very nice. She also has that indefinable quality of all the students I see, the ability to make you feel liked.

Cazamian's class consisted of a paper on Shelley's lyricism given by a young man who seems clever and funny. I didn't follow it too well, but I *felt* that what he was saying was full of passion and poetry. Cazamian's praise confirmed my intuition. But I didn't

2 Sparkenbroke, a character in Charles Morgan's novel of the same name, is, like "Charlotte Brontë" and "Stalin", a nickname for a student friend.

have the patience to listen to the end. I left at 11.15. I went to the office to have my card renewed and then home.

After lunch, Maman came with me in the car to see Dr Redon, who cut a few slivers of skin from my finger to get rid of the invisible blob of pus, and then I walked down boulevard Saint-Michel beneath the glorious sun among the milling throng, and by the time I got to rue Soufflot all my usual marvellous joy had returned. From rue Soufflot to boulevard Saint-Germain I am in an enchanted land.

So I was scarcely surprised when after leaving Maman at the S bus stop I bumped into Jean Pineau. He shook my hand, and I extracted my damaged finger without his noticing. His face was quite pink, perhaps from the pleasure of the encounter, who knows? For my part, I was delighted. But it was only afterwards that I realized what was magical about this meeting. He grabbed the book I was holding – by Hugo von Hofmannsthal – which I actually intended to show to Sparkenbroke. He was brusque but happy, undefinable. We parted almost immediately, he went up the boulevard and I went on to the English Department. It was 3.10 and I was planning to go to Delattre's lecture.

I went into the lecture hall and saw Sparkenbroke in his booth. I sat down in my usual place next to a moody girl. Delattre was talking about each of us in turn; I didn't listen, I watched my shadow in the sunlight. On the half hour there was the shuffling that precedes the practical criticism exercise, and the girl next to me crossed in front on her way out. I stood up to let her pass and I saw Sparkenbroke signalling to me, asking: "Are you staying?" I shook my head no, and we went out into the sun together. I felt a bizarre wave of relief. I would have been really disappointed not to have seen him; it was the only glimmer of peace in the hell in which I live, the only way to hang on to real life, to escape.

He said: "Shall we go to the Luxembourg Gardens?" I glanced at my watch; Françoise Masse was coming to tea. But I didn't hesitate. He went back into the lecture hall to get his bag and off we went. A strange walk along well-known streets that now seemed unfamiliar, rue de l'Ecole-de-Médecine, rue Antoine-Dubois, rue de Médicis. He talked about his plan to write a *Chantecler et Pertelope*, and his casual voice, his intonation and my usual shyness brought things back to normal. In the gardens we stopped at the edge of the pool where dozens of toy sailing boats were floating. I know we talked, but all I remember is being fascinated by the sun glinting on the gently lapping and rippling water, the gracious shapes of the sailing boats in the wind and, above all, the great blue shimmering sky. I was surrounded by a crowd of children and grown-ups. But I was drawn to the sparkling, dancing water. Even when I was speaking, I now realize, my mind was on the water. All the same, I wanted to argue because Sparkenbroke was telling me: "The Germans will win the war." I said: "No!" But I didn't know what else to say. I felt I was a coward, a coward not to defend my convictions, so I pulled myself together and shouted: "But what will become of us if the Germans win?" He made an evasive gesture. "Bah! Nothing will change" (I *knew* he was going to say that) . . . "there'll still be the sun and the water . . ." What irritated me most was that in my heart, in that instant, I too was aware of the utter nothingness of all these disputes in the face of such beauty. And yet I knew that I was yielding to an evil spell, that I was denying myself; I knew I would come to resent this cowardice. I forced myself to say: "But they won't let everyone enjoy light and water!" Fortunately, I was saved by that sentence. I did not wish to be a coward.

For I do now know that it is cowardly. We do not have the right to think only of poetry on this earth. It is magical, but it is utterly selfish.

Then he began to talk about the sailing boats, about the trees at Aubergenville, about his childhood games, and my unease evaporated. At the gate he met a comrade, I kept walking, and soon I saw Jacques Weill-Raynal and spoke to him for a moment. Spark caught up with us and we left the gardens. He said: "That's funny, when I meet a friend, you do too." Afterwards, he told me he didn't want to meet his wife. As he had always spoken about her to me very casually, I tried to adopt the same tone and asked: "Why not? She would be cross." But then he told me she was pregnant and rather agitated.

That is when something broke, the something that always threatens to ruffle this strange, magical and limpid atmosphere, the something that might suddenly make me see all this "from other people's perspective", because I now know that I do not have the right to carry on this way, and although his wife has no reason whatsoever for jealousy, it could still cause her pain. And if I knew she was in pain, that would perhaps upset all my ideas and tarnish the ideal beauty of it. So something has come to an end.

As we walked back down boulevard Saint-Michel, he spoke about his friends, who were all married now and parents. He said yes, all the men marry young. And the conversation continued along those lines. At one point I said: "Basically, it's not very hard to marry; what's hard is finding true happiness . . ." At that point I stumbled, lost for words. He responded: "I have never believed in all that stuff." I responded vigorously: "But I still do, and I don't want you to rob me of my illusions." I suddenly felt alone. The truth of it was that he too is very different from me. At the bottom of boulevard Saint-Michel we were talking about our views on life and he was explaining that for him everything and anything was interesting . . . "That's not the way it is for me. I'm not a butterfly; I seek beauty and perfection, I discriminate between things that are beautiful and those that are not. I still have values, I haven't got to the point where everything is worthy of attention." Then we talked about the impossibility of communicating thought and about the possibility of communicating thoughts. We parted at the steps down to the métro; the sun was in my eyes. He said: "I'll be back tomorrow." I hesitated. I suddenly felt it would be useless to see him again, or rather, I could no longer find within myself any desire to see him again. I said: "I think . . . I'll be back as well." He went off. I realized all of a sudden that I hadn't got any money or a métro ticket. I had only one option, so I ran after him. He was walking slowly, as if lost in thought. I caught up with him and explained, laughing, what had happened. He smiled his sly smile and got out a pack of tickets. Suddenly everything switched back to the way it had been before.

But this evening I feel that even that is slipping away, that dissonance has crept in. And the only thing that now seems pure, healthy and fresh in the whole day was the encounter with Jean Pineau.

And yet I am still young, and it is not fair that the limpid surface of my life should be disturbed. I do not want to "gain experience", I do not want to grow blasé, worldly-wise and old. What will save me?

I talked a lot, for hours, with Françoise Masse. I showed her my books and my school certificates. Now and again I was aware of the despair that threatens me. When she told me that Georges had written to say that Gérard was becoming increasingly misanthropic, I was cut to the quick because my feelings are raw. Why did she have to turn up and confirm that I had dragged someone else down, that my actions no longer affected only me, that I was no longer a free agent? Being free to suffer alone is itself a consolation.

Sunday, 19 April, noon

I've just written this letter. A bout of crying has washed me clean.

And my finger provides physical suffering for which I am grateful.

I've just been to rue de la Chaise. Redon made another small incision because it was hurting too much. He says it's nothing.

This afternoon I worked vaguely on my chapter on *Anthony and Cleopatra*. All of yesterday evening's gloom had dissipated. Lisette Léauté, who obviously muddled up one Sunday with another for orchestra practice, came and chatted with me in my bedroom. I hadn't done my hair or put on my stockings, but the Léautés don't care about such things. It was very agreeable.

Then I went to see Denise at the Jobs' apartment. She, François and Breynaert were playing the Schumann trio. Sennizergues, Job's and Daniel's friend, came along shortly afterwards. Tea was lavish, there was wonderful ice cream. I left at 5.30 to drop in on Francine Bacri. The métro was suffocating and sweaty. At the

Bacris' I saw Francine's father in his dressing gown, Jeanne Audran and her parents, and a friend of Francine's I know by sight, along with Francine herself.

Monday

When I went to bed last night, my finger again felt as if it was in the grip of a lobster's claw. I only managed to sleep with the help of some aspirin.

But it is odd: the physical discomfort makes it seem as if all my nastiness and moral unease are contained in my finger. It takes them away; it is a salutary pain. It corresponds to a major change. I do not know whether I love Gérard or not, but all malicious thoughts about him have vanished. When I think of him, it's almost like thinking of something sacred which I no longer wish to touch.

———

I spent all morning finishing off my chapter on *Anthony and Cleopatra*. After lunch I went back to see Dr Redon with Maman; my finger was not a pretty sight. He gave me four injections to anaesthetize the area. It was not pleasant. When I stood up to go and wait in the office for the ten minutes it would take my finger to go numb, I felt quite dizzy. When he began to cut, it could have been happening 10 kilometres away; I didn't look, but Maman did, and by the expression on her face I understood it looked rather nasty. At one point I saw him extracting things with a pair of tweezers. But my finger was no longer part of me.

Then I went to the library to do my duty hours. I aroused a lot of interest, of course. But Vivi Lafon was so kind that I was filled with gratitude. They pampered me like a baby. Nicole and Denise came by. I had a lot of pain when the anaesthetic wore off, but then it calmed down.

After dinner, from my bed, I dictated the beginning of my chapter to Denise. We spent a pleasant, not to say excellent, evening.

Tuesday, 21 April

This morning we carried on with dictation and typing. Denise says it's very good. I'm very glad, but at the same time I feel frightened. Then I went to the Sorbonne. Jas came for lunch. I thought that a fight might break out over lunch given how badly Maman's conversation with him went.

This afternoon I am struggling against sleep and sinking into mindlessness. Is it the stormy weather? Is it a reaction to my finger? Odile would laugh if she were there, because today is Tuesday, and all year Tuesday has been a wasted day. But Odile is not here. I fell asleep at my desk while I was working, and I really feel like dropping off again. I wasn't up to rereading *Coriolanus*. I went out and saw about having my violin case repaired in rue Saint-Dominique. I drank some tea to try and wake myself up. But it was no use. I've gone completely numb.

Wednesday, 22 April

I received two postcards.

The whole week has been spent working on my thesis in the mornings, whiling away my afternoons, worrying myself sick about my studies in the evenings, typing after dinner and feeling alarmed at my inability to express myself. I wake at 7.00 in the morning, and when I get up, all the mental freshness I've been holding back so I could work properly has vanished.

I'm living in a bad dream, it seems. I don't know what day it is or what I have done with my time.

Friday, 24 April

I went to lunch with Jean and Claudine, and it was the only bright moment in the week. I stayed there until 4.00 in the afternoon playing violin. Jean read two chapters of my thesis, and he's never been nicer. All the same he intimidates me a bit, and I'm aware I intimidate him too. But he's wonderful.

I came back here, and in mid-afternoon, as always, I felt completely at a loss. I went out again at 6.00 to see Dr Redon. On boulevard du Montparnasse, among the crowds sitting at café tables outside or bustling noisily by, I felt horribly alone and downcast. My spirits only revived when I saw the magnificent trees in the Petit-Luxembourg garden.

Saturday, 25 April

I received a postcard from Gérard; he seems really upset. All of a sudden something serious has come between us. How will it end? I can only think of him now with a kind of distant affection.

Lunch at La Reine Pédauque. We went to Aubergenville. Denise stayed home because she had invited Jean Vigué and his wife.

The lilacs are in bloom, the grass is growing, but I stopped myself enjoying it all because I now see myself as an idiot, having grasped how much I irritated Gérard with my descriptions of nature.

Sunday, 26 April

Orchestra practice: Job, Breynaert, his sister, Françoise Masse, Annick Bouteville. Denise played her Mozart concerto and we accompanied her, with François conducting.

Monday, 27 April

At the library I saw that boy with the grey eyes again; to my great surprise he asked me to listen to records on Thursday; we talked music for fifteen minutes. We were still chatting when Francine Bacri came by to tell me what she thought of my thesis after reading it through. I know what he's called. His name is Jean Morawiecki. Before knowing it I thought he looked Slavic, like a Slavic prince. It's a pity he has a voice like that.

Since Maman saw nothing wrong with the invitation, I also thought it quite natural, and I wrote a note accepting it.

Tuesday, 28 April

I went to play a violin duet with M. Lyon-Caen. Afterwards I went for tea at Miss Day's. I accepted both these midweek invitations so as to *avoid* Tuesday. And it worked. First because I was both frightened and pleased to visit the Lyon-Caens, and it was something novel, at any rate. Moreover I did not realize what I had done in accepting the invitation until I had walked all the way to rue de Longchamp. The same route I had taken on my own, first of all, every Thursday, and then together with Gérard on Sundays. That was when I realized I was going to his parents' place, to his home, and suddenly I became afraid. And I always feel a bit low going up their staircase and waiting at the door.

But it all went off fine. M. Lyon-Caen is extraordinary. When he came in, I hardly dared look at him because the shape of his face suddenly reminded me of Gérard. But I soon saw that he doesn't really resemble him at all, and I could look at him without emotion. He is extraordinarily youthful in his manner, even in his gestures. To begin with, it seemed presumptuous to play with a gentleman of his age whom I hardly knew. Fortunately Françoise was there. Then I became absorbed by the music and thought no more about it. When we had tea with Mme Lyon-Caen and Claude, I was no longer uneasy: I was visiting people no different from any others.

Wednesday, 29 April

I awoke very early after dreaming about Gérard. I carried on thinking about him until I got up, and I was very happy. I didn't try to challenge the feeling; it was new and unknown. I knew I would receive a postcard this morning.

I received it, it didn't say much, and I specially didn't understand the allusion at the end.

All day, and for the first time in a long while, I was, in a sense, his. Is it going to stay that way? Is it an illusion?

I passed the Faculté de Droit on my way back from taking a parcel to M. Boisserie at the Lycée Henri IV. And I thought with a kind of nostalgia that if he were there now, it would be all right for me to go and collect him when he came out of class. Whereas in the past I would rather have been swallowed up by the earth than even *think* of going that way. For me it would have been the nadir of the "Awkward Age"; and anyway I would never have been brave enough to do it. If only he knew that I had been thinking of him that long ago – it was the year war broke out! How things have changed!

Thursday, 30 April

I had a wonderful afternoon.

I felt very shy about going to listen to records with that quite unknown young man. But as soon as I saw him coming into the courtyard of the English Department where we had agreed to meet, my awkwardness vanished. Everything was very simple.

He took us – me and one of his classmates, whom I knew by sight, a very ugly boy but also nice – to the Maison des Lettres in rue Soufflot.

We listened to records until 6.30. To start with, there was a student nearby playing Chopin incessantly, which distracted us. But after that we had some peace. I listened to a quintet by Johann-Christian Bach, the beginning of the Eighth Symphony, the adagio from the Tenth, which I asked for and which was a marvel, a concerto for clarinet and orchestra by Mozart, a Bach cantata, two Bach preludes and Mozart's "Funeral Ode", which is a magnificent piece.

It was very funny. They brought me tea and toast; the tea was undrinkable, but the kindness was touching.

Jean Morawiecki walked me home. He's going to come on Sunday and bring a Beethoven quartet.

I found things all abustle at home. Maman's friends had just left, Papa had just come in, Nicole and Denise were overexcited, and Tante Ger was there too.

M. Périlhou came to dinner. Afterwards, he tried out my violin. We played the Bach concerto and a sonata for two violins. He kept on saying what nice kids we were. I don't know if he knows what we think of him.

Sunday
An extraordinary day. But I didn't do anything.

This morning I took some lilacs to Grandma and Françoise Masse. The morning was so lovely and sunny, with the chestnuts in festive bloom and a blue sky, that I forgot all remorse and gave myself up to the beauty of my surroundings. I had to stay at the Lyon-Caens to chat with Mme Lyon-Caen. That always irritates me.

Mme Lévy came to lunch. Afterwards there was the tea to get ready.

François didn't come to make music with us. Annick brought a very quiet but charming boy who played the viola. We tried Mozart's "Sinfonia Concertante", but it was too difficult. Breynaert arrived in the middle. We played the Bach concerto for two violins, but he annoyed me because he played *forte* throughout.

I stopped at 4.00. At 4.30 the doorbell rang and I went to open it. There were François and Jean Morawiecki. I think he's won everybody over.

It was amazing to think that a young man I hardly know, whom I met at the Sorbonne, whose name I didn't know last Monday, was standing there in front of me. There's something miraculous about the whole story.

Now that everybody thinks he looks a little Slavic, it annoys me. I don't want that to be the reason I find him charming. I found him charming for no reason, because he is who he is. There was no sophistry or affectation on my part. He brought the Corelli and the Quartet No. 15, the one that's playing when Spandrell kills himself in *Point Counter Point*. The "*Heilige Dankgesang*". The windows were all open, the sun was flooding in, the miracle of light fell on us; I felt as if we were all under a spell.

Monday, 4 May
What a night! I dreamed all night long. As I awoke this morning,

I thought about the dream and all that it might suddenly mean for me, and I sobbed.

And now it comes back to me that this afternoon, with Jean Morawiecki, whom I did not even know last week, I read Heine's poem *"Ich hab' im Traum geweinet"*. And it all seemed strangely beautiful to me but with a tragic beauty, where there were tears.

Because I spent another afternoon with him today: I knew I would see him again, he told me so yesterday, I was certain of it. He came around 3.30. And settled down at the back of the library. I had to work nonstop for an hour. I despaired of being able to talk to him. But around 4.30 he came over to ask me to look after his briefcase while he went out to do some errands. In fact he didn't go out at all but stayed with me until 5.45.

This evening a strange sadness takes hold of me. Am I letting myself be misled? Am I once again becoming crazy and passionate?

I think that with Gérard I would have missed everything that is supposed to be so beautiful – the arousal, the magnificent blossoming, gradually, deeply, silently! There's something too normal about him, and yet it is I who am bringing things back down to earth. Will I tear up these pages one day because I have chosen Gérard?

What will become of me? I do not know where I am going or what tomorrow will bring.

Thursday, 7 May

I saw Jean Morawiecki again today at Delattre's lecture. After class we walked along rue de l'Odéon and in the Luxembourg Gardens. I sat on a bench beneath the chestnut trees in the main walk until

5.00. It was quiet there, and shady. In the full sun the heat was unbearable.

He was even paler than usual. He can't take the sun. Is he ill?

I think I've found out who he is. His father must have been something in the diplomatic service. He told me today that while in Barcelona his father met all the celebrities who were passing through (on the subject of Paul Valéry). On Sunday he told me that his father had never spent more than three uninterrupted months in the same city. Jean's distinction and refinement are essentially aristocratic.

At this moment I can hear his voice, it's a little high-pitched, with a slightly affected intonation. Every time I looked at him he turned away.

He has invited Denise and me to listen to records of Russian music next Thursday.

Saturday, 9 May, evening
I think I was crazy today.

I was completely out of my mind. I told Nicole things I should never have said.

On the other hand, right up until dinnertime, those things seemed real to me. This spell seemed real; I knew that from now on he would be there, waiting for me at every turn.

But this evening I am so tired that I can only see things as if through a thick haze; I feel nothing, I can't even understand how I could have been so overwhelmed. I am cold and feel like an idiot.

There was Gérard's letter, then lunch with Simone, the Beethoven quartet and the conversation with Nicole, leaning on the windowsill, looking down at the chestnuts in bloom. What did I say? What did I think today? Will the same drama begin all over again tomorrow?

I think I'm going to sleep.

Sunday

All of yesterday's tragic atmosphere has gone. I don't understand what came over me. I shall never let myself go like that again. Day at Aubergenville. Stormy, suffocating. After lunch I was so worn out I fell asleep on the stone bench there. It was too tempting.

Thursday, 14 May

After yesterday's to-do, I was both downcast and enervated as if it was the day after a ball.

I finished my thesis as best I could. Ascension Day felt vaguely like a Sunday. Papa at home, the memory of yesterday, it all made for a strange atmosphere.

I hardly had time to prepare myself for the afternoon, which was much better. We had a date: Denise and I were to meet him outside the Department. The Latin Quarter was as empty as on a Sunday. Jean Morawiecki was waiting for us with a classmate of his. Someone threw a glass of water at me from the hotel on the other side of the street. We went to the Maison des Lettres. There were crowds on boulevard Saint-Michel. I told Morawiecki about all that had happened yesterday; it was like a dream. It provoked less incredulity than it had yesterday with Sparkenbroke. He is certainly closer to me than Spark is. The Maison des Lettres was supposed to be shut, but Morawiecki's friend Molinié, the chap who had come last time, had a key, and he opened up for us, with another girl who had also been there last time. We had the place to ourselves. First we listened to Beethoven's Quartet No. 14, which I think I like more than No. 15. Then it was time for Russian music – *Prince Igor*, gypsy music, popular tunes, Chaliapin; I really loved it. They served us a wonderful tea with frothy milk chocolate, and Jean Morawiecki handed round Egyptian and Russian cigarettes. It was exceedingly agreeable.

He took us back on the métro as far as Sèvres-Babylone. This evening, as always, I pine for the day just passed. And don't understand a thing about this week. Including yesterday's event and the nervous excitement of the last hours of writing my thesis. Tomorrow will be just the same. Maybe things will return to normal on Monday.

Wednesday, 20 May

Francine du Jessay has just been to see me. I hadn't seen her for three years.

I enjoyed it a lot, and there wasn't the slightest friction despite our disagreement about the eventual outcome of the war.

She looks stunning; she really is the only friend from secondary school whom I still enjoy seeing. Unfortunately she returns to Limoges on Monday.

Her visit awoke a host of memories of school.

Thursday, 2.00 p.m.

I am in process of doing something very hard.

I am not sure what absurd power moves me to act in this way all of a sudden. Yes, I do know: the abrupt realization that I ought not carry on, because I will hurt Jean Morawiecki. Up till now I found it all marvellous; there's no other word for what I felt. And then there was last week's crisis, which quickly blew over, and which made me question my motives, look further ahead. And in the distance I saw, amidst the unknowns, brief "intimations" of a negative kind. I do not know if these things are true or just figments of my imagination. I do not know if it is true that he is not meant for me or that it was just a fleeting crisis, because I do not have enough distance yet. But I feel it vaguely and I obey without question.

But I realize that it will be hard. It isn't hard because I am turning him down, it is hard because I do not want to cause him sorrow, not for anything in the world. He must be very sensitive, like Jacques, almost like a girl, and I know how important even tiny little things can be for a girl. And then I can also see that I am in a way sacrificing myself. I must have the courage to go all the way and renounce all the magic it has, give up what made Mondays so pleasant, and Thursdays too.

And every so often I jump up in revolt and wonder: Why do I bother to make everything so dramatic?

A voice answers: It has to be done; I am not overdramatizing, for this young man will suffer; this isn't something simple and ordinary.

I am impartial: I am not making a sacrifice for Gérard, I want to deal with this in a fair manner.

But I am like Brutus. And I fall back on instinct; in essence I am moved by the thought that I belong to Gérard and that I would therefore cause sorrow to this other young man. And that is what I do not want to do.

I was supposed to see him at 3.30 this afternoon. There was no way of avoiding it because he was bringing me a copy of the *agrégation* syllabus. But as I was on my way back from seeing the Department secretary this morning, I bumped into him in rue des Ecoles. I was sure I would meet him; I was relieved. That way I would not have to come back specially for him at 3.00. But I was burdened by *what I knew about my decision*. It felt the entire time as though I was hurting him. He came back to the Department at 11.30. He sat down opposite me. I don't know what I was doing when I thought to give him the master-class schedule. He said he would go, I don't think he specifically said tomorrow. He is too shy and well brought up to say it. He asked me what time I usually went. And I know the way his mind works; I think he will go.

So then I decided I would not. Quite apart from everything else, that irritates me, because the programme looks interesting. But I do not want to go; I know very well what effect the music will have on him, and maybe on me too. And I do not want to see him too frequently.

Only as all that is very complicated, I am staying away from home, and this afternoon I am going to run as many errands as possible just to get through the day.

Thank goodness for *Beowulf*.

7.00 p.m.

I came home so agitated I could have cried.

This is what happened. I did errands all over Paris. The *Artisanat*, then the American Library, then to rue de Passy for shoes, one pair, and so on. I arrived at Grandma's at 5.00. I found Jean-Paul in the lounge with Nicole S., and that calmed me. But afterwards, during tea, Nicole asked me if I was going to the concert tomorrow, and I realized that she was going. That touched a sore spot. I believe I felt jealous at the thought that others would see him, because he *is* nice to see. The same thing happened when Nicole told me that Jean-Paul had asked her for the name of the "handsome blond chap". It felt as if she was talking about something in the past. At the same time I was aware of a voice speaking to me through clenched teeth, promising that if I won this battle I would be purified – of what, and why, I know not. Sometimes I wonder why I gave it up so abruptly, so wilfully.

The breakdown was sparked by my outrage at the cobbler's dishonesty. I'd had him put rubber soles on the wooden clogs I had just bought. He charged me 30 francs for the soles. When I went back to pick up the clogs this evening, he demanded 30 more francs for fitting them. I'm no good at cornering people; I just walked out, leaving the clogs behind. I hadn't any money left, and I wanted to cry.

I got back on the métro at La Muette; the carriages were packed, hot, oozing and smelly. And I had but one thought in my mind: Let there be a postcard from Gérard when I get home. In mid-afternoon, exactly when I was in rue Chernoviz, the future suddenly brightened as I thought about him for a long while.

But when I arrived at home I found a postcard from Vladimir, as well as one from Jean-Pierre Aron that was utterly grotesque in its lyrical self-dramatization. In spite of all that I wrote to Gérard. Maybe I should not have done so.

When Maman came in, I poured out my story about the shoes. It calmed me to speak of material things. For the moment I feel better. But there's still tomorrow to get through.

Friday, 22 May

He wasn't at the concert. My first thought was: "I have to begin again." The second: an extraordinary relief.

———

The afternoon was hard to get through; quite apart from the fact that I returned from Pierre Vincent's wedding at 2.15 and found myself dressed to the nines for the whole muddled day.

I stayed on at the wedding with Francine. She was a safety net and protection against Lemerle, Viénot and their clique. I felt safe. Anyway I like Pierrette a lot, and her husband is a tremendous man. And the atmosphere was warm.

Saturday, 23 May

Morning: was at the Department at 9.00. Met Jacques Ulmann, Roger Nordmann (the one whose brother has just been shot) and his fiancée, Françoise Blum, whom I vaguely recognized. They told such a highly embroidered version of last week's event that I did not even recognize the story. At the Department I came upon the floor-polishers; on Saturdays the building doesn't open until 10.00. Downstairs I met a student I have never spoken to. But he was very nice and we hunted for books together – I was after a translation of *Coriolanus* and he was searching for an Anglo-Saxon grammar. At 10.00 we went back up and I buried myself in *Beowulf*.

The musical trio went very badly. Job and I weren't concentrating properly. Jean came for five minutes. At 5.00 I came back here to work on *King Horn*. By dinnertime I was in despair at having achieved nothing.

Still no post. I am starting to get jumpy again, as I was a few months ago.

Sunday

Lunch at Aubergenville with Job, Jean-Paul and Jacques Monod. Jean-Paul is charming and an easy guest; Monod is a crass and deadly bore.

The day was pleasant, but I was bored. I am missing something most terribly.

Whit Monday

I was completely buried in *King Horn* when Papa called out: "Morawiecki is on the telephone." I was so far away from all that that it made no impression, or have I solved the problem? He wanted to know if the library was open. What an excuse! After he'd said that, there was such a silence that I was obliged to break it by complaining about Anglo-Saxon. I invited him to come here on 7 June.

But it's odd how little impact it had on me.

Saturday, 30 May

This morning for the first time since I began working nonstop I felt discouraged before I began. I was almost sure I would receive a postcard today; I had dreamt of it during the night. I dreamt that I was opening two letters, one containing for who knows what reason a discussion of Blake, and another that I could not make out. That conviction made me put up with last night's noisy alert in good humour, and I got up in fighting spirits. Yet there have been so many days when my hopes have been dashed that deep down I told myself I would receive no post today. I was just hoping that I would be able to make fun of my own doubts.

But there was no post, and I threw myself back into work so as not to think about being disappointed.

Sunday, 31 May

I stayed on my own in Paris so as to get on with my work. It's curious how little stress I feel about work this year.

Lunch at Grandma's; Decourt was there again. Claudine's remarks about yesterday horrified me.[3] She thinks Catherine Viénot is stunning etc. Jean thinks the exact opposite, and that pleases me. I came back at 3.00 and worked on Anglo-Saxon grammar until 7.30.

At one point I thought I was going to scream at my own ignorance. But it was a false alarm; I can't manage to worry about it. And I flee into my studies as to a place of safety.

Monday, 1 June

[*Refait l'Ancien Rivoli dans la matinée*].[4] Maman came to tell me the news about the yellow star, and I pushed her away, saying: "I'll talk about that later." But I knew there was something unpleasant at the back of my mind.

I came home from the Sorbonne in a terrible state. I tried to carry on studying while on duty at the library. And I did my job scrappily and didn't realize what was going on. Then Jean Morawiecki came around 3.00, as did Nicole and Jean-Paul because Pons' lecture was cancelled. I was in a glorious muddle.

When I arrived at home I found a postcard in pencil from Gérard, of no interest and not even very affectionate. But I can't bring myself to get angry even about that.

---

3   The order that all Jews in German-occupied France should wear the yellow star was promulgated with immediate effect on 29 May, 1942.

4   The meaning of this sentence has not been established.

Thursday, 4 June

I don't know where I am any more.

I had a wild morning. Maman, Papa and Denise left at 6.00 for Aubergenville. I'd asked to stay behind so I could watch my classmates take their oral exams.

First of all, I have been awake in the light and the warmth since 6.00.

I had breakfast on my own and went out at 9.00, as free as air, on a bright and still cool morning. I began by going to the post office to send Sparkenbroke his book, and that reminded me of last year and suddenly made all that seem like the past. I have no regrets, but when I think about it I do feel vaguely nostalgic.

Then I took the métro to Odéon. At the Department the exams had already started again. It felt as if all that I had experienced yesterday had made me older. At the entrance I ran into Vivi Lafon. She told me such fantastic things about the star that I felt reassured.

She is so kind and affectionate that in my mind she is the incarnation of the Department's spirit. I went back upstairs with her to the study room, then came down to see the others go in for their orals, and I was chatting with a classmate when Jean Morawiecki appeared. He stopped, naturally, and we talked on the stairs for nearly an hour. Then I went with him to the Didier bookshop and to another bookseller in rue Soufflot; he drove the booksellers to distraction, and I was almost as bad.

Then I went back to the Department, went upstairs to see Vivi Lafon and left after a conversation with Jean.

Jean walked me back to the métro. He wanted us to go to the concert together this afternoon. That was why he was looking for a newspaper. When I realized what he was planning, I said I could not.

I came back here to go down for lunch with Mme Lévy. Now I am off to see Mme Jourdan, my violin teacher.

———

It was scorching hot when I left. I took the 92 bus. At Mme Jourdan's I met [. . .] and we talked about the meaning of the insignia. At that point I was determined not to wear it. I considered it degrading to do so, proof of one's submission to the Germans' laws.

This evening I've changed my mind: I now think it is cowardly not to wear it, vis-à-vis people who will.

Only, if I do wear it, I want to stay very elegant and dignified at all times so that people can see what that means. I want to do whatever is most courageous. This evening I believe that means wearing the star.

But where will it lead?

I went to Grandma's, where I found Mlle Detraux. Grandma gave me a most beautiful brooch and an envelope. When Jean arrived, Nicole S. abruptly told me everything. I understood why she had been so distracted yesterday. I was shocked.

And then agitation, so reminiscent of the mood of 14 and 15 May, 1940, displaced the pain.

Thank goodness Grandma is deaf.

Jean came with me on the métro at 5.30, as far as La Motte-Picquet. I stayed at the Department for an hour, chatting to Maurice Saur and Paulette Bréant. The exam results were only posted at 7.00. I saw Cécile Lehmann coming in, I thought I'd caught sight of her yesterday wearing black. She greeted me, and – looking at me with her blue and honest gaze – she said without so much as a quiver that her father had died in the Pithiviers concentration camp. I don't know if the others within earshot felt as I did. It seemed to me that I was suddenly in the presence of inconsolable, unavoidable and immense pain. Every Tuesday morning when I used to see her I would ask after her father. The fact of that habit had made me see him above all as a man *alive*. This brutal sundering, the huge injustice of his end, is atrocious – especially as I like the girl a lot.

I did not feel at all like rejoicing when all my classmates came to congratulate me. The thought of that death haunted me and turned everything else into nothing.

Monday, 8 June
This is the first day I feel I'm really on holiday. The weather is glorious, yesterday's storm has brought fresher air. The birds are twittering, it's a morning as in Paul Valéry. It's also the first day I'm going to wear the yellow star. Those are the two sides of how life is now: youth, beauty and freshness, all contained in this limpid morning; barbarity and evil, represented by this yellow star.

Yesterday we had a picnic at Aubergenville. When Maman came into my bedroom at 6.15 (she was leaving early with Papa and Denise), she opened my shutters. The sky was bright but with gold-tinted clouds that did not augur well. At 6.45, on my own in the house in the early morning, I rushed into the drawing room in my bare feet to look at the barometer. The sky was darkening rapidly. There was a rumble of thunder. But the birds were singing as never before. I got up at 7.30, then washed from head to toe. I put on my pink dress, and with my bare legs I felt as free as the wind. As I ate breakfast it was already raining, but the atmosphere was still heavy. I went down to the cellar to fetch some wine and almost got lost.

I left at 8.30. I had only one thought: getting to the station without any trouble. Because yesterday the regulation came into effect.[5] The streets were still deserted. I breathed with relief once I arrived in the main hall of Gare Saint-Lazare. I waited for a quarter of an hour. The first to arrive was Jean Morawiecki, wearing a white silk jacket which made him look like an American film star. He was very handsome. Then Françoise appeared, bursting with energy. When I asked: "How are you?" she answered: "Not good", and I stopped in my tracks, because she does not usually answer like that. Then she explained, in her hurried way, averting her eyes as she always does when speaking of her father, that he had probably been sent from Compiègne to clear a station that the British had bombed at Cologne. I was speechless.

Meanwhile Molinié joined us, going off twice on errands for his mother (rue de la Pépinière). Next came the Pineaus, then Claude Leroy and lastly Nicole. We waited in the hall for Bernard until 9.30. Then we went to join the others (Nicole S., Françoise and the Pineaus, who had already boarded the train). There were the usual hesitations over places in the carriage, and I ended up at one end, with Molinié, the Pineaus and Leroy at the other, and Nicole, Françoise and Morawiecki in the middle seats. It was hopelessly rainy; the sky was grey and low. But something told me it was all going to be all right.

5 Requiring the wearing of the yellow star.

Left to right, standing: Hélène Berr, Denise Berr; seated: Antoinette Berr, Jean Morawiecki, Jacqueline Job, Aubergenville, summer 1942

A lot of people got off at Maisons-Laffitte, and Molinié and I moved to sit with the middle group. At the next station Jean Pineau came and sat next to me. It felt as if I had not seen him before. I suddenly rediscovered him.

When the day was over, I compared him to Jean Morawiecki, and the result is that, though I have not seen much of him, Morawiecki is the winner. Everyone is taken with him, even Maman and Papa, with his energy and moral strength; it's odd, but he is the only boy about whom you can say he is *morally* a rare specimen. He possesses energy and righteousness.

Monday, evening
My God, I never thought it would be so hard.

I was very courageous all day long. I held my head high, and I stared at other people so hard that it made them avert their eyes. But it's difficult.

In any case most people don't even look. The awkwardest thing is to meet other people wearing it. This morning I went out with Maman. In the street two boys pointed at us and said: "Eh? You seen that? Jew." Otherwise things went normally. In place de la Madeleine we ran into M. Simon, who stopped and got off his bicycle. I went back to place de l'Etoile on the métro on my own. At Etoile I went to the *Artisanat* to get my blouse, then I went to catch the 92. At the stop there were a young man and woman in the queue, and I saw the girl point me out to her companion. Then they exchanged some remarks.

Instinctively I raised my head – in full sunlight – and heard them say: "It's disgusting." There was a woman on the bus, probably a maid, who had smiled at me in the queue, and she turned round several times to smile at me again; a well-groomed gentleman stared at me. I couldn't make out the meaning of his stare, but I returned it with pride.

I set off again for the Sorbonne. Another working-class woman smiled at me on the métro. It brought tears to my eyes, I don't know why. There weren't many people about in the Latin Quarter. I had nothing to keep me busy at the library. Until 4.00 I whiled away the time with dreams, in the cool air of the reading room, in the brownish light seeping in through closed shutters. At 4.00 Jean Morawiecki came in. It was a relief to be able to talk to him. He sat down in front of my desk and stayed until closing time, chatting or saying nothing. He went out for half an hour to get tickets for Wednesday's concert. Meanwhile Nicole S. turned up.

When everyone had left the reading room, I got out my jacket and showed him the star. But I could not look him in the eye, so I took the star off and put in its place the tricolour brooch which I used to hold it in my buttonhole. When I looked up, I saw that this had touched his heart. I'm sure he hadn't realized. I was afraid that our friendship might suddenly be shattered or diminished. But afterwards we walked together to Sèvres-Babylone and he was very sweet. I wonder what he was thinking.

Tuesday, 9 June
Today was even worse than yesterday.

I am as exhausted as if I had done a 5-kilometre walk. My face is tense with the effort I kept having to make to stop the tears welling up for no apparent reason.

This morning I stayed at home to practise the violin. In Mozart I forgot everything.

This afternoon it all started over again. I had to fetch Vivi Lafon from her English exam at 2.00. I did not want to wear the star, but I ended up doing so, thinking my reluctance was cowardly. First of all there were two girls in avenue de La Bourdonnais who pointed at me. Then at Ecole Militaire métro station (when I got off, a lady said to me: "Good day, miss"), the ticket inspector said: "Last carriage". So yesterday's rumour was right. It was like a bad dream coming true. The train was already coming in to the platform and I got into the front carriage. When I changed to the other line, I got into the last carriage. There were no stars. Thinking about it, tears of suffering and revolt welled up in my eyes, and I had to stare hard at something to hold them back.

I got to the main courtyard of the Sorbonne on the stroke of

2.00. I thought I saw Molinié in the crowd, but as I wasn't sure it was him I went into the hall at the library. It was him; he came over to me. He spoke very kindly, but his eyes drifted away from my star. When he looked at me, he looked up, and our eyes seemed to be saying: "Don't take any notice." He'd just sat his second philosophy paper.

Then he left me and I went over to the stair. There were students idling about, and some of them looked at me. Soon Vivi Lafon came down, one of her girlfriends joined us, and we went out into the sunshine. We talked about the exam, but I could feel that all their thoughts were on this badge. When she was able to have a word with me alone, she asked if I wasn't afraid that they would tear off my tricolour brooch, and then she said: "I can't stand seeing people with that on." I realize that: it offends other people. But if only they knew what a crucifixion it is for me. I suffered there, in the sunlit Sorbonne courtyard, among my comrades. I suddenly felt I was no longer myself, that everything had changed, that I had become a foreigner, as if I was in the grip of a nightmare. I could see familiar faces all around me, but I could feel their awkwardness and bafflement. It was as if my forehead had been seared by a branding iron. Mondoloni and Mme Bouillat's husband were on the steps. They looked flabbergasted when they saw me. Then there was Jacqueline Niaisan, who talked to me as if nothing had changed, and Bosc, who looked embarrassed, but I offered him my hand to shake to put him at his ease. On the surface, I was behaving naturally. But I was living a nightmare. At one point Dumurgier, to whom I had lent a book, came over and asked when he could return my notes. He seemed genuine, but I thought he was putting it on. When at long last I saw Jean

Morawiecki come out, I don't know what happened inside me, a sudden sense of relief on seeing his face, because he at least knew, and he knew me. I called out to him. He turned round and smiled. He was very pale. Then he said: "I'm sorry, I don't know where I am any more." I realized that he was completely lost and shattered. But he smiled nonetheless, and he at least seemed unchanged.

After a while he asked if I had anything I needed to do. He said he would find me in the courtyard; he was going to get Molinié. I went back to the group around Vivi Lafon, Marguerite Cazamian and another quite charming young woman. A little later they took me off to the Luxembourg Gardens. I don't know if Jean Morawiecki came back. But it was better that I did not wait for him. Better for both of us: I was too agitated, and he would have thought I had only come for his sake. In the gardens we sat down and ordered lemonade and orangeade. They were charming: Vivi Lafon, Mlle Cochet, who was married two months ago, the young lady whose name I did not catch and Marguerite Cazamian. But I think none of them were aware of my suffering. If they had understood, they would have asked: "So why did you put it on?" They are perhaps a little shocked to see me wearing it. At times I too wonder why I do it; obviously I know it's in order to test my own courage.

I sat in the sun for a quarter of an hour with Vivi and Mlle Cochet, then I went back to the Department hoping to see Nicole and Jean-Paul; I felt a bit abandoned. But even though I didn't see Nicole, my confidence got a boost at the Department. Obviously I created a stir when I came in, but as everyone there knows [that I am Jewish], no-one was embarrassed. Monique Ducret, who is so sweet, was there, and she talked with me at length, deliberately – I know how she thinks; then the boy called Ibalin turned round (he was looking for a shelf-mark) and gave a start when he saw, but he made a show of coming over and joining the conversation (we were talking music). It didn't matter what the subject was; the main thing was to display the unspoken friendship that connects us.

Annie Digeon was charming too. I left and went to the post office to buy a stamp. Once again I had a lump in my throat, and when the man at the counter smiled at me and said: "Come on, you look even nicer like that than you were before", I nearly burst into tears.

I took the métro again, and the inspector didn't say anything this time. And I popped in to see Jean. Claudine was there too. Jean does not go out. If Claudine hadn't been there, I could have had a long talk with Jean. But she was there and put a blight on every topic, so I didn't dare go too far, knowing she would contradict whatever we said. A visit that could have been wonderful ended up being wearisome, and I came home without wearing it.

Just now I told Maman how I spent the day, and I had to rush into my bedroom so as not to cry. I don't know what's wrong with me.

Jean Morawiecki rang around 3.30 to say he was expecting me tomorrow morning at 9.45; he must have gone back to look for me. He's very decent, and I am very grateful, or rather, it's what I had hoped for from him.

Wednesday, 10 June
I went to the concert at the Trocadéro today. I didn't wear it.

It was cold and rainy when I got there. I saw Nicole and Jean

Morawiecki talking at the top of the steps. Simone came a short while after. But we ended up on our own. It's the first time in my life that I've been to a concert alone with a young man.

It's marvellous to be cared for by someone, for example when he held out my coat to help me put it on; I'm not accustomed to such things. He gives an impression of refinement, almost of luxury.

Francine Bacri came for tea.

Thursday, 11 June
We went to Aubergenville.

Left on the 7.00 a.m. for Mantes. Spent the morning gathering strawberries and cherries.

All four of us were very jolly, maybe with the feeling that for once we were all together, all that's left of the family. Also to relieve the pressure.

We returned on the two o'clock train.

Maman came with me to Grandma's to pick up the photographs. In Paris the sun had come out and it was very warm. The photos were first-rate. I was so pleased with them that I flew back here with wings on my heels.

Mlle Fauque came for tea. I gave her my first English lesson. Bit by bit I'm gaining confidence.

The five o'clock post brought two cards from Jacques, one from Vladimir and one from Gérard.

Annie Léauté came for dinner. After dinner we made jam and talked nonsense.

Friday, 12 June

I got up in a bad mood and was not nice to Maman. She asked for the postcards from Jacques. I must have responded rudely, without meaning to. Things went downhill from there.

Then before going out I went to say goodbye with the badge on my pocket. Of course it offended her. She told me to put it somewhere else. I was furious at having to wear it. I took it right off and put it on my raincoat. Then she told me to put it back where it had been. We both got into a temper and I slammed the door as I left.

I crossed the whole of the Champ-de-Mars parade ground to get on the métro at La Motte-Picquet (to buy a cake at La Petite Marquise). The Krauts were doing exercises there; the commands sounded like animal noises.

I took the métro to Odéon. Then I wandered round the Latin Quarter. I went to the library, where Maurice Saur kept looking at my star as we chatted. It embarrassed him. I bought a volume of Mallarmé in rue Gay-Lussac and went to wait for people coming out of the exam session at 11.00. Before anybody had come out, I saw Jean Morawiecki crossing the courtyard. He turned and saw me. In the end he walked me home. I talked all the way; I've never talked so much in my life. I don't remember what I said.

I also saw Sparkenbroke, who looked somewhat unkempt with his hair too long. I hardly recognized him. Next to Jean Morawiecki he looked almost effeminate. He wasn't himself.

This afternoon Françoise Masse came round. We chatted for an hour and then left for Salle Gaveau for the master class given by Marguerite Long and Jacques Thibaud. We were due to meet Françoise and Jean Pineau at 4.00. Nicole S. and Denise were there. We had a box. The concert was magnificent.

We walked home. Before parting from the Pineaus, at avenue Bosquet, we had a long talk. It's a wonderful, inspiring feeling to have *real* friends who love and understand you. I have never had that feeling before. As we were saying our goodbyes, Jean Pineau said: "In any case you are splendid young women, so, so, wonderful." It came from the heart, it's an idea that is implicit in all our conversations, it's what creates this unique atmosphere. I was so grateful that I crossed the road without knowing what I was doing.

When I review the past week I see a dark sky looming over it; it has been a week of tragedy, a chaotic jumble of a week. At the same time there is something uplifting in thinking of all the wonderful understanding I have encountered – the Pineaus, Jean Morawiecki. There is beauty in the midst of tragedy. As if beauty were condensing in the heart of ugliness. It's very strange.

Saturday, 13 June

At music practice we played Beethoven's String Quartet No. 4 and also a Beethoven string trio. I played all afternoon, and in the evening I was worn out.

Sunday, 14 June

Aubergenville with Simone and Françoise.

We were all very excited. Nicole and I, in particular, reverted to our magical silliness of old – I don't know why, but it comes on especially when we're doing the washing up. We call it our euphoria.

We ate striped cherries. We talked gibberish. We teased each other about Jean Pineau and Jean-Paul. We were completely out of our minds. But it was fabulous.

Monday, 15 June, evening

Life carries on being strangely sordid and strangely beautiful. There are things occurring now that I used to think only happened in novels.

For instance, this evening, on my way back from the Sorbonne, I happened upon Jean Pineau in avenue de La Bourdonnais. He stopped, we exchanged a few words; his face bore as always his fine and honest expression and a smile on the point of turning into a laugh. He was carrying a bunch of roses. Suddenly he said: "Wouldn't you like my flowers?" I accepted. I took them. Once they were in my hand, I was stunned and horrified by what I had done. But he insisted, and we both laughed and parted with a heart-felt handshake.

I read *Crime and Punishment* at the library until 3.00, and now I'm gripped. At some point the door opened and with astonishing calm I realized it was Jean Morawiecki. He stayed a while and then went out to make a phone call. The odd thing is that we had nothing to say. He had brought me some books. He started to say: "Now, what day was that? . . ." and he took five minutes to work it out; finally he told me that on Friday evening he had telephoned to invite me to dinner to celebrate the end of exams with him and Molinié. Bernadette never passed on the message.

Around 5.00 there was suddenly a lot to do. He was talking to Mondoloni. And he left before I could talk to him. When he said goodbye, I mumbled offhandedly, and he made me repeat myself three times and didn't catch it even then. He said: "It's crowded now" in English and left.

The chap we call Stalin (and he knows it) stayed to the end, perhaps to make a statement – I was wearing the star on my jacket pocket. Nicole, Jean-Paul, Suzanne Bénezech and I went by métro. In rue de l'Ecole-de-Médecine I ran into Gérard Caillé, who came home with us. He's a very handsome man, but he knows it. He turns on the charm.

When I got in, I found two postcards from Odile waiting for me.

Tuesday, 16 June

A strange day. I went to Aubergenville with Nicole S. to get the pork. We spent a morning in our "euphoria". It was super.

And so I got back here at 4.00 with a terribly heavy basket, and now I'm having tea, in a very good mood. For no obvious reason.

All of a sudden I remember that I haven't thought about Gérard for a long time and that I can easily forget him. And my heart shudders when I think that this is happening at the very time when he has left for the highlands [of Algeria]. Where he asked me to write to him often. The distance between us has trebled. I am starting to live differently again. How did I manage to forget everything like that? At times I can dimly imagine a tragic outcome. But the rest of the time I am unaware.

It is obvious that I do not love him as one ought to love someone else.

How can I write that so coldly?

It's good that I struggled to be sincere. What will come of all this? I can't see past tomorrow.

———

Wednesday, 17 June

I've never heard anything like what I heard this morning.

The concert was *fantastic*.

Also I'll never be able to listen to the Adagio from the B Minor Concerto again without wanting to weep. I found it hard to recover my balance. I only got a grip during my walk around the Latin Quarter looking for a copy of Thucydides for Jacques. I went to Gibert and to Didier, on rue Soufflot and boulevard Saint-Michel. Browsing brought me back to normal.

I finished the day at Grandma's.

———

Claude Mannheim died yesterday after two months of pain. There can be no deeper despair, no pain less easy to assuage, than losing a husband when you are young. Denise is left with two little girls. What can life mean for her now?

———

Thursday, 18 June
Artisanat, Methey.

I slept for a quarter of an hour after lunch. It reminded me of Bergerac.

Pierre Detœuf came by at 2.30.

Afternoon at Jean's. But I didn't see Jean, or hardly. First Denise Sicard came by. Then Claudine tried to make me play. Then Mme Simon came and I played with her.

I had to leave at 6.30 to give Mme Fauque her lesson.

The Brocards and Mme Lévy came to dinner.

Thursday

Have I been crazy until now, and am I finally seeing things clearly?

Have I gone mad?

Yesterday evening I received four postcards from Gérard. He cannot know what is going on inside me. He has confidence; despite my coolness he is confident. He doesn't know what else is going on. He is waiting for us to get back together. Three weeks ago that would have made me hope that we might find happiness. This evening it just makes a painful impression.

I do not know if I am right.

A month ago, I was rudderless. Now, something in me has turned in another direction, because I have tried to live normally, as if there was nothing to prevent my doing so. And now look what has happened.

I think it was inevitable. It had to happen. From the start I have been wondering if it wasn't just because I knew no-one else that I committed myself. Nobody, not even Maman, understood my anxiety. Yes, perhaps Yvonne did, but she is so far away now.

I struggled for a week. But what's the use? If that had to happen, I cannot and should not prevent it.

I don't know if the other thing is certain, only it made me realize all at once that the first time I had given nothing of myself.

Or rather, that only my head was involved. You can't love with the head and the mind.

Is it because I don't see him that I don't love him in other ways? That's the question.

I always thought that I was missing something in Gérard.

Am I right or wrong?

If he was there, and if there was nothing between us, I could choose freely. But the mere fact of being committed torments me and perhaps prevents me from seeing things clearly.

I cannot deny that I am committed. But I don't know how it

happened. It all comes from liking to write letters too much.

It should be done again, from the beginning. Now I cannot see the future at all, not at all.

Last night I went to bed in tears. I had spoken to Maman. She had come in to say goodnight and wouldn't leave. I knew she was waiting. I told her, and then regretted doing so, because I misrepresented my thinking, because I don't know if I mean what I say, because saying wrong things is unfair, because I don't want people fussing over me, because it just made me cry.

And when I awoke this morning, the argument was still there and ready to go inside my head. What's more, I am emptied out, as if after a fit of crying.

I am rereading yesterday evening's postcards. They affect me in spite of myself. But that's because they make me feel pain, as if something has been lost, as if something is over.

How did I come to allow him to write to me like that without my loving him? As I read, I tell myself I am losing something wonderful. But when I think about it, the old dualism resurfaces.

I wrote a reply.

An evasive, disappointing, discouraging message.

When I started writing it, I suddenly remembered how much I enjoyed writing to him before. It felt as if something had been broken; I was paralyzed.

I must have been blind before. I should not have written like that since I was not sure of my feelings.

But is it true that everything is clear now? Or am I blind? And if everything really is clear, am I not going to find myself facing a desert?

Singleness of mind.

———

M. Boisserie to lunch.

Music at the Lyon-Caens. I was terribly irritated and completely mindless. Françoise [Masse] noticed.

When M. Lyon-Caen left, I stayed behind to chat with Françoise, and I felt better. I went to collect Maman from Grandma's.

I forgot my handbag at rue de Longchamp.

Saturday, 20 June

I went back to collect my handbag. Françoise had forgotten to leave it with the concierge. I went up and rang the bell three times. That door had become familiar and almost hostile; I had stopped liking it. Nobody was in. On my way down, I met M. Lyon-Caen on his way up; I went back up with him, and he searched Françoise's room, to no avail. I was vaguely aware of the comic side of the situation, the two of us on our own in the apartment where I was almost a fixture. But I didn't feel like laughing.

I left without my handbag and took the métro to Saint-Augustin. From there I walked all the way to Galignani's bookshop. I bought a book of Walter de la Mare's poetry.

I was in a foul mood at music practice and wasn't even able to try to shake it off.

And now Denise is driving me to despair with her pain. She too is in pain, but she doesn't talk about it. But I know.

Wednesday, 24 June

I wanted to write this last night. But I was too shattered and couldn't manage the effort.

I am forcing myself to do it this morning because I want to remember everything.

The first time I awoke and saw the morning light through the blinds, it abruptly occurred to me that this morning Papa would not have his usual breakfast, that he would not be coming to the breakfast table to get his toast and pour his cup of coffee. The thought was immensely painful.

That was only my first waking, and gradually (I often drifted back to sleep) other thoughts came to me, making me realize what had happened. I am still waiting for the sound of keys jangling in his pocket, of him opening the shutters in his bedroom; I am still waiting for them to get up, because he's the one who turns on the gas. At those moments, I can grasp it. At this moment of writing, I am not managing very well.

It was yesterday, about the same time as it is now. I'd been out twice in the morning. The first time to look nearby for some cottage cheese for lunch – Simone was coming. The second time I took the 92 to Etoile to go to the *Artisanat*, and from there I went to the American Library. As I was supposed to return home with Papa, I thought I was too early, so I hung about in rue de Téhéran.

When I got to rue de la Baume, I found the whole Carpentier family standing in front of the concierge's office. I said hello to them and they barely acknowledged me. They looked worried, so I didn't insist, just patted the dog and, with Mme Carpentier still as silent as the grave, went into the entrance hall without another word. Haraud came in behind me; I thought it a bit odd that he should follow me but then had a second thought – perhaps he had something to do inside. What also calmed my suspicion was that when I said: "It's pleasant in here," he replied: "Yes, it's nice and cool" in a completely natural way. But when I started up the stairs, he carried on following me. And again my curiosity was excited. I asked if Papa was in; he said no. Now I recall that his answer was rather muddled. He was telling me to go and see the Chairman. I said: "Papa will come back." He said yes, but I'm not sure he really knew what he was saying. At the top of the stairs I saw Carpentier, who was on duty as doorman, and I asked a second time if Papa was in. He replied: "No, but if Miss would like to see the Chairman . . ." At that point my curiosity turned into apprehensiveness; I saw Haraud and Carpentier exchanging glances. All this mysteriousness was getting on my nerves. Yet because I did not want to seem overly dramatic, I kept my suspicions at bay with amazing ease. But when Carpentier opened the door for me into M. Duchemin's office, I thought: "Now I can let go", and I kept nothing back. M. Duchemin stood up and I said: "What's going on?"

He began by saying: "Well, Hélène, I saw your father this morning and he left a note for you." I didn't understand a word he was saying, or what he went on saying (afterwards I had to ask him all over again), but I realized that they had come and arrested Papa. I suddenly realized that I wasn't listening to anything he was saying. When I'd gone in to the office I had been thunderstruck by Duchemin's face. I knew he had eczema, but this time he looked green, with a two-day stubble, and he stank of Junoxol. All the same I grasped that he was going to take me home in his car and that he wanted to inform Maman. And the note, I kept that too. It was on Kuhlmann letterhead. I remember it was even dated, at 9.30 a.m. on 23 June, and in Papa's neat hand: "A police officer is taking me to rue de Greffulhe and from there to the German office." And then, after a blank space: "I do not know why."

Underneath that: "It may be that it is not to be arrested or interned." "I let Maire know," and then, at the bottom of the page: "My wife has not been told, as I do not know the outcome of the matter. Yours affectionately and respectfully."

I can still see it, that sheet of paper.

Then M. Duchemin closed his inkwell and folded some papers, and we left. I pieced things together in the car. But it was above all the way he told Maman: at 9.30, when he got to the office, he found a police officer taking Papa away. Papa hadn't expected to see him, which is why he wrote the note.

I was in a kind of fog, I was unable to speak. M. Duchemin twice tried to break the silence, by asking after Yvonne, and by congratulating me on passing my exams. The weather was splendid. I could no longer quite understand why the whole of Paris looked so beautiful on this radiant morning in June. The sun always shines on disasters.

When it came to climbing the four flights of stairs to the apartment, I kept wondering how I was going to tell Maman. I went up the first three flights one step at a time, but I took them two by two on the last flight, to get there first (M. Duchemin was running out of breath), and Louise opened the door, and I glimpsed her astonishment at seeing Duchemin come in without my saying a thing. Maman was at her writing desk in the drawing room. I went in and said: "Maman, M. Duchemin is here . . . I think that . . . Papa has been arrested." M. Duchemin came into the room at that instant and there was nothing more for me to say. Maman stood up abruptly. Then they sat down again, and M. Duchemin told the whole story. That's how I heard it all. When I had got it straight in my mind, I went to tell Denise, who was practising on the piano. That was when it really hit hard. Denise stood up, I tried to finish as quickly as I could, I was talking almost in monosyllables. I remember her sighing or groaning, and I had to stop her falling over. Then we went back into the drawing room.

M. Duchemin had stood up ready to leave. Maman remained seated in the armchair. She put her hand to her forehead, saying over and over: "I've gone numb, I've gone numb." I knew what she meant. The difference is that she has now realized, and I still have not. She phoned Tante Ger.

Around 12.30 the phone rang, the voice was that of a man we did not know. We understood in a flash: it was the police officer who had arrested Papa, so I took the second earpiece to listen in. It was very strange listening to an outsider telling the story. It made it true, gave it the ring of authenticity. Up to that point it could only be something that belonged to us, that perhaps did not really exist. But from then on we knew it had really happened. Something irremediable had happened.

The officer said that Papa would have been released had his star been correctly stitched on, because the interrogation at avenue Foch had gone well. I protested and so did Maman. She explained that she had put it on with hooks and press studs so Papa could wear it on his different suits. The officer went on insisting that the press studs were what had prompted Papa's internment: "At the Drancy camp all the stars are stitched on." So that made us realize that he was on his way to Drancy.

———

I'll remember lunch that day for a long time. Simone was there. We were silent. Amazingly, I was hungry and ate with gusto. Maman phoned Mme Lévy to tell her to come up. When she sat down at the table and Maman told her the news, I didn't look at her because I thought it would embarrass her. She was sitting next to me. But from the expression on Denise's face I could tell that she had gone white. Denise said: "She's going to faint." Silently we blamed Maman for not having been more gentle. But maybe it was only because we were still so numb ourselves that we were able to think about being kind to Mme Lévy.

What I will also remember is all the excitement in the household after lunch. It was like we were getting ready to go on a journey. Andrée rushed in during the meal bringing two loaves. In Miss Child's room everything was topsy-turvy. Mme Lévy was sitting in an armchair with the coffee tray beside her. Maman was in her bedroom sorting linen with Andrée. Simone had shot off to get a ham from her place. I didn't stay long because there was a list of shopping to do at Tiffereau's. I queued outside the shop in rue Montessuy for ten minutes. The pavement was in full sun, and despite the awning I was drenched in sweat. And stamping with impatience. The street was asleep as it always is at 1.00. When Tiffereau turned up, walking down the street, I didn't recognize him at first, but then I blurted it all out. After a pause he said: "Let's see, I don't quite recall, your name is . . . ?" "Mlle Berr." "Ah, yes, I thought so." We went inside his shop and he served me methodically, slowly. I controlled my impatience. I left with a heavy load – a new stopper for the thermos flask, a toothbrush, toothpaste, rubbing alcohol. Everything was nearly ready when I got home. Tante Ger had come, and so had Nicole S., though I didn't notice until afterwards.

Haraud was the one who drove the three of us there. Paris had never been so beautiful, one more time along the quais, with a view of the Louvre and the Seine. I recalled the other time all this beauty had struck me so, in contrast with tragic circumstances. It was on 16 May, 1940, the day when the Germans broke through at Laon, when we rushed over to collect Mme Lesieur. But that was over, done with, in the past. Up to that point the future remained undecipherable. But it had unfolded, and we knew what lay in store. And we found ourselves once more facing an unknown prospect. Just twelve days went by, and another piece of the future lost its aura of mystery and impenetrability, and turned out to be sad and squalid.

The car stopped by the Flower Market. We got out and took the baggage. Then a kind of pilgrimage began. I carried the rucksack and the blankets, Denise the shopping basket. A policeman stopped us at the doors of the *Préfecture de Police*. Maman began to tell our story, and as it was the first time, it made me shudder: "We've come to see an internee who is leaving for Drancy. We were told to bring these things . . ." For that moment I accepted my role completely. We tramped up endless staircases, along blank-walled corridors with small doors leading off to left and right; I wondered if they were cells and if Papa was in one of them; we were redirected from one floor to another. We saw men in the passageways with hangmen's faces, or what I imagined to be such, and clerks sitting at little desks, all very prim and proper. The baggage was heavy. Maman found it hard to get up the top flight of stairs. I told myself: "Come on now, it'll soon be over." It was close to excruciating.

After much to-ing and fro-ing along a lengthy corridor with glass doors opening off it, we were finally allowed in to room number ??, at any rate the foreigners' department, because the clerk on the telephone had said: "Fifth floor. No, he's French.

Third floor." But when we got to the third floor, he wasn't there. It was a blank room, with a kind of counter separating us from several clerks at their desks. There was a little wooden door in the partition. On the right was another door with a young, swarthy policeman standing guard. He seemed to understand. When we explained why we were there, the clerk went through that door calling out the name Berr.

The moment Papa came in, it suddenly seemed as if the afternoon was connecting itself automatically to the still very recent past when we had all been together, and that everything else was just a nightmare. It was in some sense a calming or a sunny interval before the storm. Thinking back, that was a blessing. We saw Papa again *after* the first phase of the tragedy, after his arrest. He told us about it. We saw him smile.

We saw him leave again with a smile. We know everything, and it seems to me that we are even more united now, and that he is even more tightly connected to us as he is being taken off to Drancy.

———

He came into the room smiling radiantly, seeing the funny side of the situation. He wasn't wearing a tie and to begin with that shocked me; in the space of two hours he had already been stripped. Tieless Papa: he already looked like a man "in custody". But that was a fleeting impression. One of the clerks made some excuses and said he would give him back his tie, his braces and his shoelaces. We all laughed. The policeman tried to reassure us by saying it was an order, because one prisoner had tried to hang himself yesterday.

I can still see Papa putting his things back on calmly and methodically in that room. First of all they gave him Mr Rosenberg's tie; Papa already knew the names of his cellmates. He had found out who they were, and I asked him to tell me their details, and I was cheered by something difficult to express. It seemed to me that Papa had studied them with humorous detachment and that he found it all very comical – he had not only stayed calm, he had kept his sense of humour too. Joyful gratitude welled up in my heart. But none of this can be explained.

I recall only a few other episodes from those two hours. To begin with, I sat on the wooden bench opposite Papa and Maman, who was restitching Papa's star. Denise was pouring out her indignation to the policeman, who was supportive and sympathetic. I kept my mouth shut. I was trying to get a solid grip on what was happening. Or rather, at that moment, I grasped it completely, and my mind was fixed on the present.

We chatted with the clerks and the policeman. There was a short, very dapper gentleman with a moustache who looked concerned – a Chillip-like figure who could have come straight out of Dickens. He advised Denise and me to be very cautious. He was genuinely upset by what was happening and very respectful. The youngest of the clerks swung back and forth on the swing-door and looked like he was enjoying himself. It was a rather comical scene, with Papa in the role of prisoner and the authorities expressing copious respect and sympathy. You might have wondered what we were all doing there.

But that was because there were no Germans present. The full meaning, the sinister meaning, of it all was not apparent because we were among French people.

I'm forgetting to record the details Papa gave about his arrest; they are all I know and can ever know until I see him again. He did indeed go to rue de Greffulhe, and then to avenue Foch, where a Kraut officer (I took that to mean a soldier) assaulted him and heaped insults on him (*Schwein* etc.) and tore off his star, shouting: "Drancy! Drancy!" That's all I heard him say. Papa only spoke in short bursts because of all the questions we kept asking him.

At one point I noticed more of a stir. The door to the corridor kept opening and closing. Eventually a policeman said quite loudly: "They are trying to communicate with the prisoner through cracks in the wall." A clerk then said: "Let them in, it's his mother and his girlfriend." I had never set foot inside a prison before. When I grasped the situation encapsulated in those few words, all the police-cell scenes from *Crime and Punishment* suddenly flooded into my mind – or rather, a single scene, a composite prison scene. It was as if the whole of *Crime and Punishment* were set in a police station.

The door opened and three women came in: the mother – a stout, vulgar blonde – the girlfriend and someone else who must have been a sister; then the prisoner was brought in, a very dark-skinned young man with rough-hewn good looks, he was an Italian Jew who had been charged, I think, with black marketeering. They all sat down on the wooden bench opposite us. They brought with them an element of tragedy. At the same time the four of us were so distant from those poor folk that we could hardly conceive that Papa was a prisoner too.

Friday, 26 June
Morning. Library.

My friends have been sweet. Silvia Sebaoun makes me terribly

sad. But she is too proud for anyone to be able to offer her help. She
must be starving. I told lots of classmates about it. Eventually,
while I was revising, Cécile Lehmann came, around 11.00, looking
very pretty in black. I spoke to her. I blundered when I said this
would all have to be paid for one day; she answered: "Sure, but the
dead won't come back to see it." And I realized how insensitive
I had been. Stalin came and I told him. It made him sit down. He
stayed to the end of the session and left with me. I hardly know
him, but he is very attentive.

Maman was well today. Maybe because she got some sleep.
I'm trying to do the little jobs that Papa used to do for her, to
prevent their lack from arousing too many memories: like opening
Maman's shutters in the morning and closing them at night, and
turning on the gas in the morning.

I was half asleep all afternoon. I took a parcel to Mlle Detraux
and then crossed the Luxembourg Gardens to the English
Department. The beauty and cool shade of the great trees and the
shifting patterns of their shadows exuded a calm peacefulness
which made no difference to the sadness but encompassed it.

Then I went by the evil-smelling, sweltering métro to take
the letter to rue de la Bienfaisance. I nearly wept from irritation
because I had to ask for the right number three times.

Then I went to rue Raynouard. In the métro, seeing all those
men, I suddenly remembered how elegant and distinguished Papa
looked. And I realized that what my whole mechanical life over
these past days meant, what all these recent events meant, was
that *that* Papa was gone.

When I got to rue Raynouard I learned that there was a postcard
from Papa at home. I went to get it. My fatigue had vanished.
When I read the sender details, "Berr Raymond registration

number 11 943, Drancy Camp," I didn't understand – now and
again there are flashes of understanding. I read and reread it as
I climbed the stairs trying to convince myself this was all real.

Maman was there when I got in. She wept as she read. We
stayed until 7.30 because of callers.

I phoned Admiral Vriacos. Denise had managed to insert a
cherry stone into her ear, and we all laughed about it. Mme Lévy
was there.

Friday evening, 11.30 p.m.
There was a moment this evening when I began to understand. To
comprehend the horrible sadness of what has happened. It wasn't
when I was baking the cake for Papa. Yet there I was, besieged
by memories of small things, like Papa's tours of inspection in
the kitchen, and the way he had of sniffing the cakes we used to
make. But that didn't hurt; on the contrary, they made his presence
more alive and held an understanding of present circumstances
at an even greater distance.

But it hit me when I reread passages from his postcard,
sentences that began "my little daughters", descriptions of what
he had been doing the past twenty-four hours. To begin with, I
hadn't felt sad in the midst of the joy I felt at knowing what he was
doing out there. But I realized how empty his new life was and
what his concern with basic necessities signified. At first glance
you think he's organizing a new kind of life; then you understand
what that new life means.

Yet as I looked at the postcard I still could not grasp the reality:
Papa's handwriting just reminded me of the letters he used to write
when he was away from home. I saw it recently on the postcards he

used to send to Jacques and Yvonne, in which he wrote mostly about Aubergenville. I could not manage to reconcile the handwriting with what it said, with the meaning of the words.

And now I've lost it again.

No, I've got it now, suddenly, in the dark: between the Papa of home and the one out there who wrote this postcard, a gap is yawning open.

Saturday, 27 June, morning
This morning Mme Lévy got a postcard from her husband, who had left one side blank for Papa to use.

Papa seems a lot less jolly than yesterday (he wrote this card yesterday). He mentions the monotony. We had all felt that, but only Maman dared say it out loud, and we tried to deny it or to say it was only natural. Maman noticed that he was asking for woollen clothing. She is crying as she transcribes the letter.

We made up the first parcel on the kitchen table. Then I cancelled all my other engagements so I could stay with Maman. I telephoned the Pineaus to tell them that Papa had made the acquaintance of the student. Denise left to deliver the parcel. I copied yesterday's postcard for Jacques. But all the time I have to skip passages that would hurt the young man.

I called Mme Agache to pass on the news. The nurse took the call and said that Mme Agache could not be disturbed because things were bad. The world is nothing but suffering. Why did the telephone have to ring in a house where someone is dying? I hung up quickly, as if to erase the call itself.

In fact he died this morning.

7.30 a.m.

I don't understand anything any more. The Saturday-afternoon routine went off so smoothly that I find myself back living a normal life and feeling that all the rest is just a nightmare. We had Detœuf and his family to tea, together with Annick and her cousin Legrand, Job, Nicole S. and Breynaert. The post brought two cards from Odile and two from Gérard. Everything is normal. I don't know where I am. I feel as if I have woken up after a bad night and am back in comfortable reality.

However, I was deep inside the nightmare until 8.00 and things were not good all morning. After lunch I copied Papa's postcard for Yvonne (right now, that sentence hardly has a meaning any more). Job came, he sat with Denise in the study. The Legasts were with Maman. I went in and showed them out; I think Mme Legast was weeping, she didn't say goodbye.

Then I went to see the others. Gradually, as I talked to Job, the conversation and atmosphere returned to normal. We ended up playing a bit of a trio. I had asked Maman to leave me a one-line space on the postcard for Papa. When she came into the room with it, reality had slipped away once more, and I had lost my sense of the postcard's true value.

This evening, however, I was supposed to be dealing with Gérard's messages. But something in me has gone dead as far as that topic is concerned. Metaphorically speaking, I'm not replying. Receiving them pleases only my curiosity. Is it because I have decided not to do it? Or have I really detached myself from him? Sincerely I do not think it is because of the other thing, although I thought about it often this week. I have lost my spark.

Maman has just come back in, I'll soon get back my sense of wrong.

Monday, 29 June

When we get up in the morning, there's no longer any determinate shape to the day. But there's always something unforeseen to do.

This morning I got a postcard from Gérard, not his number 1, but one dated earlier. I struggled for a moment, then forgot.

I took a letter for Mme Duc to Thérèse's place. Her cleaner opened the door; she swore the Russians would avenge me!

On my way back, walking down avenue de La Bourdonnais, I was thinking, I believe, about my shoes. I suddenly became aware that a man was approaching me, and I came out of my meditation. He offered me his hand and said, loudly: "A French Catholic shakes your hand . . . and when it's over, we'll let them have it!" I said thank you, and as I walked on I realized what had happened. There were other people on the street, quite far off. I almost wanted to laugh out loud. All the same, that was a decent thing to do. He must be from Alsace; he had three ribbons in his buttonhole.

In the street you can't avoid being a representative; going out is a trial.

When I was getting the milk from the dairy, I knocked my head hard on the steel roller blind, and it hurts. When I went out after lunch, around 12.30, the avenue was bathed in such calm and radiant beauty that I let myself go for a moment.

Jean Morawiecki came to the library around 4.00. I was expecting him. Jean-Paul dropped by as well. We walked as far as Sèvres-Babylone on the way home.

Françoise Masse told me yesterday that among the eighty women deported from the Tourelles barracks last week, one (for example) had been included because her six-and-a-half-year-old child wasn't wearing the star. In the group is the daughter of a lady doctor who knows both Jean Morawiecki (she lives in Saint-Cloud) and Françoise. She's been sentenced to hard labour for life. Apparently they're all somewhere near Cracow.

On Sunday, Denise, Nicole S., Françoise and I went to Aubergenville. At the last minute Maman didn't come because she wanted to see M. Aubrun. It's better she didn't come. I think it would have been too harsh a trial for her.

I managed not to think. First, we talked a lot on the journey. And while picking raspberries I thought about something else I can't stop thinking about. We obviously felt there was something missing, and I kept on going over to where Denise was to supervise the picking and help her. But we did not talk about what we were feeling.

We stayed in the raspberry patch all afternoon. At first we could have told ourselves it was an ordinary weekday outing without parents. But the memory of recent events lurked in our consciences. When I think back on it now, I see that we were completely isolated among the raspberries and that the rest of the garden lived its separate life, as it must do when we are not there. I can no longer manage to commune with it, to feel that it loves and welcomes me. It has become almost indifferent. It's my own fault, because when I go to Aubergenville now, I never go and greet it any more. And then we always rush in and out.

The umbellate roses were in flower, the reds and pinks. It reminded me of the garden party.

I tried to stand in for Papa. So Denise would not think of doing so. I hauled the caddy and loaded the punnets.

Before leaving we said goodbye to the Hups. They knew everything but had not told their children. When I was talking to Mme Hup, I saw her face twist into an expression of pain, on the verge of tears. It was horrible. But it only lasted a moment. M. Hup came to help us pick cherries. We spoke of what we had to do for Papa. Plans always have a material dimension that keeps your mind busy.

On the train back, we were soaked in raspberry juice. In addition I had broken an egg, which was leaking. We gave up our seats to mothers with infants. At the station, Andrée and her husband and Louise were waiting for us. There was something comforting about that. But at the same time, when you thought about the impression it made, you knew it masked something sad.

Tuesday, 30 June

Last night there was gunfire, then an alert during which we heard nothing. I vaguely remembered that during the afternoon we'd been saying that the English had stopped coming. Jean Morawiecki had told me that they wouldn't come. Maman spoke to me from her bedroom and I replied – we had had the same idea, the idea of Papa. It grabbed me in the dark, but it never comes to me during the day. In the daytime, life forms a crust on top of thought.

This morning Papa sent his clothing docket. Maman cried as she read the list, because he's asking for lots of knitwear and heavy stuff. As she went down the list, her voice broke, it was desperate. She read out a word I couldn't understand; I learned later that it meant lice powder. She waved her hand round her head. I understood.

I went down to the dairy straight away. The shopkeeper didn't have any.

This afternoon I'll go to Aubergenville to get the grey suit Papa has asked for. Will I understand the meaning of this journey? Right now I can't. It's not my fault, I can't manage to grasp it properly. I *know* Papa is at Drancy. I *know* that last week there was a living, smiling, active Papa here at home. I can't reconcile the two things.

Thursday, 2 July, 11.15 p.m.

As I was closing the shutters in my bedroom, lightning flashed across the sky. The sky is still threatening tonight. After a whole day of storms, showers, distant rumbling and nervous tension. A day designed for an unwinding tonight. I want to write these lines before I go to sleep. Because I know that despite it all I will go to sleep, and that my body will overcome my spirit as it always does.

What is happening? First, just as we sat down to dinner, a phone call from M. Duchemin. I took the call and passed the receiver to Maman. She spoke with such precision and calm that I was astonished when, having ended the call, she said: "Papa will be freed as long as he leaves." I hadn't yet accepted the idea. I was surprised when I saw that Maman had accepted it, because she asked us what we would do in his place.

To leave. That's the vague foreboding I've had all week. My response to the idea was an abrupt feeling of annihilation. And then a feeling of revolt. After thinking about it a bit this evening, I think that I am being selfish, that I do not want to sacrifice my own happiness, because every kind of happiness I have ever felt is concentrated in the life I have here. But I can tell myself to do it;

I can force myself to make that sacrifice. But there is more to it than that.

There is also giving up a sense of dignity, if I agree to go away and join those who have left already.

There is also giving up that sense of heroism and struggle that you feel here.

There is also giving up the feeling of equality in resistance, if I agree to stand apart from the struggle of other Frenchmen.

But I have to set Papa against all that. And there can be no hesitation. Apparently at the beginning of the week there was a very real fear that he would be leaving for far away. There can be no hesitation and no question. It is odious blackmail, and there are a lot of people who are going to be thrilled. People who believe they are acting out of the goodness of their hearts and out of charity, and who will have no idea how glad they are not to have to worry about us or even pity us; others who will think they have found the dream solution for us and who will fail to grasp that for us it is just as much of an uprooting as it would be for them, because they do not put themselves in our shoes and consider us as naturally destined for exile. But those are all ideas in the mind. And I can dispel them by telling myself that they are only mental figments. But that's not everything. There are also impossibilities, thoughts that pop up and make you jump, because they really are impossible: leaving Grandma and Tante Ger. Attitudes towards other internees. Leaving Mme Lévy.

She came upstairs just after the phone call. She was a bag of nerves. Suddenly she exploded. She had to tell us something she'd been told. She was ready to burst, not to burst into sobs but to burst with words, and with irritation. It's about an order for 15 July to lock up all Jews in concentration camps. She must have been mulling it over all on her own, in today's storm-laden atmosphere. All through dinner she carried on harping on it while we three were thinking of other things. Two trains of thought crossing over, or passing side by side, in silence. It made my spine freeze to think that our fate cut us off from the common lot. I could almost take comfort in the poverty of life in the Free Zone. I don't know why, but I felt a desire for expiation.

After dinner the sky darkened even more. And thunder crashed down right on top of us. But Mme Lévy gradually loosened up. By the time she left, she had calmed down. This evening Maman is pondering revenge on the cowards who made this bargain and is working out what she will say to people. But sleep is lurking now; it's weighing on my forehead, and I can no longer gather my thoughts. My mind will be clearer tomorrow morning. I don't believe this evening was real. Say what you like.

Friday, 3 July, 7.00 a.m.
I awake with a single clear idea in my head: what they are trying to make us do is an act of abominable cowardice. What else could you expect from the Germans? They are swapping Papa for what we value most: our pride, our dignity, our sense of resistance. Not cowardice. Other people think we enjoy being cowards. Enjoy! Good God.

And deep down they'll be glad not to have to admire and respect us any longer.

It's a good deal for the Germans too: keeping Papa in prison makes too many people indignant. It's bad publicity for them. In their view, releasing Papa and allowing him to resume his career would be dangerous. But having Papa vanish into the Free Zone, and the whole business go quiet, go flat, that's ideal. They don't want heroes. They want to make their victims despicable, not arouse admiration for them.

But if that's the way it is, I vow to carry on being as much of a thorn in their side as I can be.

I have two feelings that come to much the same thing, though they are of different kinds: the first is the feeling that leaving would be an act of cowardice, enforced cowardice, it would be cowardly towards the other internees, and the wretched poor; the second is that it would mean sacrificing the joy of struggle, which is a sacrifice of happiness, because – apart from the joy of heroic action – there are also the compensations of friendship and of community in resisting.

Basically I am adopting a double point of view: for me, leaving is not cowardly because it is a huge sacrifice, because I would be unhappy on the other side of the line, but I can't ask other people to think the way I do. For other people, it would be an act of cowardice.

Friday

The whole morning was odd. First, the sky was still dark and heavy. Indoors it was hot, damp and stifling. I left home late (I was scheduled for library duty) because I waited for the post to arrive. I received two postcards from Gérard and read them in the street. When I arrived at the Department, Albus told me there was no library duty during oral exams. Whole morning empty all of a sudden. I went up to the library and had to force my way through the crowd of students who had gathered on the stairs. Then it was so hot up there that I went downstairs again. On the first floor Charles Delattre was conducting the philology orals. I put my head round the door, I didn't know if he could see me, and I took refuge behind the door. But I heard a military stride coming out of the classroom, and it was him. He said good day and understood straight away that the folder under my arm contained my diploma. He asked me if everything was all right. I said: "As all right as it can be." He was about to go back into the classroom. Then he turned round and said: "Is it true your father has been arrested?" I recited the story one more time. He listened, a look of concern on his face. Then he went back into the classroom.

I went back down and waited for almost an hour for Nicole, leaning against the wall in the courtyard. I felt isolated among all the undergraduates I did not know. All the same I did know some, who came to speak to me. I chatted with Monique Ducret for quite a while. Around 10.00 Jean-Paul turned up. I was delighted to see someone from my own group of friends at last. He was as jumpy as a cat because of the oral. I went with him to room 1, Landry's classroom, to calm him down. He registered for an afternoon slot. On one of my several climbs up the stairs I saw Sylvère Monod, who is very sweet, and Annie Digeon, who is charming. When something makes her indignant, she flares her nostrils, and her nose, which is very small, swells with anger. When I mentioned her to Jean Pineau, he said: "She looks very sweet". It's true. At last I found Nicole S. upstairs, where she had joined up with Jean-Paul. So that's when I left. It was 11.00. I came home. Maman and Denise were here. There was no other news. But yesterday evening's saga was not an ultimatum. All three of us felt emptied out by yesterday's struggle. I went into the kitchen to make biscuits for tea. Louise has left, and Bernadette copes with everything. We are more united than ever.

M. Boisserie arrived at the same time as M. Duchemin. M. Duchemin – I listened from behind the door for a moment – is very optimistic and speaks with apparently unselfconscious gravitas about "de Brinon", "who has been informed" and so on.

M. Boisserie was horrified by the news. We didn't say much over lunch. Afterwards, Denise and I felt sleepy. But I pulled myself together heroically. Around 2.30 I went to the Matheys'. It was terribly hot. Françoise Masse came around 5.00. We had tea in my bedroom. Then played a Mozart sonata.

Olivier Debré, who had had his beard shaved off in a student prank in his art class, came around 7.00, at the same time as Annick.

After dinner, Maman went downstairs. Denise was at Papa's desk studying German. I was reading a life of Dostoyevsky. Maman came back around 10.00. The evening was not finished yet. The issue of concentration camps came up again. As we always do at moments like that, we alternated between laughter and serious-ness, and made jokes which won out in the end and prevented us from grasping how grave the problem is. It all ended with us in the kitchen eating cold garden peas, which I adore, and then in Denise's bathroom, discussing the respective merits of Jean Morawiecki, whom Denise does not like, and Jean Pineau.

If I'm recording all these little details, it's because life has now brought us closer, made us more united, and all these details have become enormously important.

Saturday

Dannecker has ordered the evacuation of the Hôpital Rothschild. All the patients, people who were operated on yesterday, have been sent to Drancy. In what state? With what care? It is atrocious.

Job and Breynaert came. Job doesn't want even to think about leaving. We played the "Trout" Quintet, and very pretty it was.

Sunday

Aubergenville with all the Bardiaus. Picked fruit all day, dreadful heat. There was a storm all night.

Monday, 5 July

This morning the second of Papa's postcards arrived. He describes his life, one of his days. They are lamentably empty. Reveille (he put a question mark beside that, because he can't sleep much) at 7.00. Roll call at 8.00. (The other day a certain M. Muller, who was ill and stayed in bed for once, was denounced, and when Dannecker did his round he went straight up to the man and, finding him in his bunk with too fine a pair of pyjamas on him, had him deported, age fifty-eight.) From 8.00 to 10.00, exercise and callisthenics in the yard. Papa uses some comical terms, but in the circumstances they are heart-rending. Further down he mentions potatoes. I can still hear him saying the word in English, at Aubergenville. It's both consoling, because it makes us feel really close, and poignant. At 11.30 they have soup (and again at 5.30). Then they get on with the lunch menu. Afternoons drag on because Papa prefers not to have a siesta so as to save his sleeping for the night-time. He plays draughts, Diamino, bridge. Papa, who never played games, who worked imperturbably at his desk in the drawing room at Aubergenville while Jean and the others played Diamino! He spends the evenings chatting. He sends news of M. Basch, Maurice, Jean Bloch. He recounts his visit to the dentist, who has a bunk in the same dorm. You have to get used to sleeping among snorers and without shutters; he used to be blinded by moonlight. There's one thing, a little detail, in his postcard that gave me enormous pain. He writes: "You can send me gooseberries, I saw some in parcels received." Why does that make me want to run away as fast as I can? There's something childlike about that sentence.

And all his days must be spent like that. He says he doesn't realize he's already spent a week there. And here I am, free, running this way and that as I wish, with something different to do at each hour of the day and each day of the week, without a moment to think.

Papa's handwriting, made for drafting speeches and business letters, or to send news of his travels – that precise, clean, neat and intellectual hand – hasn't changed, but it now describes a life reduced and enclosed, the life of a jailed criminal.

You can't grasp the enormity of this injustice, the infamy of the way he is being treated, because they are too great, and also because we have become accustomed to expect anything.

Papa says M. Basch is feeling rather low. He's been shut up there for six months – for six months; all hope of seeing the end of it must have vanished by now. How can you still want to go on living?

Papa lives for us. He must be thinking of us night and day. For me he is almost a stranger. It's odd and maybe bad to say that. But Papa, the Papa whom Maman knows, is very closed off. Only a few sentences in his postcards give a glimpse of him. When I read this morning's card, something inside me said that there still was an indissoluble pact between us.

Tuesday, 6 July, morning
Worries return and pile up like black clouds. It's amazing, the way I have of forgetting and not thinking.

This morning I received a card from Gérard. The longer it goes on, the more it seems to me that there is a painful misunderstanding; I know something already that he does not know and that I do not want to tell him; I feel that I've been playing a role. Because I liked writing. And yet I never committed myself.

It's just that I thought I could remain on the surface of things, and the mere fact that I kept on writing made everything seem more significant to him.

I used to really like him calling me "my dear little Hélène". Nowadays, forgetting that feels awkward, because it's as if he has taken possession of my private self, or else, when I remember that I used to like it and that I even asked him to do it, the words seem devoid of meaning, just a formula.

———

In Tennyson's *Princess*, the Prince suffers a strange affliction: suddenly he finds himself in a world of ghosts and can no longer distinguish shadow from substance.

I am like that Prince, this whole story is real and alive, I've just been discussing Shakespeare in a postcard I'm writing to Gérard, I barely raised the issue of our relationship, I thought he knew me well, that his mind was made to understand what I was writing, and suddenly I see what underlies it all. And it all becomes empty and horrifying.

That must be what happens when only the head and not the heart is engaged.

———

Denise, Nicole and I all went to the U.G.I.F. in rue de Téhéran to register with this charity. We all got the giggles, but it was I think more like a kind of exhilaration, a state of exaltation. M. Katz told us: "You've no business here! If I have one piece of advice to give you, it's: Get out!" To which I replied before he had even finished speaking: "We do not want to leave." Then he said: "Then you absolutely must have something to do."

We were issued a rather distasteful certificate. Nicole hasn't stopped being angry about it, saying it's a concession to the Germans. I treat that as the price we have to pay for staying here. It is a sacrifice, because I detest all those more or less Zionist movements that unwittingly play into the Germans' hands; and in addition it's going to take up a lot of our time. Life has become very peculiar.

———

After lunch – Mme Lévy was there – a telephone call from Françoise Pineau asking us to come round on Saturday, and also from Claude Leroy, who very kindly came by to see me around 3.30.

I waited all afternoon for Cécile Lehmann, who never came. I had tea with Nicole S., just back in a nervous state from seeing Jean. Then I went to Hudelo's. Denise gave Jeanne Fauque her lesson in my place, I fixed two appointments at the same time,

I think it will sort itself out. I've lost my ability to conduct an argument. I've got a rheumy eye, it's a bother to look after.

———

After dinner made cakes for Jacques.

The twins went away at last. If Marianne says one thing, Emmeline says the opposite. It must be hell.

Thursday, 9 July

I slept badly last night. It's not surprising after an evening like that. I'd been out to Aubergenville for the day with Nicole S. and Françoise. We picked raspberries and gooseberries in the silence of the orchard. It was peaceful and relaxing despite our having brought our thoughts with us. We understand each other perfectly; Françoise is going next week, and I have the feeling she will never come back. My sense is that the irrevocable is coming to pass; I don't know if I'll ever see any of the people who are leaving me again.

When I arrived back here, I found Gisèle waiting for me. There was a tremendous muddle. Mme Périlhou was in the drawing room. Françoise and Nicole had helped me bring the baskets up. Then M. and Mme Jacobson turned up and, on their heels, in short order, Mme Léauté, M. Mathey, and Maman's young protégé. There were Nicole and Françoise to say goodbye to, there was the fruit to sort and also Gisèle to listen to. She's leaving too, and it throws her into despair. The feeling that "the end of the world is nigh" fluttered over me. At the same time there was a postcard from Gérard waiting for me that I couldn't bring myself to read; I went downstairs with Gisèle on my way to Tiffereau, and on the way I did read it. It was very sad. But I didn't have time to think about it.

It was afterwards, when M. Mathey had left, that I began to reflect. The scales were evenly weighed once again yesterday evening. Before I went to sleep, I suddenly wondered why I didn't accept everything on offer, why I didn't let myself go. With my mind only half awake, I almost yielded. I had lost track of my daytime reasoning, which has come back to life this morning. The problem is becoming acute, and I want to believe the opposite; he writes that his plans depend on me. And I don't want that. I want to be free, I do not want other people depending on me.

———

Went to get the photographs and took them to M. Katz.

Spent the afternoon at Budé's bookshop, for Jacques. Bought Suetonius and Wordsworth (for me). Dropped by the Department, nobody there, it was dead; I'd walked all the way across the Luxembourg Gardens, it's full of memories now.

From Grandma's I went to Mlle Fauque's, where I found Denise.

Found a postcard from Gérard dated the 22nd, which brought me much closer to him. Is this the truth or not?

Friday, 10 July
At the library I had nothing to do. I almost finished *Eyeless in Gaza*. Remarkable.

Nicole S. came to collect me.

Mlle Detraux for lunch.

A new order's been issued today, about the métro. In fact, this morning, at Ecole Militaire, I was about to get into the front carriage when I suddenly realized that the harsh words of the inspector were addressed to me: "You there, in the other carriage." I ran like a hare not to miss the train, and when I got into the last-but-one carriage, tears were pouring from my eyes, tears of rage, and of protest against this brutality.

In addition, Jews are no longer entitled to cross the Champs-Elysées. Theatres and restaurants are off limits. The news has been couched in normal and hypocritical terms, as if it was an established fact that Jews are persecuted in France, as if it was a given, accepted as a necessity and a right.

When I thought about it, I boiled with such rage that I had to come into this bedroom to calm myself down.

Went to the Charpentier gallery with Nicole and Bernard, who took us back to his place for tea.

Saturday, 11 July
Music practice. Afterwards, the Pineaus and Françoise Masse as well as Legrand were here. Played the "Trout" Quintet. I wasn't the hostess I wanted to be. Around 6.30 . . . the corset-maker and Mlle Monsaingeon called. When I returned to the lounge, it was too late. Everyone was leaving. The Simons came after dinner.

Sunday, 12 July
Aubergenville with Mme Lévy.

Monday, 13 July
Jean Morawiecki at the library. He walked back here with me without waiting for his exam results.

Tuesday, 14 July

It's grey and heavy. I don't know where I am. I've just written three spiteful postcards. I wonder if all my "scruples" are real or if I am not in the process of destroying my own happiness.

I'm also wondering if it isn't the other thing that is making me nasty. I am more divided than ever. I received three more postcards this morning. Every one of them is a torment now, because each one asks the question more pointedly. I acknowledge his right to be brutal and to resent me. What astonishes me is that he has not been like that more often.

Will I not *wake up* one morning and realize that all this is just fantasy, and that I've lost my chance to be happy?

Wednesday, 15 July, 11.00 p.m.

Something is brewing, something that will be a tragedy, maybe *the* tragedy.

M. Simon came round this evening at 10.00 to warn us that he'd been told about a round-up for the day after tomorrow, twenty thousand people. I've learned to associate the man with disasters.

Day began by reading the new order at the shoe shop, also ended the same way.

A wave of terror has been gripping everybody else as well these past few days. It appears that the S.S. have taken command in France and that terror must follow.

Without saying so, everybody disapproves of our staying. But when we broach the subject ourselves, disapproval is expressed in no uncertain terms: yesterday, it was Mme Lyon-Caen; today, Margot, Robert, M. Simon.

Saturday, 18 July

I am resuming this diary today. On Thursday I thought life might have ground to a halt. But it has gone on. It has resumed. Yesterday evening, after my day at the library, it had returned to such normality that I could hardly believe what had happened the previous day. Since yesterday it has turned again. When I got home just now, Maman announced that there was a great deal of hope for Papa. On the one hand, there's Papa's return. On the other, this departure for the Free Zone. Each of these things brings its own trial. The departure gave me a feeling almost of despair, I can't work out why. I came home geared up for the struggle, united with the good against the bad; I had been to see Mme Biéder, that poor mother of eight whose husband has been deported; she lives in Faubourg Saint-Denis. Denise and I stayed with her for a quarter of an hour; as we left, I felt almost glad to have plunged myself into real suffering. I definitely felt that I was guilty, that there was something I hadn't been *seeing*, and that this was reality. This woman's sister who has four children has been taken away. On the evening of the round-up she had gone into hiding, but fate had her come back down to see the concierge just when the policeman was coming to get her. Mme Biéder is like a hunted animal. She's not afraid for herself. But she's afraid they'll take her children away. Some of the children they took had to be dragged along the floor. In Montmartre there were so many arrests that the streets were jammed. Faubourg Saint-Denis has nearly been emptied. Mothers have been separated from their children.

I'm noting the facts, in haste, so as not to forget them, because we *must not* forget.

In Mlle Monsaingeon's neighbourhood, a whole family, the

father, the mother and five children, gassed themselves to escape the round-up.

One woman threw herself out of a window.

Apparently several policeman have been shot for warning people so they could escape. They were threatened with the concentration camp if they failed to obey. Who is going to feed the internees at Drancy now their wives have been arrested? The kids will never find their parents again. What are the longer-term consequences of what happened at dawn the day before yesterday?

Margot's cousin, who left last week, and we knew she hadn't succeeded in her attempt, was caught at the demarcation line and thrown into jail after they'd interrogated her eleven-year-old son for hours to get him to confess that she was Jewish; she has diabetes, and four days later she was dead. It's over. The prison matron had her moved to a hospital when she went into a coma, but it was too late.

On the métro I met Mme Baur, looking as gorgeous as ever. But she was worn out. She did not recognize me straight away. She seemed amazed that we were still there. I always want to be proud when responding to that. She told me we would have lots to do at the U.G.I.F. She didn't hide the fact that it would soon be the turn of women who were French citizens. When she mentioned Odile, it seemed like something very far away.

But if we have to leave, to leave and abandon struggle and heroism in exchange for dullness and despondency – no, I'll do something.

The common people are admirable. Apparently quite a lot of factory girls lived with Jews. They are all coming forward to request permission to marry to save their men from deportation.

And then there's the sympathy of people in the street, on the métro. Men and women look at you with such goodness that it fills your heart with inexpressible feeling. There's the awareness of being above the brutes who make you suffer, and at one with real men and real women. As the misfortunes are heaped up, this connection deepens. Superficial distinctions of race, religion and social class are no longer the issue – I never thought they were – there is unity against evil, and communion in suffering.

I want to stay on longer, to get to the bottom of what happened this week, I want to do that so that I can preach and shake up people who don't care.

As I say that, I think of Ibsen's *Brand*, which I began reading last night. And I am drawn back to Jean Morawiecki, who lent me the book.

I also know, and I am not trying to hide this from myself, that it's because of him that I do not want to leave. I know I don't want to see Gérard again. All this week I thought about just one thing: seeing Jean again. I saw him on Monday; on Thursday morning he wrote me a letter describing the result of the task he had asked Papa to perform for him.[5] I replied on the spot. As I was sealing the letter, Denise came up from the dairy quite out of breath and said: "It's happened, they've rounded up all the women and children, don't tell Maman." But I'll recount all that in detail

5 Tamara Isserlis (1918–1942), a Jewish friend of Jean Morawiecki, had been arrested for refusing to use the last carriage on the métro. Jean Morawiecki was trying to find out from Raymond Berr if she had been interned at Drancy. But she had already been deported to Auschwitz, in convoy 3, on 22 June, 1942.

later – I added a P.S. to my letter to say so. I wondered if it would be like Victor Hugo's *Last Day of a Condemned Man*. There was something uplifting in that feeling, because I did not quite grasp what the prospect of catastrophe might mean.

And then yesterday, all through that endless Thursday and yesterday's ruined morning, I went to the Department. I didn't know if he would come. I thought I had a foreboding that he would not. And I became gloomy. I realized that he was what the library meant to me. Fortunately Monique Ducret was there, and that was a comfort. To begin with, I was still in a haze, dulled by my strange night and not entirely normal. Gradually the calm and familiar atmosphere overcame me. At 4.00 Morawiecki was still not there. At one point Mondoloni came in; I don't know why, but my hopes were raised. Someone was blocking my view, but, turning round, I recognized the back of his waterproof coat and his hair. I calmed right down. We said nothing to each other for a long while. I was busy and so was he. And I am always very shy, because I was waiting for him. It felt like all of yesterday's nightmare was melting away. If he hadn't come, I don't know what would have become of me.

I am not ashamed of writing all that down. I do so because it is the truth; I'm not going out of my head. It's probably that I've got into the habit of seeing him, and as the days I spend with him are the only fine things in my life, I don't want to miss out. On Tuesday I was completely divided and torn, after Monday, and during and after the trip to rue de Longchamp. On Wednesday morning my sole thought was to see Jean Morawiecki. I didn't have any trouble testing the firmness of that thought.

8.00 p.m.

A new order, number 9: no admittance to shops except between 3.00 and 4.00 (a time when all the small ones are shut).

Maman has just phoned Mme Katz: tomorrow morning there'll be a mass departure from Drancy; one reassurance: no French army veterans will go, only non-nationals (including veterans) and women. They are being sent unfortunate children from all over, from Belfort, Monceau-les-Mines.

Françoise [Bernheim], who came round this evening, told us that at the Vélodrome d'Hiver, where they locked up thousands of women and children, there are women giving birth, infants bawling, all of them lying on the ground with Germans guarding them.[7]

We played music as usual. It seems unbelievable to see François still here. He laughs all the time and makes a joke out of everything. Underneath he is perfectly aware. But his courage has something mad and tragic about it. We are on a tightrope that is getting tighter hour by hour.

Around 7.00, Françoise Pineau came round with the course books Jacques needs for the Ecole Normale Supérieure. She looked normal, but I feel she couldn't say what she wanted to say. She did tell me quickly that she would run any errand at all for us, and that her mother would supply the food.

Sunday, 19 July, evening
Other details.

One woman lost her mind and threw her four children out of

7 The guards at the Vélodrome d'Hiver were in fact French policemen.

the window. The policemen worked in teams of six, with electric torches.

M. Boucher gives us news of the Vélodrome d'Hiver. Twelve thousand people are incarcerated, it's hell. Many deaths already, sanitary facilities blocked up etc.

News of Papa yesterday evening.

For two days now confined to their 1.5 square metres. Has seen atrocious sights. Eugène B. laid miserably low with rheumatism all over.

Spent the morning with the Pineaus. I went to collect Françoise at 9.15 and we took the métro together. It was pouring with rain. She is so calm and poised she makes you feel refreshed.

Jean [Pineau] was waiting for us at the Ecole Normale Supérieure. I sat in on student presentations in history, French and philosophy. To begin with, I was very intimidated. It wasn't much worse than a school-leaving certificate exam. But the fact of being invited by Jean Pineau to see something that was his intimidated me. Some students wearing spectacles. But the school is empty except for those who are either preparing for the *agrégation* or sitting it. We walked home through all the streets I like; we came out on to place du Panthéon all misty and wet but all the more lovable for it.

Crussard went past on his bicycle. I only recognized him when he had gone by; but he could have got off.

I was wrong to become overexcited when writing about the horrors of Paris and my own horror of the Free Zone. Because Jean said almost in a whisper: "That's why doing nothing is hard for a twenty-one-year-old boy like me. It revolts me." I know what's in his mind, I'm afraid of him dying a young and glorious death. Chivalry is his nature. It's magnificent, but at the same time it fills me with sadness. I can't define the feeling.

———

The friendships that have been made here this year will remain marked by a kind of sincerity, depth and grave affection that no-one will ever know. It is a secret pact sealed in struggle and in suffering.

———

I came home at 12.30. Maman's and Denise's eyes were red. I didn't ask what the matter was, I waited for it to come out. Denise was crying simply to cry; she's right. But the indirect cause was the news that we really would have to leave. Maman went to see René Duchemin this morning; he's always been extremely calm and optimistic; only today he said we had to think about leaving.

This is more or less what happened on Thursday:

Since French workers refused to leave for Germany, Laval sold Polish and Russian Jews, thinking nobody would protest. The workers are disgusted and even less inclined to go. There's yet a third consignment of Jews (Turks, Greeks and Armenians), and after that, it will be French women.

6.00 p.m.

I am blank, I don't understand anything about today.

After lunch, Denise and I went to [the U.G.I.F. in] rue Claude Bernard. They gave us a severe dressing-down. On leaving I felt it was so well deserved that I didn't even want to fight back. I thought about this all the way home. We were walking side by side. I must have looked fierce. Our thoughts led to a decision to write a letter to M. Lefschetz. Beforehand, I dropped in at the Department, where Mlle Moity passed on a message from M. Cazamian that I should not wear my jacket in the library, and one from Denise Keuchelievitz, that she was leaving [for the Free Zone]. In other circumstances that would have upset me a bit. But I felt I was living inside a bad dream and that everything had changed, all the familiar surroundings of the Latin Quarter and the Department, and that I didn't care.

Tuesday, 21 July, evening

Other details, from Isabelle: fifteen thousand men, women and children at the Vélodrome d'Hiver, so crowded together they can only squat, they get trodden on. Not a drop of water, the Germans have cut off the water and gas mains. The ground has turned into sticky, gluey mud. Among them are sick people hauled out of hospital, people with tuberculosis wearing "contagious" signs round their necks. Women are giving birth right there. No medical help. No medicines, no bandages. It takes an infinite number of applications and permits to get inside. In any case first aid is being stopped tomorrow. They will probably all be deported.

On Thursday Mme Carpentier saw two goods trains at Drancy in which men and women had been stacked like cattle, without even any straw, for deportation.

———

Mlle Fauque just came by. She doesn't have the time for her lesson. I prefer it that way. A lesson would have returned us to normal, as of two weeks ago.

She knew everything; from her I also heard that a woman had

given birth in the gutter in boulevard Saint-Michel, and that a man whose wife was being taken away tried to follow her, and that the German got out his revolver and four passers-by managed to drag the man away.

Wednesday, 22 July, morning

Got Papa's postcard. It is dated 12, 13, 14 [July]. I've just copied it out for M. Duchemin. Maman wouldn't be able to read it to him without weeping. There has been talk of a convoy. As I read it, I lived a day of Papa's life. I'm transcribing here the last half page, written on the evening of the 12th, in a slightly shaky hand. He described his life up to then:

> 12 July, 9.00 p.m. I've learned that a long journey is possible, indeed probable. Know that images and thoughts of you all, my dear wife, my two dear little girls Denise and Hélène, my dear big girl Yvonne and her adorable Maxime, dear Daniel and my dear little boy Jacques, never leave me and never will. Whatever happens, I will do what has to be done to endure, and I hope the Good Lord will allow me to see you again. Dearest darling Antoinette, I know you will have the strength and the faith to bear this trial, that you will be up to leading and inspiring our children. And you, my dear children, I know you will remain intimately united and will support each other whatever happens to one or the other. I am also sure, dear Antoinette, that you will make the decisions required by circumstances for yourself and for our two Denden and Lenlen [Denise and Hélène]. I don't

doubt that Kuhlmann, to which I have given all I could, will do whatever is necessary for you whom I have so warmly protected, and I have every confidence in M. Duchemin and as the case may be in his colleagues.

13 July, 7.00 p.m. If it's still possible and if there is time (??), try to add to the next clothing parcel my brown overcoat with its lining, and two tubes of gardenal.

13 July, 8.00 p.m. Since 11.00, news different. Henri says that pending further orders he is staying with Paul. This shows importance success Hup trip because Henri not comfortable about vintage which is missing one.[8]

14 July, 11.00 p.m. Nothing to report. Slept very well despite the air-raid warning, after previous bad night. Morning spent on very light tasks. Love to all three of you, plus those away, with all my soul and heart. Papst.

This morning I went to [the U.G.I.F. in] rue de la Bienfaisance with Maman to take things for these unfortunate people. On pont de l'Alma I met Jean Pineau, and in rue de Miromesnil I encountered M. Eissen; Mme Katz and Mme Horwilleur told me to come and help them this afternoon, in any case every morning.

At last I've found something to do which will stop me being too selfish. I am glad.

It feels as if last Wednesday was a whole year ago.

8 This sentence is in code. Raymond Berr was trying to find out the result of the attempt to have him released. Convoys were supposed to consist of a thousand people each; when a given load was a little short of the target, the S.S. often added "makeweight" internees chosen at random. Raymond Berr was referring to this fearful possibility by using the expression "vintage . . . missing one".

Thursday, 23 July

I worked at [the U.G.I.F. in] rue de la Bienfaisance from 2.00 until 5.30 yesterday and from 9.00 until 12.00 this morning. Shuffling papers. But I am almost happy to bury myself in this atrocious reality. Yesterday evening when I got to Nicole's and told her what I had heard, I was all floppy; down there, people talk about deportation as if it was just an ordinary thing. As far as I could understand, there are women and children at Drancy. Every day some of them leave, are deported. The Vélodrome d'Hiver has been cleared, and everyone has been sent to Beaune-la-Rolande.

The women who work there are admirable. Mme Horwilleur, Mme Katz and the others. They are exhausted, but they are managing. All day long there's a continuous line of women who have lost their children, men who have lost their wives, children who have lost their parents, people coming to ask for news of children and women, and others offering to take them in. Women weep. Yesterday one of them fainted. I don't see it all because I am in the back room. But I gather snippets.

Yesterday a full trainload of children from Bordeaux and Belfort came in; trains like they use for holiday-camp outings, but it is horrible.

Some women at Drancy are in their nightdresses.

A girl came to say her father and mother had been taken away, she had nobody left.

At the next desk Françoise Bernheim is on the telephone all the time to hospitals to get news of children whose parents and brothers and sisters have been arrested.

When I left rue de la Bienfaisance I went to see Mme Baur; she is charming and full of youth.

Friday, 24 July

Morning: rue de la Bienfaisance. I worked a lot with Françoise Bernheim. Sorted the things these poor folk send back[9] – wedding rings, keys, scissors; there was even a pair of tailor's (tailor's?) scissors: maybe someone who was leaving thought he would be made to ply his trade. Among all these more or less scrappily made parcels there was one very clean small white box; I don't know why, but I had an intuition that it was Papa's. Indeed, it was his eye-glass that he was sending back for repair.

Mlle Detraux.

Library in the afternoon. It brought me back to normality. Jean Morawiecki came, so did Jean-Paul and Nicole. Jean Morawiecki made a present to me of *The Brothers Karamazov*; how ironic.

I left at 5.00 to go to Nicole's, where the Pineaus were expected. I invited Jean Morawiecki for Sunday. All the way to Sèvres-Babylone I was wondering if I would do it. Just as I decided not to, it burst out all by itself, I was launched. I was glad that the irremediable happened. He accepted straight away.

Sunday, 26 July, evening

Life is extraordinary. This is not an aphorism. This evening I feel exalted. It's as if I am living in the atmosphere of a novel, I can't explain it. It's like having wings. Yesterday Denise and I went to Jean Morawiecki's place at Saint-Cloud. We spent a marvellous afternoon in the library listening to records, with the windows open on to an infinitely tranquil yet buzzing sun-drenched garden.

---

9 Before being deported to Auschwitz, internees at Drancy were searched and stripped of possessions. Valuable items were mostly stolen by the P.Q.J.; remaining pieces were sent back to the U.G.I.F. for return to families.

Denise played. Molinié was there as well as another very nice boy.

After dinner, at 9.00, Jean Morawiecki telephoned to say he would not come over today; his parents must have made a scene, I don't know why.

I was so disappointed, more than disappointed, I was in greater pain that I have ever been over anything of that sort. I didn't sleep all night. My sorrow was spontaneous and irresistible. I thought my day was ruined. I had decided to be sad.

But thanks to Jean Pineau it has been a splendid day, without anything changing. He is so sensitive and chivalrous that he brings me out of myself. After tea, sitting on the steps outside, we had a big conversation. I let myself go without fearing that it might be a bad thing to do. Everything is easy and normal with him. And I am neither muddled nor divided. I am enchanted. There is an enchantment in my life at present. I am grateful for it with all my heart.

Monday, 27 July

Worked this morning at rue de la Bienfaisance.

News from Papa. He mentions harrowing and hallucinating scenes. Since 16 July walks outside are not allowed. Paul likens it to Dante's Inferno. Compiègne seems like paradise in comparison! Attended the first administrator-training day; I struggled silently from the beginning. Lefschetz gave a lecture about the Jewish Question which drove me to increasing exasperation. What he said about the Jewish nation, and this is true, was that we did not know why we were being persecuted because we had lost our traditions, and we had to return to the ghetto.[10] No, I do not belong

10 Presumably in total ignorance of German actions in Eastern Europe, Hélène Berr, and perhaps Lefschetz too, use the word *ghetto* loosely, to mean "traditional community life".

to the Jewish race. If we could live in the age of Christ . . . There were only Jews and idolaters then, believers and the unenlightened. That's where any reasoning has to begin. Those folk have got narrow sectarian minds. And what is really serious right now is that they lend credence to Nazism. The more they huddle in a ghetto, the more they will be persecuted. Why create States within States? He recalled one of the principles of the French Revolution, which recognized Jews only as individuals, not Judaism as a race. Surely it's the only principle that still stands. Judaism is a *religion* and not a race. Anyway, in order to identify who is Jewish and who is not they can't avoid talking about the religious issue.

All this talk makes me dizzy. My mind isn't clear enough to follow the argument through. I just feel that I do not share their opinion and that their reasoning is flawed at its heart.

When we came out, we went to the Léautés' place in rue des Ursulines. It is delightful. So pretty. I really felt ill before allowing myself to re-adapt to the "Léauté atmosphere", which now seems to be a thing of the past.

Got card from Odile, one from Françoise Masse and one from Gérard. The only one I feel like answering is Françoise's; she's the only one who understands.

Gérard makes me cross with his jokes. I can feel a degree of hostility in him, and in me too. This will end badly.

Tuesday, 28 July
This morning there was a rumour that the husbands and fathers of the women working at the U.G.I.F. would be released. I think they were all astounded by my lack of excitement, including Mme Katz.

It was nice at rue Claude-Bernard, I learned some outdoor games; on leaving, I stopped in to see Mme Jourdan, but she had just gone out. Came home and tried to read *The Brothers Karamazov*. I was so tired I dropped off. After that I was completely lost.

After dinner sight-read Schumann's second sonata, with Denise.

Wednesday, 29 July, 2.00 p.m.

After a morning spent doing nothing in particular at rue de la Bienfaisance, I raced around in a frenzy from 12.00 to 12.15. Four men in the U.G.I.F., including M. Rey, have been released, and I have to admit the fact. But I still can't share the good ladies' enthusiasm, because I think it is unjust, because of the others who have as much and more right to their freedom. But I made myself look glad, otherwise they would think me ungrateful. I raced over to rue de Téhéran and rue de Lisbonne to get André Baur's I.D. issued and stamped. I was terribly hot; I just flew down the street. Which may have been taken by Mme Katz and Mme Franck as a sign of enthusiasm.

When I arrived at home, I found that Maman had had a ghastly morning. She had just been visited by a poor woman whom Papa used to look after and who had been treated like a dog by M. Lemaire. Maman sobbed as she thought of all of Papa's charity work turned upside down.

Out of duty I went to see Mme Lévy to give her what little news I had managed to get from Mme Rey. She reacted just as I would have expected, with even more bitterness than I could believe; I told her she was right, and that I thought it was almost a personal reproach.

Thursday, 30 July

Rue Claude-Bernard this morning.

Mathey, Grandma.

Music with Job in the afternoon.

Friday, 31 July

Rue de la Bienfaisance in the morning.

Library in the afternoon.

Jean Morawiecki came. He also agreed to Sunday. Straight away. From the beginning I hadn't dared to ask him round. Then, suddenly, I forced myself, and it just popped out of my mouth. I said: "Tell me, would you like to come round on Sunday?" He replied straight off: "With pleasure." He walked me back as far as Sèvres-Babylone.

Saturday, 1 August

Afternoon at the Jobs', exceedingly hot. Couldn't wait for tomorrow.

When I got home, I received a *pneu* from Jean-Paul, who's not coming. I was sorry. Nothing was going well. The barometer was falling, the sewing machine was not stitching properly, my skirt wasn't finished. I was sure it would be awful.

Monday, 3 August, evening

I really don't know what's happened to me, but I have changed from top to toe. I am living in a strange mixture of memories of yesterday and today. Since Friday there have been neither days nor nights; at night I've not slept, or rather, for the last three nights, I've awakened after a few hours, I think about him and can't go back to sleep. I am not tired, I am even happy during these strange nights.

When I saw him again this afternoon, he asked me if I had slept well; I answered: "No, I slept very badly. How about you?" – I knew anyway that he'd slept badly too. It seemed to me that we hadn't parted and that he knew that too. It all seemed natural. He said he dreamt of me as [Thomas Hardy's] Eustacia. Eustacia, Egdon Heath, the windy plateau at Aubergenville yesterday, today's black sky over the dome of the Institut [de France], the wet and shiny streets, and my certain, magnificent, unwavering happiness throughout; I almost feel like I have wings. I don't even think about him as a separate person. He has become a vague idea because of my happiness.

Yesterday at Aubergenville was the happiest day of my life. It passed like a dream. It was such a happy, transparent, pure and unmixed dream that I knew no regret, nor even the fear of seeing it come to an end.

Wednesday, 5 August, evening
I've just written to Gérard. In reply to his two postcards received Monday. It was horribly difficult. I put off writing the card every day and every hour. Especially because I wasn't sufficiently clear-headed. Yesterday evening sleeping sickness overcame me; I went to bed at 8.30 and fell asleep straight away. The other reason is much more serious: I was evading the reply because I did not *know* what to say. Because I haven't thought about it, and because I know I am up against a very, very serious matter. I don't know what to tell him (1) because I can't accept that things have got to this point (2) because I am afraid of being hypocritical because of the other matter – and yet this evening I can manage

to keep the second matter out of it entirely. I don't *see* myself at all as someone false and hypocritical just because I have managed to forget the other matter for a moment.

On the one hand, when I think that this is a complete break, I realize I am very attached to Gérard, in spite of myself. The relationship is based on the letters we exchanged all last winter.

On the other hand, at the other extreme, I see him as a stranger, I see the whole thing as a matter over which I had no control, and I realize almost with terror that the final decision has been made outside of myself.

And then I sink back into my usual mindlessness.

Thursday morning

There were two letters in the post this morning: one from the bank, the other a bulging envelope for me. I was sure that it was the real thing.

A charming letter half in English and half in French, funny, ending with a poem by Meredith. But after reading it I was shaking all over. I had a go at explaining things to Maman before leaving for rue Claude-Bernard, and another go after lunch. She keeps on saying I am going to be ruined, that she can see it coming, that I'm getting carried away. I was apprehensive about coming home. But in the evening, when I was in bed, we talked about it calmly: it all ended in giggles, I showed her his letter and my reply, and suddenly the mood became light-hearted, affectionate and comforting; since then I've only talked about it to myself. Sunday's perfect happiness is gone; I've no memory of that day, because I haven't thought about it again. But I'm afraid that next Sunday there will be a whole flood of memories.

Friday, 7 August

Last training day at rue Claude-Bernard.

Tea at Nicole's with the Jobs.

A letter from Papa this morning, I found it terribly sad. I wanted to copy out passages, but Maman took it back. Aubergenville is in his every thought, how he loves the place; he knows which tree bore each piece of fruit we send him. At the end of his message, he agonizes over whether he did the right thing by staying [in Paris]. He too is now prey to these sterile problems which bring you to doubt the validity of moral principles, such as staying where you are. People will not understand why we stayed. We don't have the right not to want to escape. But is evading an inevitable fate a real escape? As for me, I'm still convinced. It's just that all you have by way of approval is your own conscience.

Saturday, 8 August

An empty afternoon, for once. I read *The Eternal Husband* and then I went to Gilberte's.

The four have been released, but not Papa, as I thought. I was hardly cheerful about it. But it must have been a terrible disappointment for him.

Tuesday, 11 August

Yesterday morning, I really wasn't expecting it, another letter – all of it in English this time, and there was also an edelweiss.

All morning I thought about the afternoon without having the faintest idea what I would say or what would happen.

And it happened, almost immediately, despite long pauses; from rue de l'Ecole-de-Médecine we went back up towards the

Ecole de Pharmacie and then down along streets I've forgotten and back here on foot. I was calm and almost devoid of ideas. Talking was terribly difficult, I didn't know how to answer. What's marvellous is that there's no embarrassment, apart from the difficulty of speaking. Here we had tea on the small table, listening to the "Kreutzer" sonata. It's odd, but I had nothing more to say. I couldn't take in what had happened between us. When I thought about it, waves of joy and pride swept over me. He sat at the piano without being asked and played some Chopin. Afterwards, I played the violin. Everything was very simple and easy. I walked him back to pont de l'Alma through the golden evening. When I got home Maman gave me a dressing-down for having done that. But in the evening, after Mlle Monsaingeon and Perez had left – he stayed until 11.00 – she spoke to me so sweetly that I felt entirely comforted.

Obviously I hardly slept. But that doesn't matter.

———

Went to Grandma's. Saw Thérèse.

Finished writing my letter when I came back.

Wednesday, 12 August
The Léautés for tea (Gilberte, Annie).

M. Périlhou.

M. Simon.

Thursday, 13 August
Didn't go to rue de la Bienfaisance today, stayed at home writing letters and reading.

Job and Breynaert; we ended with Beethoven's first string trio. Very pretty.

Friday, 14 August
He's accepted for tomorrow.
　　Went to Grandma's. Saw Marie-Louise Thyll, Nicole S.'s friend.

Friday, 14 August
I received my letter.

———

A heart-rending letter from Papa. He ended with the words: "But I still thought that my clever Lenlen would get me out of my hole." That means he trusted me. But I didn't. He was relying on me.
　　He writes about the sights he sees, separations, departures, luggage left behind. Pestilential smells.
　　He *has* to be got out of there. He's not the type who can cope.

Saturday, 15 August
Second day at Aubergenville.
　　I was afraid that by doing it again everything would be spoiled. I was also afraid that after what had happened only last Monday the miracle of the first time would not happen twice.
　　We left with Mme Lévy in glorious weather. All the way to the station I was *afraid*. Apprehension grasped at my throat and made my heart thump.
　　We stood all the way. Gradually that horrible shyness disappeared.
　　When we arrived there, we peeled the potatoes first, then I

Hélène Berr and Jean Morawiecki,
Aubergenville, summer 1942

went with Jean Morawiecki to pick fruit in the upper orchard. When I look back on it, it seems like an enchantment. The dew-soaked grass, the blue sky, the dewdrops sparkling in the sunlight and the joy flooding over me. The orchard always has that effect. But this morning I was completely happy.

After lunch we went for a walk on the plateau, over towards Bazemont.

But all afternoon I was obsessed by the time, by the feeling that it was going to end. I showed him round the house just before we left.

The journey back was magical. At the station, he asked me quickly if he could see me again on Monday; I was taken by surprise and said yes. It gave me a beacon of light that was very near, the day after tomorrow.

Sunday, 16 August

Our first outing with the children [from the U.G.I.F.]. We went to Robinson.

It was a tiring day, the children were adorable and very endearing.

Monday, 17 August

Half past three, at the Department. He was dressed all in white. We went for a walk along boulevard Henri-IV and then came back here along the quais.

When he left I felt frightened because it was too beautiful and too unreal.

Tuesday, 18 August

Went to Grandma's.

Wednesday, 19 August

Stayed at home on my own all afternoon, something I haven't done for two months now.

Torrid heat.

I did a bit of work on my blouse. But I was so steeped in my own thoughts that I tried to read, *The Brothers Karamazov*, then Meredith. In the end I played the violin.

Thursday, 20 August

A letter from Papa. He is completely downcast.

What is to be done?

Cécile Lehmann and the Pineaus came round. When Jean Pineau left, I really thought I wouldn't see him again when he came back. But time has passed nonetheless.

Friday, 21 August

Rue de la Bienfaisance. I helped Suzanne process the people coming in to the office. It's lamentable, almost everybody gets stopped trying to cross the demarcation line. And that means instant deportation. What a pile of troubles for each of these people. And when we opened the parcels that had been returned, and they saw the rings or their mother's or father's watches, it was unbearable.

All the children at the Beaune camp have been brought to Drancy, probably for deportation. They play out in the yard, their sores and lice making them quite repulsive. Poor little souls.

Saturday, 22 August

We have been informed of the despicable blackmail on Papa's behalf.[11]

Went to the Breynaerts'.

Monday, 23 August

Outing to La Varenne.

It wasn't a success. No way to make the children follow instructions.

After lunch I told them *Rikki-Tikki-Tavi*. They sat in a little circle. My favourites among the children. Herbert listened as well. I was very nervous to begin with. But by the end I was very happy because one of the children, his eyes still moonstruck, kept on repeating mechanically: "Tell us another, miss, tell us another!"

———

11 Etablissements Kuhlmann had agreed to pay a ransom for the release of Raymond Berr.

Monday, 24 August

Nicole S. had told me to bring Jean Morawiecki round to her place. The Pineaus and the Jobs would be there. When I went out, I wasn't sure what I would do. I caught up with him at the library. I saw Sparkenbroke. Seeing him arrive made me feel funny. He was very handsome. But it felt as if I had known him for centuries. When I asked what he was doing, he told me: "I'm going to be a father." It was strangely awkward, and I was relieved to get away.

We walked back up to Nicole's. It was very nice. But I wasn't happy with my day.

Tuesday, 25 August

Went to rue Raynouard.

Thursday, 27 August

Job, music practice. Breynaert came round too. M. Périlhou came by at the end of the evening.

Friday, 28 August

Rue Raynouard, where I was alone with Grandma.

Then to Cécile Valensi's. Back into the old familiar atmosphere, talking English and music. But it feels almost painful, because it seems to me now that this was all in the distant past. And yet it was only in June.

Saturday, 29 August

Took the parcel to Mme Schwartz. In rue de la Tour-d'Auvergne, a quaint old street that felt friendly and hospitable.

In the afternoon, in heavy, damp heat, we went to the S.'s; it felt almost like Aubergenville, because Tante Ger and Oncle Jules were there. Denise and I played. It was a strange Saturday but a pleasant one.

In the evening M. Olléon stayed until 8.00. He told me the story of the Rosovskys' arrest; the scene haunted me, its memory haunts me. I visualized the evening with this White Russian man and his wife, *resigned to their own arrest*, entrusting their little boy to Olléon; the wife is a beautiful blonde lady, now sick and wan, lying on the sofa staring into space; they were trying to make the man drink so he would change his mind; and afterwards . . . Drancy, deportation, the woman probably dying en route.

Maman came home in a state of high dudgeon because she had heard that "undeportable" people were now being sent to Pithiviers.

She has changed even more over the last week. Thinner, and as edgy as a child.

Nosley came after dinner. The atmosphere settled a bit.

Sunday, 30 August

My fine Sunday. It makes me think of Kipling's *My Sunday at Home*.

For two weeks I've been yearning for this day at Aubergenville.

There was Jean Pineau, Job and Lancelot of the Lake. The miracle happened again. Why would it stop? In the light-drenched upper orchard, after lunch on the windy plateau, and coming back on the train.

But when I arrived at home, there was a struggle between the enchanted memories flooding through me and the sadness of a letter from Papa, once again entirely downcast.

Monday, 31 August

M. André May and his wife have been caught. Probably denounced. When they were at the station.

The number of people who are at Drancy for having tried to cross the line! Papa saw the Thévinis come in, they are cousins of the Schwartzes and had been to Aubergenville, to the wedding. This is the second time Papa has seen them. It's tragic. Mme Lévy is the wife of a general!

And the countless Polish men and women whose relatives come to rue de la Bienfaisance. This morning there was a man who could barely speak, asking me if they'd returned "the little one's things". He was talking about a child of four who had died at the Pithiviers detention camp.

Tuesday, 1 September

I'd said I wanted to see Jean Morawiecki today so the week would seem less long. It was a marvellous afternoon. We did the grand tour of Paris by way of place du Carrousel, the Champs-Elysées and avenue Marceau. I felt immense pleasure at walking down the Champs-Elysées with him. We came back here to drink raspberry cordial and listen to the last movement of the Fifth.

In the morning I'd had a letter from Jean Pineau which I'm a bit afraid to understand.

Wednesday, 2 September

The outing with the group from rue Claude-Bernard that I was worried about went off very well. There were seven of us with Cassowary, who was nice, in charge. I was very glad. I put on a pair of Cassowary's gym shorts. I was a bit frightened, but Nicole S. thought they suited me. We spent the day at Montmorency, doing gymnastics and first aid, and playing games and charades.

Thursday, 3 September

Job came. We practised the Triple Concerto.

Friday, 4 September

I didn't go over to rue de la Bienfaisance. I'd decided not to, so as to read the *Wolf Cub's Handbook*. But I spent half the morning replying to Jean Morawiecki's letter.

Saturday, 5 September

Outing with the eight Sixers. Robinson.

Pleasant, but it exhausted me.

Little Bernard told me his story, stammering, in his child's voice. His mother and his sister were deported, and he made a statement that seemed so old on the lips of a mere babe: "I am certain that they will not come back alive." He looks like an angel.

Sunday, 6 September

Aubergenville.

Job, picking blackberries.

A man in the room next to Papa's committed suicide.

Monday, 7 September

I got some information from Mme Rhey. It was a Frenchman by the name of Metzger. Arrested with his wife and daughter because they had not left La Baule. His wife and daughter had been deported. He stayed at Drancy (aged sixty-three), tortured himself with remorse and slashed his carotid artery.

This morning we saw a very young woman whose father was deported six months ago and her mother one month ago, and whose seven-month-old baby has just died. She has refused to work for the Germans, even though this might result in her mother being freed. I admired her, and yet, at times, I almost doubt the value of moral principles, since everybody defaces them or responds to them by killing.

———

I had arranged to meet Jean Morawiecki at the library at 3.00. The place was packed. He was sitting at the back, opposite Mondoloni. It seemed to me that I was emerging from a different world. Saw André Boutelleau, Eileen Griffin, Jenny. We left together to go to rue de l'Odéon, then to Klincksieck's bookshop, then to Budé's bookshop; and when we came back here, we had tea with Denise listening to Schumann's concerto and the Mozart symphony. But time goes by too fast. I leaned over the balcony; these last two days we've had wonderful autumn weather. The sky is so gently luminous that it fills you with longing. I wanted to grasp the ungraspable. Everything is so unreal and we speak so little of the real thing that at times I believe there is nothing.

I walked him back to the métro. But there was something not right today, not as right as on Tuesday, I can't explain it.

M. Olléon called.

Tuesday, 8 September

I had an attack of doubt and fear, but I felt better after calling in at Nicole's. And quite well again on leaving Josette's, where I fell back into the old Sorbonne atmosphere with her and one of her friends, Madeleine Boudot-Lamotte, who works at Gallimard and who also knows Chardonne and André Boutelleau. Josette always perks me up in any case.

I finished *Daphne Adeane*. This book made me feel strangely awkward, because I'm afraid of finding my own story in it. I *take books too seriously*. All the same it is a fine book but insufficiently worked out.

Wednesday, 9 September

When I came home from my day at Clamart, Denise opened the door with the announcement of the birth of Yves. I didn't *take in* the news. I can't truly see the fact that there is another little fellow in the world, a son of Yvonne. It's all happening so far away from us. I can't imagine.

Thursday, 10 September

I remember the birth of Maxime at Blois. I wept when I saw him at the age of fifteen minutes. If I looked in my diary I could find the page. That was two years ago already, it's unbelievable.

I've not got the time to think about that. I'm not thinking any more; there are days and nights with dreams that are only a continuation of reality.

I'm not even keeping this diary any more, I've no willpower left, I'm just putting down the salient facts so as to remember them.

As for young Pironneau, Maman has got the details of his execution. It was on the day of the great parade, he was taken off at

7.00 a.m., with another man, in the prison van, with their coffins. There was nobody there to shoot them; they had to wait until 3.00 in the afternoon for a "volunteer" to come and shoot them, obliging one of them to witness the other's death.

———

Friday, 11 September, morning

I dreamed of Yvonne last night, and on getting up I felt as if I had really seen her and suddenly spent a whole day with her. Now she has gone, but the feeling remains.

I wasn't expecting any post, reason told me that it was not possible. And yet when the bell rang a wild flame of joy surged up inside me. I thought: "No, I am not hoping", and yet I hoped. I thought: "I must remember that I was not hoping", and yet behind that there was a ray of hope. And everything lit up when I saw the envelope.

It's the letter he wrote last Saturday and which he didn't want to send because it was too long.

On reading it I am borne up as if by wings; all my faculties of feeling and loving are multiplied by ten.

After that, it leaves a very gentle sensation which is simultaneously an exaltation, which convinces me again that I am different, that I do not want to come back down to earth, as if something unknown were on fire inside me.

And then I drop back, as I have done all week, into doubt and mistrust of myself.

———

I spent the whole afternoon wandering around (boulevard Saint-Germain, to the Sorbonne, to Cité Condorcet) and then went to synagogue for Rosh Hashanah. The service was held in the oratory and the community hall, since the synagogue itself has been destroyed by Doriotistes.[12] It was depressing. Not a single young person. Only old folk; the only representative of our "old times" was Mme Baur.

Saturday, 12 September

Nicole and I went to Aubergenville with Jean-Paul and Jean Morawiecki. As we were about to leave, my joy was almost spoiled by Maman's worrying.

We stood all the way on the train. The weather was marvellous. If we had gone for a walk straight away, we would have seen the mist rising from the earth.

We had a walk after lunch (a lunch with foie gras, Chartreuse and American cigarettes).

There was a magnificent storm, and I was soaked before I got back to the house.

I can no longer write this diary because I no longer belong entirely to myself. So I am simply noting external facts, just to remind myself.

Sunday, 13 September

Went to Saint-Cucufa with thirty-five children, it was a hot and tiring day. Laure wasn't there.

12 The Synagogue de la Victoire (1874; restored 1967), the largest and grandest in Paris, was damaged by a bomb in 1941, then ransacked and desecrated in 1942; the congregation attending Rosh Hashanah service in 1943 was rounded up and interned.

Jean-Paul kept his word and we were stunned to see him emerge into our clearing around 4.00.

Monday, 14 September

The most beautiful things that happen are those I don't foresee. All my life I will remember this afternoon that was so rich and full. I went with him to rue Saint-Séverin, then we sauntered along the quais and sat in the little garden behind Notre-Dame. There was infinite peace.

But we were shooed away by a park attendant because of my star. As he was with me I didn't take the insult in, and we carried on wandering on the quais.

The looming storm broke in the end. And it is the storm I will remember, the sound of the downpour splattering over the steps of the Tuileries, the dark sky and the pink lightning. I could have stayed like that for centuries.

Tuesday, 15 September

Tante Ger has broken her leg. I heard about it when I arrived at rue Raynouard; we waited for Dr Redon. She left this evening for rue de la Chaise.

Wednesday, 16 September

A day out at Robinson with Cassowary, without Nicole S.

Lots of gymnastics.

José, one of the girls who comes with us, was afraid of being arrested, because there's talk of arresting Belgians.

Nor were we very sure of having the right to cross into Seine-et-Oise since the arrests that occurred the other day.

Papa had written a desperate letter. He's talking about never seeing us again. Maman had spoken to him about Jean Morawiecki. He raises no objection, but he's behaving as if it were all over and far away.

Thursday, 17 September
Rue de la Bienfaisance.
Revised some German, music practice with Job and Breynaert.
Got Jean Morawiecki's docket.

Friday, 18 September
When I got back from rue de la Bienfaisance this morning (Roger was here), Maman had been crying. Papa has sent a *pneu* this morning saying: "Negotiations must conclude urgent. The Elyane Hébert[13] are beginning to leave". I had vague apprehensions all morning; people were saying they were wrong to stay at Drancy, they would be taken to fill the quotas in the convoys of deportees.

Belgians and Dutch have been picked up – José? I think it's all going to begin again just as it did in June.

A man called Dr Charles Meyer was arrested because he was wearing his star too high up . . . One of the ladies at the U.G.I.F. exclaimed: "That really proves their bad faith!!!" How can you believe they'll respect the laws they have set up when those laws are illegal from start to finish, a mere product of their whims; those laws are nothing more than a pretext for making arrests, that's their only aim, not to legislate or regulate anything at all.

13 Coded phrase for "French Jews".

Sunday, 20 September

Never have I had any sense of foreboding until now. All this week it has hovered over me. Yesterday I understood why. Yesterday morning there was a lot of excitement at rue de la Bienfaisance. There was a lot to do. I was set to leave at 11.30 to fetch the letter from avenue de la R. When I mentioned Papa's *pneu,* the ladies all said: "Yes, we know (that they're starting to deport Frenchmen from Drancy)." There was nothing but urgent requests for certificates or warm clothing. At 11.45 I was still there. M. Katz arrived. I had something to ask him. He was talking to his wife. He turned round and said: "Warn all the people who have loved ones at Pithiviers to be here by 10.00 tomorrow with warm clothing etc." I understood, with horror, that that meant "mass deportation from Pithiviers".

This morning as I left, the concierge told me that as a consequence of an "outrage" the entire population was to be punished and would only be allowed on the streets from 3.00 p.m. until dusk, 116 hostages have been shot, and there will be "mass deportations".

So that was what it was.

6.00 p.m.

I find myself wishing that this day would be over and that time would move on; suddenly I realize that there is *nothing* to hope for and everything to fear in the days to come and beyond.

At times my awareness of imminent misfortune is muted. At all other times it is acute.

M. R. described to Denise what goes on prior to a deportation. Everyone is shaved, they are parked behind barbed wire, and then they are piled into cattle wagons without any straw, and the doors are sealed.

Everything is being got ready and everything is waiting, as for the last act of a play. Pierre Masse was transferred from the Santé prison to Drancy on Friday. Apparently he said he knew what that meant. So they are all brought together and prepared for this horrible thing, for this event that will be felt as a worrying silence, a distant exile and uninterrupted suffering from the moment it occurs.

A strange day. Everyone is staying indoors. In the maids' rooms up at the top of the building, people are looking out of the windows. There's a strong wind sweeping clouds across a blue sky.

A lady called during lunch. She had come out of Drancy yesterday, and she came to give news of M. Lévy, who is unstinting in his devotion to others. He took care of the children in the camp and took them for walks. The camp has to be emptied by Wednesday. What are they going to fill it with now?

In eight days this woman who ate nothing and slept on straw has seen horrible things. Convoys leaving, two girls who had been arrested at the same time as she been were deported last Wednesday wearing summer frocks and canvas shoes.

This morning I set off at 9.30 to collect Françoise Pineau on our way to Mme Cohn's to get the letter. We walked by way of rue de Sèvres.

I came back up here and then went down to post a card from Maman to Jacques. At the post office I met Denise. I saw she had been crying because she had read Papa's note (the letter from Mme R.). M. Geissman said that *everyone* would go.

I couldn't really make out Papa's note because Maman was sobbing so hard that it stopped me concentrating. For the time being I can't cry. But if misfortune does come, I shall be sorrowful enough, sorrowful for all time.

It was an adieu, it rips us apart from all that had made our lives happy.

Yesterday morning as I got up I noticed that I had never felt so fit, I was surprised at the sensation.

But everything changed suddenly. It could only have been an illusion. Jean Morawiecki was due to come in the afternoon – an inexpressible weight of oppression bore down on that afternoon. But I would have blamed myself for feeling happy. The minutes passed, I could see them flying. M. Olléon came and stayed for three-quarters of an hour. In addition there was a kind of barrier between us which didn't even lift when we had tea for two at the table with the blue cloth. There was no escape. But that is of no importance, I have no right to be happy.

———

Tomorrow is Yom Kippur. Today we are so empty it's as if we had fasted.

Monday, 21 September, 11.00 p.m.
Papa is coming home tomorrow at noon.

At 9.00 this evening M. and Mme Duchemin came round. I went into the drawing room, they kissed me and said: "It's for noon tomorrow."

I was so sunk in the slough of despondency, so haunted by the thought of what was going to happen during the night of Tuesday to Wednesday, of the horrifying wait those people were experiencing, that I felt not a spark of joy. I thought only of the others. I felt an injustice was being done. Which I could never call joy.

Tuesday, 22 September, morning
During the night, probably, I became accustomed to the idea. Now I am thinking of all that Papa's return home means, what it must mean to Maman, what will he say when he finds out? He still knew nothing last night, he must have spent yet more hours in anguish and final despair.

When I came in at 6.00 yesterday evening, I too was in despair. I had no more feelings, only a featureless memory of these two dark days. I didn't fast. I had made up my mind to fast, but when I was washing God knows what impulse made me abandon the plan, and to go instead to help at rue de la Bienfaisance, I made up my mind in a flash. I can't remember what my state of mind was at the time, but I know I almost wept several times in the métro at the thought of all this misery. We worked all day as if the Last Judgement had *already* happened; we could feel that something irrevocable had been done. Mme Schwartz was there; she was fasting, as were Mme Katz and Mme Horwilleur. Apart

from that, the building was empty and miserable; I returned home
by métro at noon with Mme Horwilleur. Maman was at home,
and that's when I heard about M. Duchemin's very noble last
gesture. Mme Lévy was lunching with us.

Tuesday, 22 September, evening
Papa is here, at home. It'll soon be six hours since he arrived, and
he'll be sleeping here tonight. We're going to spend the evening
with him. He's here, he's walking up and down in the drawing
room, with a distracted look on his face. But he's so little changed
in his body that it is a great comfort just to see him.

When he arrived, it seemed that two fragments of life had
suddenly slotted back into each other exactly, and that all the
rest didn't exist. God be praised, this impression didn't last very
long, because it gave me a strangely distasteful feeling, because I
do not want to forget. It didn't last because I know what Papa
has seen, because I am in the thick of others' suffering, because
nobody can forget what has happened and what is going to happen
tonight and tomorrow.

———

Mme Jean Bloch was just here: we didn't want to tell her, her
husband and M. Basch and the three hundred who were not let
out of Pithiviers on Sunday arrived at Drancy this morning and
will leave on tomorrow's convoy; they were in the barbed-wire
compound this morning. She's going to go mad. She speaks in a
mechanical, monotone voice. I know from experience (I'm writing
it down here, nobody will see this) what state her nerves are in,
only hers will get worse, to the point of madness. When she speaks
you can feel irremediable, infinite, unnameable, inconsolable

misery. I reckon that for her we are no longer among the living; we are just ghosts in her world, an immense barrier shuts us off from her. When she left, I could see that she was taking her burden of freezing gloom and pain with her, in such despair that not a glimmer, not a shard of struggle remained.

———

Going over the day's events I remain completely lucid and awake; in my dreams I have often told myself I was awake. And yet I have awakened from those dreams. It's the same thing. As late as this morning I still had my true normal consciousness, when I rushed first to the Francks', then to K.'s to get woollens for Mme Cahen's nephews, who will perhaps leave tomorrow, then took them to rue de Chaumont, and then back to the U.G.I.F. to work. But since Papa has been back, with all these visits, from M. Maire, Duchemin, L., Chevry, Frossard, Nicole, Job, and my errands for the U.G.I.F., all that remains is this abnormal hyperawareness.

———

When I came in I found tea roses from Jean [Morawiecki]. In my mind he became Jean when I received the flowers. My first thought was: How did he know? Then I reckoned that he did not know. And that these flowers were a shared thought. And I was touched to the very core of my being. Each time I think of them, I am overcome with sweetness, it's the only sweet thing there is in this atmosphere. And the strange thing is that I enjoy this sweetness without reservation, because it does not seem to me to be illegal, it doesn't betray everything that is tragic in this day.

———

Wednesday, 23 September, evening

We are all obsessed by this morning's departure. Basch and Jean Bloch have left, it's all over.

There is something even more horrible about this deportation than the first one; it's the end of the world. How many gaps there are around us now!

I nearly lost my equilibrium today, I thought I was sinking, reaching the point where I could no longer control myself; I'm beginning to recognize that feeling. But this is not the time to let myself go. It came over me on my way back from André Baur's, where we had taken Papa. He is very pessimistic. Then I went to see Mme Favart and to the PoW Centre. When I got back, I found a man sent to me by Decourt and who nearly drove me mad; he forced me to discuss the future, but I was not in a normal state of mind. Everything he spoke about, all the questions he asked seemed to come from another world to which I would never return. There's a kind of bell that tolls inside me whenever I hear talk of books and Sorbonne professors.

———

Also, I've been trying all day to read Jean Morawiecki's letter as in a dream in which the letter you're reading slips forever out of your grasp. I still haven't taken it all in.

———

This evening in the kitchen we were making a cake for Yvonne. Such a short time ago it was for Papa. Papa who is here. Life has stayed so much the same since *before* his arrest that I can't believe it lasted three months.

I am too tired to write this evening.

I am stopping.

Thursday, 24 September

Finally reached the goal which seemed to recede even further. We met at the Department. The nightmare is gone, and I could not recover the atmosphere of these last days.

We came back and had tea with Job and Denise in our bedroom. Visitors obliged us to retreat there.

Saturday, 26 September

He came to collect me from home. We listened to a record, had tea and went for a walk in avenue Henri-Martin. It was already cold.

Sunday, 27 September

To La Varenne with the Cub Scouts. It was a grey day and rained the whole time.

Monday, 28 September

Simon came for tea. We played music together.

Tuesday, 29 September

Madeleine Blaess and Josette.

Wednesday, 30 September

Mme Jourdan.

Tea at Nicole's with the Jobs. They sang *Véronique*.[14]

---

14 A comic opera by André Messager.

Thursday, 1 October

We walked for two hours; we began talking in rue Guynemer and didn't stop until the Alma métro stop. From Les Invalides I talked as if in a dream. I saw nobody in the streets, though they were crowded.

Friday, 2 October

Went to Dr Redon to have a whitlow lanced.

Job here. I didn't practise violin and pottered the entire afternoon getting ready for tomorrow's walk round Paris.

Saturday, 3 October

Nicole and I each had four children to walk round Paris between 9.00 and 11.00. My route was from Palais-Royal to rue Claude-Bernard. I showed them the Louvre from all sides. I got quite excited about it. From pont des Arts I watched the sun break through the grey mist, like a promise of joy.

The afternoon, on the premises, was quite long. I left before the end to hear Jean Vigué, but he had already gone.

Sunday, 4 October

Marvellous.

I spent the morning writing my letter.

In the afternoon after an obscure meeting at rue Vauquelin I came back up here with Nicole. We listened to the quartet, and I flicked through my Stefan George. I walked Nicole home; she was scarcely less excited than I was.

Monday, 5 October

I've resumed my old job as librarian. I didn't think I ever would. It gave me back my equilibrium.

As I did three months ago, I began to hope that Jean Morawiecki would come in. I couldn't remember what had happened between us. When it did come back to my mind I felt triumphant in a way. As 3.00 came and went, I began to feel afraid, and very disappointed. But at 3.45 he came in, and joy and calm swept over me. I looked at all the other readers to see if they knew. But nobody knows, and that's what's marvellous.

Afterwards I walked him back to Gare Saint-Lazare by way of the Grands Boulevards. It was becoming dark and the streets were packed with people. We were swathed in mist. To the west there was a livid yellow glow in the sky. A strange memory: crowded boulevards and a sky so low and grey.

He gave me a recording of Schumann's *Frauenliebe und Leben*.

Tuesday, 6 October

Went to see Delattre at 3.00.

He advised me not to do anything, and since the interview I am starting to understand that he let me down.

Afterwards, to the Léautés with Nicole and Job. Job had forgotten his score. Instead of music, we played ping-pong.

In the evening I prepared a batch of "cat heads" for Denise. I organized a secret tea party for her birthday. Invited the Léautés. The Pineaus, Job and the Vigués.

Wednesday, 7 October

Spent the morning shopping for Denise in the neighbourhood. My heart was singing within me. Never had I been so happy at the thought of seeing him again, I had the same feelings I had before, almost as if it was "the night before the ball". But on top of that was distilled and inexpressible joy.

When I'd made all the arrangements here, I left for the Sorbonne. Coming up the steps from the métro I turned and saw him. We went together to rue de l'Odéon, then to the Comité du Livre, where I felt all hot and bothered.

Job was already here when we came home.

When Denise came in, all of us except Annick hid behind the curtains and the furniture, then we all came out together, saying: "Happy birthday".

Thursday, 8 October
Rue Raynouard, then Simone for tea. I was waiting for tomorrow.

Friday, 9 October
We had arranged to meet at the Palais-Royal métro station. I was much too early.

We went to Dalloz to buy books, then we walked to Gare Montparnasse and home. I was tired from walking. At home he asked to listen to Schumann *Lieder*. But the music had no effect. He wasn't listening.

Saturday, 10 October
I was all at sea today; I didn't go to rue de la Bienfaisance in the morning, that felt like sacrilege. I just pottered all morning long. In the afternoon Job came to play a trio with us.

Sunday, 11 October

A meeting at rue Lamblardie. Berthe, Nicole and I are going to found a new Wolf Cub pack. But we left the children at noon, and the poor little things were really upset.

The sun was shining as we left the orphanage; suddenly I had an idea that filled me with pleasure: I would phone him and say I was free that afternoon.

But thought soon quashed my joy. As I neared home, it started to rain. I fell into a kind of lethargy for no reason I could think of. I smoked two cigarettes, practised the Beethoven concerto, then went to rue Raynouard, where I froze in Nicole S.'s bedroom despite the memories it brought back.

Thursday, 15 October

I can't see how to summarize the beginning of this week. I didn't notice the days passing by. It was one long wait after another. On Sunday evening I thought I still had two more days to wait. We were supposed to go to Aubergenville on Wednesday. Together, alone. Maman didn't object, to the point where I wondered if she had really understood.

But on Monday afternoon, when my role as librarian suddenly felt burdensome, boring and long, in he came. He wasn't supposed to, as he was sitting his law exam the next day. I was overcome with joy. For a long while we couldn't speak. In an instant, while I was in the library, he came silently up the stairs. Then he sat down in front of my desk. Then he came to help me tidy the books at closing time. Never has the library closed so late. I had lost all notion of time in the poorly lit stacks.

When I arrived at home, Louise told me that M. Lévy had

been released. For the first time I had a few moments of total and unalloyed joy.

On Tuesday I went to fetch him when his exam ended; I sat in the Department courtyard for an hour, whiling away the time. The courtyard felt lonesome and sad. Fortunately around 5.00 I came across a classmate. That cheered me up. I met him in rue de l'Odéon. He had been whiling away the time just like me! We went for a walk under a setting sun that cast a golden light over old Paris. It was a very fine October evening. We leaned on the parapet of the quai near pont des Arts. Everything was shimmering, the poplar leaves, even the air. When I walked home alone, cours La Reine was dark, night had already settled over it though the sky was still completely pink.

Tuesday night to Wednesday morning was interminable.

Wednesday was marvellous. This evening, though, I'm not myself; this morning I was still newly born, and I hoped I would stay that way. But I've become the old Hélène once more. Absence is a curse.

Thursday

When I awoke, reality was still as beautiful as it was yesterday. The whole morning was strange and marvellous, I couldn't bear to stay at the U.G.I.F. At 11.30 I dashed out as if the devil was on my tail and rushed back here to write.

Afternoon, went to the library to see Cazamian, proposed doing a thesis on Keats.

Friday, 16 October

Nicole S. came with me to buy shoes and a shawl, then visited rue Raynouard.

Saturday, 17 October

Jean Morawiecki came round towards 3.30. We had tea with Maman and Papa and Job; it was mildly irritating. He came into this room afterwards, then I walked him back to the métro.

Sunday, 18 October

Meeting at rue Vauquelin with Berthe and the others, by the end I was finding it profoundly boring.

   In the afternoon we played music with Job at the S.'s place. The twins were there too.

Monday, 19 October

The library was glum and cold. A feeling of loneliness. He didn't come, and that gave me a foretaste of what it will be like when he is no longer here [in Paris]. I had a brief visit from André Boutelleau; Nicole S. and Jean-Paul also came by. I returned home feeling empty and worn out, nearly fell asleep before dinner.

Tuesday, 20 October

I had a rendezvous with Jean at the Faculté de Droit to see his exam results posted. But he had got the day wrong. He was cross about it, and there was something else on his mind which spoiled the day. We went down to the Seine near pont des Arts, where two men were fishing. Afterwards I went with him to his tailor in avenue de l'Opéra, and then to the railway station. I was suddenly afraid of losing him in the station crowds. Then he took my arm. I couldn't explain why I was so grateful for that small gesture.

Wednesday, 21 October

He rang to tell me his results while I was at rue Raynouard, I rang back after dinner.

Thursday, 22 October

A quite maddening tea. Simon, the Lévys, Mme Roger Lévy, the Biéder girl, the Rehs were all there at the same time, I was in a complete whirl.

Friday, 23 October

Woog and Day for tea, an English tea party, with the last pot of Dundee marmalade. It was really nice.

Saturday, 24 October

In the morning I dashed from the Sorbonne to rue de Téhéran, where I waited for Nicole and then Berthe.

At 3.00 I went to meet Jean Morawiecki at the station. Something was wrong. Was it the low grey sky? Was it me? Was it the dreary moodiness that often weighs me down and turns me inwards? Was it disappointment at not being able to see him alone because Job was there? We played some music together, but it seemed like I hadn't seen him, and that we were a thousand kilometres apart. I had a good cry before dinner.

Sunday, 25 October

An aborted outing with the little ones. Rue Vauquelin. I hadn't expected to have other things to do in the afternoon. When I left them at noon, I was sure the day would end badly. Rechtmann was loitering in the corridors after the morning's scene.

I came back feeling very low. The Ponceys were here having lunch.

Monday, 26 October
Library. I knew he wouldn't come and yet I was hoping. The hope came from heaven, because he did come, in fact at 4.30. Everything was illuminated; as there was another librarian on duty, I left at 5.00. He was due to take his oral exam in the morning. We walked through the rain to rue de Rennes, and then walked back to the métro station at Les Invalides; night was falling, I was thinking about the next day, we arranged to meet at the Faculté de Droit.

Tuesday, 27 October
I was wrong to get too excited, because I felt sorry for him, he failed the oral. Yet he wasn't expecting to fail. When I arrived at the school at 10.30, he told me to return in three quarters of an hour. I went to get my I.D. renewed and then went back. We waited for the results; I couldn't believe it, I don't want to think about it. Because I can feel his pain when I think of him coming out of the examination room.

We walked back in silence, in the rain, holding hands, that was all I could do for him. At 1.00 the rain-drenched streets were empty. Paris was ours.

And despite our sorrow that silent walk in the rain is a marvellous memory.

All day long I hung about waiting for tomorrow. I didn't want to do anything that would take me away from him. I went to the hairdresser's, I went to see Grandma, and at the end of the day I went with Denise to Josette's.

Wednesday, 28 October
From the Sorbonne we came back here, to this room. We listened to the Schumann recordings, just as I wanted to.

Thursday, 29 October
And suddenly it all fell apart. He talks so much about leaving[15] that I have become afraid. As long as I was with him, because he believed in it, I believed as well. He said: "This is perhaps the last time we will see each other." And although I was certain that once I was alone I would no longer understand, I believed. It was pouring with rain, and we spent an hour in a corridor at the Sorbonne. He was in a bad mood and hardly said a thing. We parted in the métro, at Ségur. I came home and did a jigsaw puzzle with Simon.

Thursday, 5 November
I waited for a telephone call all weekend. From Saturday night on, I stopped fearing it. But I was in a dreadful mood.

We were supposed to meet again on Tuesday, if everything remained normal.

All the same, on Monday, All Saints' Day, I went to the library.

15 Jean Morawiecki was planning to escape so as to join the Free French.

Nobody came. That was lamentable. Icy cold. Darkness fell, and he did not come.

Tuesday came. In the morning I got a letter, the one I had been waiting for for days, and it was the waiting that was largely responsible for my bad mood; it was short, and if I hadn't also seen him that afternoon, there would have been room for deception.

On Wednesday I wrote a letter.

Thursday

Went to rue de la Banque.

Thursday and Friday, I was tormented by the story of the telephone call that Andrée hadn't understood.

Sunday, 8 November

A strange day, I don't understand it at all.

Yesterday was marvellous. Even the thought of his departure, confirmed for Thursday, could not darken yesterday. I went to meet him at the station, and we came back here along the Champs-Elysées. I wore my fur coat for the first time.

Job came around 5.00, he'd had too much to drink and was very funny. Last night I dreamt of Jean Morawiecki the entire time. In the end the idea of him leaving woke me up.

I left for rue Vauquelin in radiant weather under a fragile, golden sun, a deep-blue sky, and in an atmosphere as clear as crystal. As I write, the sun is boiling hot, adding to the strangeness of the day.

The other thing that makes things odd is the news. Everyone seems to be bubbling over with excitement. Maman and Papa are very agitated. I *should* be, but I can't seem to manage it. My lack of enthusiasm does not come from excessive scepticism but rather from an inability to adjust to this sudden burst of news. I haven't adjusted to it yet. All the same it is perhaps the beginning of the end.

Monday, 9 November

The library was about to shut when Jean appeared, it was like a dream. I had so much wanted it to happen that I had given up waiting; as in a dream we walked through the dusk via place du Carrousel and avenue de l'Opéra to the Gare Saint-Lazare. The Louvre was like a great dark vessel against the pale sky. We are going to see each other three days in a row.

Tuesday, 10 November

The parents have gone to Aubergenville. Denise stayed behind. At 2.35 I met him at the station. We walked back here by way of cours La Reine. It was a fine day but cold, our last time alone together. Tomorrow we are going to Molinié's.

He brought Beethoven's D-major concerto and the "Sinfonia Concertante". We had tea on my bed.

Wednesday, 11 November

In the end he didn't leave. Events made that inevitable. He told us when Molinié, Geneviève Loch and I met up with him at Gare du Nord.

A very cosy day at Molinié's at Enghien, listened to Bach.

Thursday, 12 November
First day of classes at the Sorbonne.

Cazamian, 11.00, room 1, suffocating; I was drowned in sweat and stunned to be back after so many *external* and *internal* events.

Delattre at 2.00. The lecture theatre was full.

Saturday, 14 November
We were supposed to go to a concert at the Madeleine together. At the last minute Papa said no. I still went to the station to meet him at 2.25. We came back here after a long walk. Listened to the Concerto in D. Job was here, tea in the drawing room; afterwards we moved to the study.

Sunday, 15 November
Rue Vauquelin this morning.

Job and Annick Boutteville.

Monday, 16 November
Library.

Tuesday, 17 November
Three o'clock, Mme Jourdan, the lesson lasted an hour and a half. We sight-read Bach's first sonata and a part of Quartet No. 13.

Wednesday, 18 November
Rue de la Bienfaisance in the morning.

Afternoon at Saint-Cloud. I was terribly excited about going there. At 1.30 he phoned to say that the train was early. M. Lévy came up to tell me, and I laughed.

There were Nicole, Denise, Molinié, Savarit and Jacques Besse and Max Gaetti (two composers).

He's leaving on Monday. He said so in front of everyone; I felt overcome by panic.

Thursday, 20 November

Went to the Sorbonne for nothing. Cazamian didn't lecture. At 3.00 I went to meet Jean Morawiecki at the station. We went to his tailor. It was already past 4.00 when we got back on the métro at Saint-Augustin.

That was the penultimate time.

He brought the Quartet No. 15.

He agreed to come for lunch on Saturday.

Friday, 21 November

Dashed to rue de Buzenval, then to Galignani's to buy a book for Jean.

Was at rue de la Tour. They are practising the Ravel trio.

Saturday, 22 November

The last day.

The morning went like the wind; I'd gone to rue de Téhéran to see M. Katz about Cécile Lehmann and to take him a parcel. Came back here and began to write the letter I'll give to Jean this evening. I didn't believe what I was writing because I knew he would soon be here. At noon I still wasn't properly dressed.

And the rest of it passed like a dream. Parents had prepared a magnificent meal and gave him a magnificent reception. After-wards we listened to some records. He left for a short while to go to rue Montessuy, he'd misread the time. I thought it was 2.45, but it was 4.00; an hour of our time had been stolen. And when Jean-Paul and Nicole burst into the room, Louise having opened the door, it all ended abruptly, because I'd invited lots of people for after – the Pineaus, Françoise, the Digeons, Jean Rogès, Job – "after" the end. I was reckless (because of the curfew) and walked him back to the métro. The guests were still here when I got back. That stopped me from thinking.

Sunday, 23 November
Rue Vauquelin in the morning.
  Job and Breynaert.

Monday, 24 November
Library.
  Saw Savarit.
  Françoise de Brunhoff.

Tuesday, 25 November
Pot-black Tuesday, stayed home all afternoon wrestling with John Middleton Murray, lost.

Wednesday, 26 November
Letter from Jean. He only left this morning. He could have seen me on Monday.
  When I got back from the U.G.I.F., I found a magnificent bouquet of carnations from him. They came from our shop in rue Saint-Augustin. The sun was shining. I was overwhelmed with pleasure, and yesterday seemed like a nightmare.
  Went to the Sorbonne to register.

Thursday, 27 November
Dropped in on Nicole.

Simon for lunch. He stayed until 5.30; when I came back from Mme Jourdan's, he was still here.

Friday, 27 November
When I came back from Nadine Destouches, I found a postcard Jean had written on the train on Wednesday.

Saturday, 28 November
Afternoon at the Sorbonne library, to transcribe an article for Jacques. Came back on my own, did a bit of work.

1943

Wednesday, 25 August, 1943

Ten months ago I stopped writing this diary; this evening I have taken it out of my drawer to have Maman put it in a safe place. Once again I've been told that I should not be at home at the weekend.

Almost a year has passed, but Drancy, deportations and suffering continue. Many things have happened: Denise has married; Jean left for Spain without my being able to see him again; all my friends at the office were arrested, and it was only by an amazing chance that I wasn't there that day; Nicole S. is engaged to Jean-Paul; Odile has come; a year already! The reasons for hope are enormous. But I have become very serious, and I cannot forget the suffering. What will have happened when I resume this diary again?

Sunday, 10 October

I am resuming this diary tonight, after a year's interruption. Why?

Today, on my way home from Georges and Robert's apartment, I was abruptly assailed by the feeling that I had to describe reality. Just the walk back from rue Margueritte was a whole world of facts and thoughts, images and reflections. Enough for a book. And suddenly I understood how banal a book is, basically. I mean: what else is there in a book but reality? What people need in order to write is an observant spirit and a broad mind. Otherwise everyone could write books; I recall, or rather, I looked up this evening a quotation from the beginning of Keats's *Fall of Hyperion*:

> Since every man whose soul is not a clod
> Hath visions, and would speak, if he had loved
> And been well nurtured in his mother tongue

Yet there are a thousand reasons stopping me from writing and which tear me apart even now, and will trip me up again tomorrow and thereafter.

First, a kind of laziness that will be hard to overcome. Writing, writing the way I want to – that's to say with complete sincerity and never thinking that others will read me, so as not to affect my attitude – to write all the reality and the tragic things we are living through, giving them all their naked gravity without letting words distort them, is a very difficult task and requires constant effort.

Then there is the considerable repugnance I feel at thinking of myself as "someone who writes", because for me, perhaps mistakenly, writing implies a split personality, probably a loss of spontaneity and abdication (but maybe these are prejudices).

And then there is pride. I do not want any part of it. The idea that you can write for other people, so as to be praised by them, horrifies me.

Maybe there is also the feeling that "other people" won't understand you completely, that they make you dirty and mutilate you, and that you let yourself be cheapened like mere merchandise.

Uselessness?

At times too the sense of the uselessness of it all paralyzes me. Sometimes I have doubts and tell myself that this feeling of uselessness is just a form of inertia and laziness, because set against it is a significant reason which, if I convince myself that it is valid, will prove decisive: I have a duty to write because other people must know. Every hour of every day there is another painful realization that *other folk* do not know, do not even imagine, the suffering of other men, the evil that some of them inflict. And I am still trying to make the painful effort to *tell the story*. Because it is a duty, it is maybe the only one I can fulfil. There are men who know and who close their eyes, and I'll never manage to convince people of that kind, because they are hard and selfish, and I have no authority. But people who do not know and who might have sufficient heart to understand – on those people I must have an effect.

For how will humanity ever be healed unless all its rottenness is exposed? How will the world be cleansed unless it is made to understand the full extent of the evil it is doing? Everything comes down to understanding. That truth fills me with anguish and torment. War will not avenge the suffering: blood calls for blood, men dig their heels into their own wickedness and blindness. If only you could manage to make bad men *understand* the evil they are doing, if only you could give them that total and impartial vision which ought to be the glory of humankind! I've argued with people too often about this, with my parents, who certainly have more experience than I do. Only Françoise [Bernheim] shared my opinion. Just thinking of Françoise makes my heart burst with sorrow. When I came home this evening I was thinking about her and about how well we got on. When I was with her I felt alive, and a world of marvellous possibilities lay before me just when she was torn from me. It has always been like that: people who seemed a whole world, the only world in which I might have developed, have been taken before I could enjoy them. Afterwards I blamed myself; I reckoned it may have been because I wasn't truly able to know the people around me, and that I wished they had remained only once they had gone. Since this last sorrow, I have turned more to my parents; I talk to them more, and I think that a fine prospect lies ahead in that direction too. This evening, in the stairwell, when I had just come in, I heard the sound of a piano; I thought it was the lady on the ground floor playing. But the sound grew louder as I climbed the stairs. On the second floor it occurred to me that it was Maman playing, perhaps with Tante Ger. I smiled. And when I reached our landing and was certain it was Maman, I felt my smile turning, involuntarily, into a stupid grin. If Maman had seen me, she would have called it "beaming over" like she did when I was a little girl and got myself into a glorious mess with Jacques. I was suffused with utter, pure, unexpected joy on seeing that Maman had gone back to playing the piano, for me, in order to play with me, and to wake this house from its silence. For a second I felt sorry for her because it struck me that she had wanted it to be a surprise and that if I rang the bell she would know I had heard her already. I don't like spoiling other people's pleasures. But that kind of pity is no good. I don't want to feel sorry for Maman. Anyway, it wasn't regret but affection, and a billowing wave of pleasure made me ring the bell firmly and loudly, greet Maman and sweep aside everything that was not my own pleasure.

But none of that stops me from missing Françoise and Jean a great deal.

I'm getting carried away, that's not what I wanted to say.

So I must write to show people later on what these times are like. I know that many others will have more important lessons to teach, and more terrible facts to reveal. I am thinking of all the deportees, all those in prison, all those who set off on the great adventure of escape. But that should not make me a coward; each of us in our own small sphere can do something. And we can, we *must*.

Only I don't have the time to write a book. I haven't got the time and I haven't got the necessary peace of mind. Nor do I probably have sufficient distance. All I can do is note down the facts, which will help me remember if one day I want to tell or write about it.

In addition, in the hour that I've been writing this, I realized what a relief it is, and I am determined to put down on these pages everything in my head and in my heart. Now I am going to stop so I can spend the rest of the evening with Maman.

Sunday, 10 October, 9.00 p.m.
Outing. Cubs and women with stars. Jean O., Edmond B., Thibault.

Monday, 11 October, morning
A sharp ring on the bell at 7.00 a.m. I assumed (correctly) it was a *pneu* from Mme M. Hélène brought it up and put on the lights to give it to me. She hadn't been able to get in touch with Anna, but her letter contained something else, a bit of news that unleashed such an insistent flood of thoughts that I have to write to calm myself: Mme Löb's husband and daughter have been arrested in the south of France. She had thought them safe, and it had been so hard for her to part with her daughter. Now she is looking on powerlessly as they are tortured.

Once again I sank beneath those familiar waves of bitterness. I lay in bed for nearly an hour going over the same dreadful questions again and again. I thought about Jacques, Yvonne, Daniel, Denise, and also about Papa, because I fear for Papa too, and I broke out in a cold sweat.

Why? It's all so pointless: what use is it to arrest women and children? Isn't it a monstrous stupidity for a country at war to have to do that sort of thing? But everyone has such scales before their eyes that they cannot even see the simple point of asking such a question. It's a frightful machine; now all we can see are its results. On one side, a rational, organized, considered evil (I'd like to know whether B. has become a fanatic, or if he is coldly self-aware), and on the other side, frightful suffering. No-one can see the monstrous pointlessness of it, no-one can see where it all began, the first cog in the infernal machine.

Maman's anger had turned against Mme Agache. And, through her, against the inertia of the Catholics. And she was quite right. Catholics no longer have the freedom to follow their conscience, they do what their priests tell them to do. And the latter are weak, often cowardly and unintelligent. If there had been a mass uprising of Christians against these persecutions, would it not have won the day? I am sure it would have done. But the Christians would have had to protest against the war in the first place, and they weren't able to do that. Is the Pope worthy of God's mandate on earth if he is an impotent bystander to the most flagrant violations of Christ's laws?

Do Catholics deserve the name of Christians when, if they applied Christ's teaching, religious difference, or even racial difference, would not exist?

And when they say: The difference between you and us is that we believe the Messiah has come already, and you are still waiting. But what have they done with their Messiah? They're as evil as men were before he came. They crucify Christ every day. And if Christ were to return to earth, would he not answer them with the same words as before? Who knows if his fate would not be exactly the same?

On Saturday I reread the chapter about the Grand Inquisitor in *The Brothers Karamazov*. No, Christ would no longer be wanted, because he would give men back their freedom of conscience, and that is too hard for them to bear. "Tomorrow, I will have you burned", the Grand Inquisitor tells him.

On Saturday I also read the Gospel according to St Matthew; I want to speak the whole truth here, why should I hide it? What I found in the words of Christ was no different from the rules of conscience which I have instinctively tried to obey myself. It seemed to me that Christ belongs much more to me than he does to some good Catholics I could mention. I sometimes used to think I was nearer to Christ than many Christians were, but now I can prove it.

And what's surprising about that? Should anyone ever be anything except a disciple of Christ? The whole world should be Christian, yes it should, if you have to use labels. But not Catholic, not what men have done with Christianity. From the beginning there has been only one stream. But unfortunately, wherever you turn, incomprehensible pettiness stops people seeing that. On the one hand, there were those who rejected Christ, despite his having come for everyone's sake, and those people weren't "the Jews", since at that time everyone was Jewish; they were just stupid, nasty people (nowadays you could just as well call them "Catholic"). And their descendants persevered on their narrow path and took pride in their perseverance: they became what are now called "the Jews". On the other hand, there were those who adopted Christ; at the start they were men of conviction and pure heart, but later on they made him their personal property, even though they had slipped back into being as evil as before.

So there was nothing but unity, uninterrupted flow, evolution.

As I read the Gospel I was struck by the word *convert*. We have given it a precise meaning that it did not have. The Gospels say that "ye shall be converted" – that is to say, changed and made good by listening to the word of Christ. But nowadays, conversion means going to a different church, following a different sect. Were there different sects at the time of Christ? Was there anything other than the cult of God?

How men have become petty while believing they have become clever!

Monday evening

I went to Neuilly this morning, and in the afternoon I sorted books at the library.

Mme Crémieux came to dinner. What anguish it is just to think of her! The imposition of these general measures means a whole world of suffering specific to each individual affected by them. She is very young, all alone in her flat, childless. For eighteen months already.

Tuesday

I took five youngsters – the prettiest and the nicest – to Lamarck.

If only the people who help me on and off the métro knew what these children are – children for whom a train always reminds them of the one that took them to or from the camp, children who point at a policeman in the street and say: "He's like the one who brought me back from Poitiers." "Suffer the little children to come unto me," Christ said.

At 2.15 Robert [Dreyfus] was buried at Montparnasse cemetery. It was the second burial I've been to recently. His red gown had been laid on the coffin. Julien Weill read the prayer over it. The last time I saw him was at Denise's wedding. What a muddle of joys and miseries life has become! – I say "has become" because I think that the birth of awareness at my age consists exclusively of discovering the indissoluble unity of joy and sadness. I'm thinking of Keats's "mansion of Many Apartments".

Keats is the poet, writer and human being with whom I commune the most immediately and the most completely. I am sure I would manage to understand him very well.

This morning (Wednesday) I copied out phrases from Keats which could be topics for essays, for pages into which I would pour all of myself.

Last night I almost finished *Les Thibault*. Jacques Thibault haunts me; his end is so sad and yet so inevitable. This is a beautiful book, for it possesses the beauty of reality, like Shakespeare; and it is on this topic that I would like to write about Keats's statement that "the excellence of every Art is its intensity".

Thursday, 14 October

I took the children and Anna to the Hôpital Rothschild, for her adenoid operation. I came home for lunch at 2.00 and missed

François. Went out again at 2.30 because I'd had a letter from Sparkenbroke asking to meet me at the English Department so he could give me back *Peacock Pie*.

The Sorbonne is starting up again. But this year it's harder for me to summon up the joy I used to feel at seeing students return at the end of the holiday period, during which, these last two years, all life around me has seemed to stop. I no longer belong among the studious.

I had a word with a recently promoted *agrégée* while waiting for Spark, who was with Cazamian. For a moment I fell back into the magic kingdom. But I am no longer my whole self in that kingdom. I feel as if I am betraying the new kingdom to which I belong.

Thursday, 14 October, continued
The Léautés came to tea.

Friday
German lesson.
    Hospice. Gave Simon an English lesson.

Saturday
In the morning, Hôpital Saint-Louis. Performed and observed treatment for scabies. A three-year-old girl. She cried because she wanted me to carry her. But I was repaid by the angelic smile she gave me every time I spoke to her on the métro.

The Blonds for tea, very distant; she makes you feel you are in the petit-bourgeois world of a novel by Balzac or Flaubert. Quite quaint to begin with, but it soon gets too boring.

Sunday, 17 October
Georges for lunch.

Rue Raynouard. Played music in Denise's room. Breynaert walked me back to the métro. That man really lives in a different world from ours! He's just back from a holiday on Lac d'Annecy. I'm not jealous of anyone, and I am too proud to even try to make them aware of their insensitivity (which would be difficult in any case), because I don't want their pity. But it is painful to see how distant from us they are. On pont Mirabeau, he said: "So, don't you miss being able to go out in the evening?" Good God! He thinks that's all we're up against! That was something I left behind ages ago. I never even thought of making a point of it, perhaps because I've never liked parties, but especially because I knew that there were more horrible things.

I am indignant at his lack of understanding. But sometimes I try to put myself inside the skin of someone outside all this. What might such a person make of our plight? For someone like Breynaert, it just involves being deprived of social pleasures. And he's been seeing us every week for the past two years! That is proof, I think, of his being impermeable, impenetrable and selfish.

Tuesday, 19 October, morning
I awoke worrying about other people's lack of understanding. I've come to wonder whether what I wanted was impossible. Yesterday at the Sorbonne I had a talk with one of my very nice classmates, Mme Gibelin. There was an abyss of ignorance between us. However, I believe that if she knew, she would feel the same anguish as I do. That's why I was terribly wrong not to make a real effort to tell her everything, to shock her, to make her understand.

But so many obstacles inside me stop me making the effort: first of all, distaste at arousing the pity of others (and yet I always try to grab hold of their understanding and to make them a little ashamed of themselves). It's just that that brings you up against a serious problem: human nature is such that people only understand if you present immediate evidence, evidence which concerns *you*; they aren't upset by stories about other people, only about *your* personal fate. You only succeed in creating a little understanding by describing the misfortunes that have befallen you yourself. And then? I realize with disgust that I have become the centre of interest, while the only thing that matters is the torture others are experiencing; it's a question of principle, it's the thousands of individual cases that make up this question; horrified, I see that the person I am talking to pities me (pity is much easier to get than understanding, for that requires the gift of one's whole being and a complete reconsideration of oneself).

How to escape the dilemma?

There are very few souls sufficiently generous and noble to face the issue itself, without seeing the person telling the tale as an individual case, and to see through that person the suffering of others.

Souls like that must be endowed with great intelligence, and also great sensitivity, because seeing is not sufficient; you have to be able to feel, you have to feel the anguish of a mother whose children have been taken from her, the torture of a wife separated from her husband, the huge stock of courage that every deportee is going to need every day, and the physical suffering and misfortunes that he must endure.

I end up wondering if I shan't simply decide to split the world in two: the world of those who cannot understand (even if they know, even if I tell them; nonetheless I still often think the fault is mine, for failing to convince them), and the world of those who can. Make up my mind to concentrate my affection and my preferences on the latter half. In short, to renounce a part of humanity, to stop believing that all men are perfectible.

And in the preferred category, there will be a large number of ordinary folk, of working-class people, and very few of those we call "our friends".

My great discovery of the year is isolation. The big problem: how to bridge the gap that separates me from everyone I see.

———

The more attachments you have, the more people there are who depend on you because you love them, or just because you know them, the greater is your suffering. Suffering for yourself is nothing; I will never complain on my own behalf, because personal suffering is, for the time being, an opportunity to triumph over myself. But what anguish for others, for loved ones, for other people! "Health and Spirits can only belong unalloyed to the selfish Man – the Man who thinks much of his fellows can never be in spirits." (Keats, Letter to Bailey)

Monday, 25 October
Yesterday evening I read this in the epilogue to *Les Thibault*:

> He launched into a masterly summary of the course of the war, beginning with the invasion of Belgium. Presented thus, with the successive phases summarized in clean-cut patterns, the march of events was seen to follow an

amazingly logical sequence, move following move as in a game of chess. For the first time Antoine saw this war, in which he had taken part day after day, in full perspective, under its historical aspect. In Rumelles's eloquent résumé names like "Verdun", "the Marne", "the Somme", pregnant till now for Antoine with trivially vivid personal associations, were suddenly stripped of immediate reality and became landmarks in a technical epitome, chapter headings in a handbook for the use of history students.

This is a question that has always worried me, this difference between the present and the past, the movement from present to past, the death of so many living things. At present we are living through history. People like Rumelles[16] who package it in words can huff and puff if they like. Will they ever know how much individual suffering lies behind a single line in any of their speeches? How much throbbing life, tears, blood and anguish lies behind their dry words?

Thinking of the future makes you dizzy. Since earliest childhood I have been tormented by the problem of the annihilation of the outside world that follows the loss of self. I'm expressing myself badly. It would be clearer if I said (and this is the only form in which I can still summon up the sharp feelings I had at that time): "And if I were to die, would all this still exist?" The question quickly leads to a terrible feeling of isolation. When I was little, I felt it very acutely. Now I am more accustomed to living among others, its intensity has weakened.

I think about history, I think about the future. About *when*

16 Rumelles is the fictional speaker of the quoted passage from Roger Martin du Gard's saga of World War I, *Les Thibault*.

we will all be dead. Life is so short, and so precious. And now that I see it being squandered criminally or pointlessly all around me, on what can I rely? Everything loses its meaning with death constantly staring you in the face. I was thinking about that this evening as I walked past the German-occupied hotel in avenue de La Bourdonnais. I thought: "All you need is for a man to throw a bomb through that door, and twenty innocent people will be shot, twenty blameless people will suddenly have their lives taken from them, maybe it will be us, a round-up in our neighbourhood, like the one at Neuilly . . ." And the bomb-thrower won't have thought of that because he could not think of it, because his mind was clouded by the passion of the instant, because you just can't think about everything.

I fear that I won't be here when Jean returns. It's a very new feeling. I still imagine him coming back and I still think of the future. But when I am fully in reality, when I see it clearly, I am gripped by anguish.

But it is not fear as such, because I am not afraid of what might happen to me; I think I would accept it, for I have accepted many hard things, and I'm not one to back away from a challenge. But I fear that my beautiful dream may never be brought to fruition, may never be realized. I'm not afraid for myself but for something beautiful that might have been.

And when I think about it, I see that it is not a vague and groundless fear, it's not an "affectation", a fear that would make sense in a novel. There are so many dangers lurking in my path, what's strange is how long I have escaped them. I am thinking about Françoise; the feeling I had at the time of the mass arrest has lost none of its sharpness: why not me?

It's odd: this confirmation of my fear, which gives it foundation, reason and force, instead of making me more upset calms my nerves, strips fear of its mysterious, horrible nature and endows it with sad and bitter certainty.

Wednesday, 27 October

On Monday morning twenty-five families were arrested on boulevard Beaumarchais without the slightest "reason". Their apartments were sealed straight away. If that happens here, I would want to save my violin, the red folder into which I put Jean's letters, and the few books I've not been able to part with.

Sometimes I tell myself it's stupid to keep them here, but I object instantly: "Those things at least." Those things are precious to me for one reason or another. There's *The Brothers Karamazov*. The thought of the few lines on the fly-leaf is infinitely precious. I know they are there, living proof, and that I will be able to look at them. Sometimes I suddenly remember that they are there, on my bookshelf, and it is like a warm, bright glow in the enveloping coldness.

There are some other books I cling to because they are indispensable. I can see them through the middle glass door of the bookcase: Tolstoy's *Resurrection*, Shelley's *Prometheus*, *Jude the Obscure* and, on the lower shelf, *The Freelands* by John Galsworthy, *Island Magic* with its fine descriptions of children's lives, *The Wind in the Willows*, the two Morgan novels, *A Farewell to Arms*, *Gone to Earth*, Pourtalès' translations of three Shakespeare plays, Hofmannsthal's prose writings, *Tales from Chekhov*, Dostoyevsky's *Adolescent*, the Rilke volumes, my Shakespeares and, on the mantelpiece, *Alice in Wonderland* and the Shakespeare *Sonnets* that Denise and François gave me when they got engaged.

I wrote "the two Morgan novels". But I recalled with a jolt that *Sparkenbroke*, which I loaned to Mme Schwartz, was kept in her office, in the lower drawer. It's not the loss of the book that made my heart sink, it's remembering Mme Schwartz. The memory of that office and of the friends I had there never leaves me. But sometimes a small detail may make me jump and feel it with greater intensity, or rather, feel it differently, as if I was suddenly able to see the situation through a different window. For instance, the other day, as I was thinking about little André Kahn and his mother at the same time – I was holding the boy by the hand, he's one of the Neuilly children I adore, with black eyes, golden hair and pink cheeks – I suddenly realized that Mme Schwartz's young children were now in exactly the same situation, that both father and mother had been deported, had been made equal; I found it hard to bring them together in a single thought.

And that's probably how the *past* will be *made*: the misfortune of the children I was looking after was a fact, something accepted as real, as "having happened", but the misfortune of Pierre and Danielle [Schwartz] had not yet been grasped. Later on I'll probably see no difference; the two things will acquire the appearance of facts that have occurred.

Often as I'm walking along the thought of Françoise catches me unawares, despite the fact that I never stop thinking about her and that a great part of the sadness that has become my usual state of mind is due to her absence. She wasn't ready for that, she did not want it, she was so attached to things here, she seemed to love life so much; I do not think of her in the context of my own sorrow, and I tell myself that she must be unhappy, she must be suffering a great deal due to this attachment. I don't know why I am so sure that she was expecting it less than me, and why she will be more outraged than I will be.

Will I rise up in protest against my fate some day? Fatalism is not what enables me to put up with it but rather a vague sense that every new trial has a meaning, that it was intended for me and that it will make me more pure, more worthy in respect of my conscience and, probably, in the eyes of God. It's something I have always felt: I have always turned my back almost with embarrassment on the person I was *before*, a year or six months *before*.

It's strange, but thoughts of Françoise divide into two alternating kinds: the thought of her physical and moral suffering, and then my *own* sorrow, the feeling that I have lost something very precious, because I gave all my affection to Françoise and I know that she liked me a great deal too. This mutuality was something very sweet, and it was also full of light and life.

Now I am in the desert.

Nobody will ever know what this summer and autumn have been like for me. Nobody will know, because I have carried on living and acting, but not a single one of my deep thoughts – thoughts in which I felt myself really to be me – hasn't been a source of pain. I've not suffered physically yet, and God alone knows if such a trial awaits me. But in my soul, in my affections and in a general sense, I have lived and am living in perpetual pain.

Nobody will know, not even those closest to me, because I do not talk about it, not to Denise, or Nicole S. or even Maman.

There are too many things that *cannot* be spoken about. What I suffer in respect of Jean, nothing can make me talk about that, probably because I keep it to myself and because nobody else has the right to be involved, and maybe also out of a kind of shyness which often stops me even talking to myself about it. I'm going to try to explain how I feel: sometimes I won't allow myself to be in this new place at this new stage of my life out of lack of self-confidence and an instinctive repugnance at showing off, at making *more* of myself than I am.

And yet that is only one part of the truth. The truth is that since Jean went away a year ago, I have been suffering with such intensity that the fundamental change Jean brought to my life must have been real, I am not simply adopting a pose or an affectation.

I've very few solid things to rely on. Externally, I have none. When I think of putting it into practice, I instinctively turn away. Before, I did that because anything practical seemed likely to tarnish my dream. Now I do it because I know, because I have an acute and scalding memory of my penultimate conversation with his mother, when, apart from discussing religion, which I was expecting to do, and which does not frighten me, she hurt me in a way I shall never forget by telling me I had been to Saint-Cloud on trust two days previously, whereas her husband knew nothing about it and thought I was just one of Jean's "flirtations". How much that word hurts! It was not my pride that was wounded but everything I knew myself to be and that I knew to be the most worthy part of me, the purity I have strictly maintained through constant effort. Perhaps, in fact I think certainly, she did not do it consciously, especially because up to that point she had spoken to me in a manner consistent with her thinking me a mere . . . I shan't write that word again. I think it just slipped out because she had suddenly "realized" and in the same instant saw all the struggles she would have with her husband. In that case, however impartial I may be, I am obliged to acknowledge that she is clumsy, that she lacks the sense that allows you to guess the full impact on another's soul of what you are about to say; she hasn't got the ability to "put herself in someone else's shoes". She is too impulsive and maybe too headstrong for that. I have other evidence of that: the way in which, when Jean is not present, she insists on trying to make me agree to have the children brought up as Catholics (which I find unfair on Jean, irrespective of my religious convictions) surely proves her lack of concern for others as individuals. I don't believe she is bad, I even think she likes me up to a point, but I think she is missing one of her senses. I would never try to convert anyone, I have too much respect for other people's consciences.

So, on the outside, I have virtually no support. As for here, I don't know about Maman. We never talk about it. Maman and Papa never mention Jean or my future. Presumably because I don't talk about it either, presumably because they do not know what I am thinking, presumably it's better like that.

On the inside (in the inner temple constructed in the few months that he was here), many things are missing; I hardly know him. What's more, there'll be all the new things that life will have brought him, and which will surely be numerous and decisive. But there is a magic castle which, when I enter it, is full of sunshine and warmth – it's the thought of our profound resemblance, of how we communicate. It is in this domain that I store my memories of those three months of last year.

As for the other part of my sorrow, Françoise's departure, I can't talk about that either, because it is a distillation too rare to allow me to define it.

There remains a further huge part: the sufferings of other people, of the people I know, of those I do not know, of the world in general. I cannot speak of that suffering either, because people *would not believe me*. They would not believe that it has haunted me and haunts me every hour of the day, that I put the suffering of other people above my own. What else has dug such a gulf between my best friends and myself? What else creates this awful malaise, this terrible separation that I feel when I talk to everyone? This malaise, this impossibility of communicating fully even with my comrades, even with my friends, is it not the price I pay for my awareness of those who are suffering?

God knows what the price really is, because at the depth of my being I have always aspired to give myself entirely to others – to my comrades, to my friends! And now I have to admit that it is impossible because life has put a barrier between us.

There's a last part of my suffering, but it isn't really, because in this respect I accept the sacrifice since I know I have to make it, although I am perfectly aware, if I think about it, of what this loss means to me – giving up on a whole side of myself, giving up on work and not going more deeply into music. But that is nothing. It's not hard for me to bear.

———

Will there ever have been many people who, at the age of twenty-two, were aware that they could suddenly lose all their potential – I feel unembarrassed saying that I feel I have immense potential, since I think of it as a gift, not as something I own – that it could all be taken away from them, and not rise up in revolt?

———

A strange contradiction.

When I put my mind on the same level as other people – people who can "afford" to wait for the end, "normal" people – I think the war will soon end, that there are perhaps six more months to go. Six months – what's that compared to what we have been through?

But in my inner world, all seems dark and I see only anguish ahead; I have always in my mind the thought that a trial awaits me. It feels as if a huge black corridor separates me from the moment when I will come out into the light again, and Jean will be back. Because Jean's return will be not only my own resurrection but also the symbol of the rebirth of happiness, of happiness for everyone. For me there is deportation, and for Jean there are all the dangers in his path.

And when I suddenly find myself looking at things like normal people (which does not happen often any more), I feel as though I am raising my head and seeing the light. I don't dare believe in it, and I wonder: "Is such joy possible?"

———

Perhaps it is only since Jean left for good that I feel so rudderless. I feel that anything could happen to me now.

———

Yesterday I went to the Léautés. I put on my old me like an overcoat, but I was all messed up inside, how distressing that was!

I know why I am writing this diary, I know I want it to be given to Jean if I am not there when he comes back. I do not want to vanish without him knowing what my thoughts were during his absence, or at least a good part of them. Because I "think" all the time. I count the perpetual *awareness* in which I exist as one of the discoveries I have made.

When I write "vanish", I am not thinking of my own death, for I wish to live; to live as much as I am able. Even if I am deported, I shall think ceaselessly about coming back. If God does not take my life, and if (and this would be so nasty, and proof not of God's will but of human evil) men do not take it either.

If that should happen, and if these lines are read, it will be clear that I expected my fate; not that I had accepted it but, because I do not know how my physical and moral resistance will hold up under the weight of reality, that I was expecting it.

The reader of these lines may be shocked at this moment, just as I have been when reading an allusion to the author's death in the work of someone long dead. I remember reading the passage in which Montaigne speaks about his own death and thinking: "And he did die, it did happen; he forethought what it would be like afterwards", and it seemed to me as if he had outwitted Time itself.

As in these gripping lines of Keats:

> This living hand, now warm and capable
> Of earnest grasping, would, if it were cold,
> And in the icy silence of the tomb,
> So haunt thy days and chill thy dreaming nights
> That thou wouldst wish thine own heart dry of blood
> So in my veins red life might stream again,
> And thou be conscience-calm'd – see, here it is –
> I hold it towards you.

But I'm getting carried away, I am not morbid as these lines are. And I don't want to hurt anyone.

I shall give these pages to Andrée [Bardiau]. And when I have handed them to her, I shall be obliged to imagine Jean reading them as reality, as something that can happen. So I cannot stop feeling that I am writing for him; I must stop writing in the third person and start writing the way I used to write letters to you, Jean. Using "*vous*" and other similar formulae seems a lie, it makes me feel straight away that I am play-acting, being what I am not, and yet if he were here, I would find it quite natural to say "*vous*" to him. But in the present moment, at the bottom of my heart, I think, or rather I *feel*, even before any actual words come to mind, I can feel my Jean, and I say "*tu*" to him, and it would be lying to myself to do otherwise.

Now I have written the word, it seems just as far from the truth. In reality, when I think of Jean I am in a domain prior to thought and words, and I don't know what I call him or how I think of him.

If I wrote "darling Jean" it would feel as if I was acting the role of a heroine in a novel, it would remind me of Miss Thriplow's "darling Jim" in *Those Barren Leaves*, and I would laugh at myself. If only I could laugh! Jean liked laughing so much. Before, I used to laugh. Nowadays a sense of humour feels like sacrilege.

———

I note below the passages from *Summer 1914* which gripped me, like Keats's hand:

P. 917: He's talking about the war and what was happening between Mondidier and the Oise: "But will I still be here to see it? The appalling slowness (from the individual's viewpoint) of the events that make history is something which has often been brought home to me during these last four years."

P. 928. 1918: "The future of the world which, when the war ends, will be cast into the melting-pot. All will be jeopardized – and for heaven knows how long! – if the peace that's coming doesn't remould, reconstruct and, above all, unify this stricken Europe of ours. Yes, if armed force is to go on being the principal instrument of policy as between nations, if each nation is to go on regarding itself as sole judge of its conduct and free to indulge its appetites for 'expansion' as and when it chooses, if the Federation of European States does not bring about an *economic* peace, as Wilson desires [. . .]; if the age of international anarchy isn't violently cut short [. . .]; this war will have served no purpose, all the blood that has been shed will have been shed in vain.

"But just now – there is no limit to one's hopes . . ." (!!!)

If this passage was written at the time (and even if it wasn't, as long as it faithfully reflects the thinking of that time), then I was right to say to Jean Pineau, on Saturday, when he gave me the last part of *Summer 1914*: "Things are desperate." Doubly desperate for us and, in that last sentence above, with a despair that can only be felt by those who can put themselves in the writer's shoes, who can give themselves over to him (or am I being naïve?).

"(I write of this 'better world' that is coming, as if I were going to be here to see it!)" (p. 929).

I know it's only a work of fiction, that the author wasn't observing himself dying like Antoine, but I accept it as a vision of another person's state of mind. I think Roger Martin du Gard produced something true, that his talent gave him a sharper awareness than we have, and that he did not invent anything. I believe that "the novel" can be a vehicle of psychological revelation.

P. 950, to Paul: "But especially I ask you to be on your guard against yourself. Always have in mind the risk of forming wrong ideas about your character and being misled by appearances. Practise sincerity at your own expense [. . .] Another thing you should try to bear in mind: in the case of young men of your stamp (I mean the educated type, whose minds are shaped to a great extent by books and heart-to-heart conversations with intelligent companions of their own age) theories on life and the human sentiments always precede experience. Their imagination enables them to conjure up mentally a host of sensations with which, so far, they have had no direct personal contact. But this they fail to realize; they mistake *knowing* for *experiencing*." (Cf. Keats, "sensation with and without knowledge".) "They believe that they personally experience cravings and emotions which they merely *know that others feel*."

P. 957: "For Paul. Don't worry overmuch about inconsistencies. They are vexatious, but a healthy sign. I have noticed that it was precisely when my mind was tossed this way and that by contradictory ideas that I felt nearest that Truth, with a capital T, which always lies just around the corner.

"Could I have another lease of life, I'd like to live it under the sign of Doubt."

Shakespearean impartiality.

P. 966: "He must safeguard his personality. He must not be afraid of making mistakes and contradicting himself time and again. He must take stock of his deficiencies so as to gain an increasing insight into himself and ascertain the task that fits him – his duty."

I've just had spectacular proof of that. Hélène interrupted me to go and see a Mme Sarbor (?) who had been waiting for Papa to see her for a long while. I curse under my breath, my resentment of Hélène crystallizes around the image of Mamizelle Agatha in Axel Munthe['s *Story of San Michele*]; I know I am in the wrong, yet I cannot deny that I am irritated. It was Mme Sartory, that good woman from Alsace who adores Papa. My irritation subsided immediately (I thought it would) and I was ashamed of my "partiality". I spoke to her. Her sister, who has five children and has lived in Alsace for forty years, and whose husband is in Savoie, is only allowed to come to Paris for a week, and meanwhile her children are being held hostage.

We always ought to be able to see things from the perspective of a judge higher than us who can see both sides of a question.

P. 967: "Newspapers. The English are making little progress. We are hardly doing any better, despite some small local advances. I write 'small local advances', following the communiqué, but I can picture what those words mean for the men making them; I see them crawling up the communication trenches, shells bursting round them in no-man's-land, first-aid stations packed with wounded."

P. 933: "I have never had the time or the (romantic) inclination to keep a diary. I regret it. If I could hold between my hands today, in black and white, all my past life since my fifteenth year, I'd have a better impression of having lived. My life would have specific bulk and form – historical concreteness. It wouldn't be the shapeless, shadowy thing it is, vague as a half-remembered dream."

From the preceding paragraph: "Impression of having fallen down an open manhole. I didn't deserve this. I deserved (pride?) the 'fine career' my teachers and friends predicted for me. Then suddenly, at the corner of the trench, the whiff of gas!"

And this passage, for its beauty:

"It was so hot that at about one I rose and pulled up the blind. Back in bed, I feasted my eyes on the marvellous spectacle of the night sky [. . .]

"Suddenly it struck me – and I'm certain I was right – that an astronomer, whose spiritual home lies in the interplanetary spaces, must find dying a much less painful process than it is for other men.

"Meditated for a long while on these things, gazing up at the sky, the boundless firmament that always recedes a little farther as our telescopes grow stronger. A wonderfully soothing meditation. That fathomless immensity in which a host of stars like our sun run their slow courses, and our sun itself – a million times, if I'm not mistaken, larger than the earth – is no more than a tiny unit of an untold multitude.

"The Milky Way, stardust, a cloud of suns, round which wheel billions of planets, hundreds of millions of miles distant from one another. And all the nebulae from which new broods of suns are born. And the discoveries of astronomers that all this teeming mass of worlds is a mere drop in the ocean of infinite space, in an all-pervading ether traversed by radiations, waves of energy, of which we know absolutely nothing.

"Merely to write it down makes one dizzy. A healthful dizziness. Last night for the first time (perhaps the last) I managed to think about my death with a sort of serenity, with vast, superb indifference. All regrets fell away and I felt already free of the frail husk of life that is my body [. . .]

"Resolved to gaze at the sky each night to recapture this serenity" [pp. 967–8].

———

Infinitesimal magnitude of man in the discoveries of modern science, yet prayer exists.

It's magnificent, the ending of the Thibault saga, where the story no longer occupies any space at all, and where a man's soul (Antoine's, but it could be anyone's, since it is a soul) becomes the exclusive focus of interest, to the extent that any reader feels personally, individually affected, because *it could be you*.

On the train when I was going to fetch Charles the other day I discovered two more reasons why I am so attached to this book. First, that devastating end of an era, that depiction of the holes the war tore through that family and its entire circle, is so much like what doubtless awaits us too, *after*.

Then there was the poignant realization that Antoine *could* have understood Jacques but only after his death. An acute sorrow that I feel so often – just when our closeness could have engendered something marvellous, Yvonne, then Jacques, then Françoise and Jean were taken from me.

There are two parts to this diary, I realize on rereading the beginning: the part I write out of duty, to preserve memories of what will have to be told, and the part written for Jean, for myself and for him.

It makes me happy to think that if I am taken, Andrée will have kept these pages, which are a piece of me, the most precious part, because no other material thing matters to me any more; what must be rescued is the soul and the memory it contains.

To think that Jean might read this. But I don't want it to be like Keats's hand. I'll come back, you know. Jean, I will come back.

At the thought that the envelope in which I am putting these sheets will only ever be opened by Jean, if it is opened at all, and when the realization of what I am writing flashes through my mind, something swells up inside me, I wish I could write everything about him that has been piling up for months.

But I have only just realized; I shall try to grasp the precise moment when it does occur.

Thursday, 28 October, evening

I've just spent a marvellous afternoon here with friends I love: Mme Lavenu, M.-S. Mauduit, Jeanine Guillaume, and Catherine came too to hear us speaking English.

Today I managed to glimpse the atmosphere in which I think I could show the full measure of my potential. M.-S. Mauduit – how she reminds me of Katherine Mansfield! – brought me a print of a Rockwell Kent illustration for *Beowulf*. My instinct had not deceived me when I was struck by the illustrations to *Moby-Dick* in the American Library edition. Now I have a better sense of Rockwell Kent, because she also lent me a travelogue of a voyage to Greenland that he wrote and illustrated.

Mme Lavenu is a true friend, she really is, a friend who understands; our friendship was sealed when she came to see me when I was so upset the day after the round-up.

François also called. Chatted enthusiastically with Jeanine Guillaume. She borrowed a section of my thesis, *The Hunting of the Snark* and *The Wind in the Willows* – I love exchanging things that way.

And now I am thinking of Jean. How I miss him, how I would blossom if I were with him.

————

A strange day, symbolic of my life now. At 9.00 this morning I was at the Enfants-Malades to get news of one of my charges. I walked through the ward with its little white beds and all those young children with their heads on their pillows. Doudou recognized me first; I recognized him by his radiant smile, because he was much more beautiful than before, with his ginger curls.

After that I went to Saint-Denis to see Keber. As I was ferrying the packages I spoke with a woman of the lower classes, and it was so hurtful because she did not *know*. She reckoned there were a lot of Jews in Paris, obviously, you notice them with that label stuck on them, and then she said: "But they don't bother French people, do they, and anyway they only arrest people who have done something."

The type of encounter that causes so much pain. On the other hand, I can't hold it against the woman; she did not know.

After lunch I went to rue de la Bienfaisance to talk to Mme Stern; our office has become so dreary now that the legal department has taken over. Nobody there knows me. I don't mind. They don't know what I have seen, and the memory of the women who were my friends remains intact inside me. Happened upon Mme Dreyfus, same as ever, she's all that remains of our sunken ship. She told me that Léa had been taken with her entire family – Léa, who had survived so many close calls as well as the 30 July round-up. That was a real blow.

We talked about Mme Samuel. In the end she was deported. She had been left behind because she was a half-Jew and a pregnant mother. But they deported her from the clinic in a hospital car; that cannot be true, because how can cattle-car trains include hospital cars? And what more flagrant proof could there be of the monstrous stupidity of Nazi policy than to deport people in ambulances?

And what possible use is it? I wrack my brains. Answer: They have set a frightful machine in motion that keeps on going without thinking.

Each time, it catches and consumes prominent people. At the moment there's a convoy leaving every week.

Mme Samuel talked to me about what would happen after the war, and she's the only person I've encountered who has said that what we would have to do first was *make the Germans understand*, open their minds. She has gone, leaving a one-year-old born when his father was at Drancy and whom she hardly knew because she spent six months in hospital, as well as the young husband who was released thanks to her.

On the métro today I wondered: Will anybody ever be able to understand what it was like to live through this appalling tempest at the age of twenty, at the age when you are ready to grasp life's beauty, when you are completely ready to trust in humanity? Will they ever acknowledge the *merit* (I say it unashamedly, because I am aware of exactly what I am), the merit there was in preserving a sense of fairness in the mind and softness in the heart throughout this nightmare? I think we are a little more virtuous than a lot of other people.

Saturday, 30 October

I spent today walking, all day walking. I walked back from my German lesson along rue Saint-Lazare, rue de la Boétie, Miromesnil, avenue Marigny and the Seine.

I walked right at the edge of water, which had its magical effect, calmed me down and lulled me, not making me forget but refreshing my overburdened mind. There was nobody about. Two barges went past slowly and noiselessly; there was just the faint lapping from the spreading ripples of the wake as they struck the riverbank and died.

I was thinking about Jean. I was thinking that I had dreamt about him last night. I do that very rarely; such dreams are very precious to me, because they are like visitations. It feels as though, when I see him again and look back on this long separation, I will vaguely remember having seen him in the interval, in a world above and beyond the everyday world.

If these dreams were true apparitions, they would leave me terribly disappointed on waking. But a vague underlying sense of reality persists in my dream, because *there is always something* that stops me from seeing him completely; so I must still be clinging to the memory of reality at the back of my mind. In last night's dream, I had gone out (for some urgent reason), I can't remember why, and Jean had stayed alone at home. I was hurrying back, impatiently, but I also knew that something would stop me, because underneath it all I knew *that it was not true*. And so the dream took on a shape imposed by that awareness: the lift I was going up in went all the way up to the sixth floor and then came down again without my being able to make it stop. Then, when I did arrive at home, my guests were coming up at the same time as

I was, and from that point on I knew I would not see him again. I came into this bedroom: he was standing by the window. He turned round, and then, for the briefest moment, I had him; I can still recall the sensation of his arms round me, his broad shoulders enfolding me, and the warmth. Then there is a gap, I am sitting on my bed, and seated around the games table set up in the middle of the room (as for Simon's lesson yesterday) are my guests (why did I have guests? Just like when he came here for the last time, when I felt I was desperately trying to make time slow down). Nicole S. was there. I took her by the arm to show her out and to make her understand that I wanted to be alone with Jean. But Jean had gone. The dream was over.

Presumably I dreamt about him because his mother telephoned yesterday; I didn't know what to say, and her voice was wavering too. She had no news; she began by saying she hadn't forgotten me. I was wrong to give up hope about the photographs; she has been taking care of them.

When I arrived at pont de l'Alma I was still looking at the water, and suddenly, without prompting, I began to think what life could be like as a couple, that I would be able to make him happy. I hadn't taken my thoughts in that direction before, this was something new. But the dark abyss we had to cross first? That's why I can never let myself go in that direction; it seems to me to be a fallacy.

At lunch there were Mlle Detraux, Denise and François. Afterwards I escaped again, went to Galignani's to get a book for Annie Digeon's wedding. I wanted to continue my walk, and I was drawn back to the Seine. I didn't go right down to the river but stayed on cours La Reine, close to the parapet, trudging through pungent autumn leaves. The sun had broken through and the sky turned blue. There was a wealth of golden hues, the last leaves on the chestnut trees were copper-coloured, the lawns were emerald green, the sky was clear, bright and airy, there was a clinging smell of trampled leaves and, all around, the tart autumnal odour of dead leaves smouldering on bonfires. The shimmering beauty of the light-speckled Seine was unreal, fragile and splendid.

At place de la Concorde I came across such a quantity of Germans! With women – and, in spite of my wish to be fair, in spite of my ideal (which is real and profound), I was overwhelmed by a surge not of hatred, for I do not know hatred, but of protest, revulsion and scorn. Without knowing what they are doing, those men have deprived the whole of Europe of joie de vivre. They clashed so sharply with the fragile and luminous beauty of Paris: men capable of committing such horrors, as we know only too well, men of a race that has spawned the Nazi leaders who have gone so far in self-abasement, despiritualization and stupidity as to become no more than brainless automata, with the responses of five-year-old children at best, that's why I will always react inside when anyone talks to me about Germans. Everything about me is the opposite of the Germanic character, bristles at the slightest contact with it; maybe it's because my temperament is essentially Latin? The glorification of violence, pride, sentimentality, the glorification of emotions of all kinds, the taste for vague and gratuitous melancholy, these are the features of the Germanic character against which my own temperament rebels. There's nothing I can do about it.

And the disgust I felt in that instant contained not a shred of thought about my own position; I was not thinking about persecution.

But when I passed under the colonnade along rue de Rivoli and felt the deep attachment, the essential affinity, the understanding and reciprocal affection that tie me to the stones, the sky and the history of Paris, I experienced a surge of anger at the thought that those men, those *foreigners* who would never understand Paris or France, dared to claim that I was not French, treated Paris as their rightful due and reckoned that this wonderful street belonged to them.

At Galignani's I bought a fine edition of *Sentimental Journey*, and *Lord Jim* (for myself). I would stay there for hours if I could.

When I came out I crossed the river by pont de la Concorde and went up to Françoise's to see Cécile. Cécile told me that when she saw the barges on the Seine on a fine day, it made her think so much of Françoise! And that thought has haunted me on my walk. With each pleasure I experience – but they are no longer pleasures, merely the *awareness that I am witnessing something of beauty* (for no true enjoyment ensues) – I think of Françoise, who loved life so much, who loved Paris so much. My thoughts never leave her.

———

Perhaps I was born to be a worrier? When I was a girl, I always found calm contentment and perfect enjoyment repulsive; I was always discontented. But after this ocean of suffering I shall never be at ease again, I shall never resume my better self in selfish joy.

Yet I do not wallow in it. I don't have a morbid streak, not like in Keats's poem: "Come then, Sorrow! / Sweetest Sorrow!" Because no-one can deny that I have experienced real suffering.

What I mean is that it seems to me there is more sincerity in pain than in joy.

———

That is presumably the reason why I do not like Gide, unlike Nicole. I read *Strait Is the Gate*, now I am reading *The Immoralist*. I dislike Gide's philosophy of the enjoyment of life as much as I loved *Les Thibault*.

———

How all my memories of last year haunt me, the small gate of the Tuileries, the leaves on the water! I live among these memories, and each corner of Paris awakens a new one.

———

Jean-Paul has come back. He returned yesterday while I was at rue Raynouard. I was so excited for Nicole S.

His return is probably what made me dream of Jean's visit.

———

Les Thibault: Summer 1914, p. 975: "There can be no security for Europe so long as German imperialism has not been uprooted. So long as the Austro-German bloc has not made a decisive move toward democracy. So long as we have not sterilized that hotbed of false ideals (false because inimical to the general welfare of mankind) which consists of a mystic faith in imperialism, the ruthless glorification of brute force, the Germans' claim that, being superior to all other races, they have a right to rule them."

P. 978, in connection with one of Victor Hugo's speeches against tyrannies: "The fact that the suppression of autocratic regimes and the limitation of armaments were already mooted as far back as fifty years ago, is that a reason for abandoning hope that at long last men will learn wisdom?"

Well, is it a reason? In 1943 you need a lot of courage and faith to put the question the way Antoine Thibault did in 1918.

P. 980, to Jean-Paul: "There is always such a temptation to shirk the strain of thinking for oneself, to let oneself be caught up in a great wave of collective enthusiasm, to embrace some comforting doctrine because it makes things easy [. . .] For it is precisely when his mind is most beset with doubts that a man is liable, in his desire to find an escape at all costs from perplexity, to clutch at any ready-made creed that offers reassurance. Any fairly plausible answer to the problems he has been brooding over, and cannot solve unaided, will strike him as a heaven-sent solution – especially if it bears the seeming guarantee of being endorsed by the majority [. . .] Turn a deaf ear to the slogans of the day. Refuse to become a 'party man'! Better to endure the torments of uncertainty than to enjoy the specious peace of mind that doctrinaires induce in their adherents."

P. 1004, to the chaplain: "Why don't the churches make a stand against war? Why do your French and German bishops bless the flags, and sing Te Deums to thank God for a bloody butchery?"

Sunday, 31 October, 7.30 a.m.
We've just sight-read a quartet, Beethoven's seventh. Annick had come. We made a dog's breakfast of it, but despite that the middle theme, the Andante, raised me up profoundly, completely. My soul feels as if it has become huge; I am filled with echoes and a strange desire to weep. I'd not heard any echoes for too long. I call out to Jean with all my heart. It was with him that I got to know the quartets, with him that I heard them.

Monday, 1 November

I finished *The Immoralist* last night, and I don't think I understand Gide: I can't manage to comprehend the meaning of his books because it is barely hinted at, the problem isn't put squarely. Why does Michel make his wife die? What does he gain from it? What is positive in his way of thinking? His doctrine is not even defined.

Gide's philosophy, moreover, runs directly counter to mine; there's something *old*, unspontaneous, over-considered and egotistical in his wish to enjoy and possess all things.

This personal bias is presented too logically; it focuses on the writer's self; it lacks humility and generosity. No, I don't like Gide.

In addition the style strikes me, rightly or wrongly, as precious, pretentious and outdated. On every page are turns of phrase that startle me with their unnaturalness.

My thought hovers ceaselessly between two poles: human torment, which is given living, tangible form by arrests and deportations, and Jean's absence. The two forms of wretchedness have blended into a single pain and will forever remain connected.

It is like a bed on which I shall twist and turn forever, only to find the same miseries facing me.

———

This morning I received a letter from Mme Crémieux, who let slip the following phrase: I am at the end of my tether. Good God, what could I do for her? Now I feel more keenly the ruination wrought on her by eighteen months of anguish and silence.

One day when we felt like taking her in our arms, Françoise [Bernheim] said this about her: "Hélène, you know, Mme Crémieux is so unhappy, she is suffering so much." Françoise's voice, in which I learned to hear sincerity and feeling behind her ever-cheerful smile, still rings in my ears. We were talking about the strength that some of the women [working for the U.G.I.F.] managed to summon up in the unspeakable trial we all faced. She spoke of Mme Crémieux as if she were a child whose every possession had been taken away – it's true, I have had the same impression of her. And now Françoise too. Her jolly voice with its high notes and her cheery laughter have also been silenced and sound only in my memory. She also reminded me of Mme Schwartz, whom we used to compare to Mme Crémieux. Such emptiness all around me! For some time after the arrests of 30 July, I had the stressful sensation of being the only survivor of a shipwreck, and a phrase kept jogging and banging around inside my head. It took hold of me without my looking for it; it haunted me, it's the line from the Book of Job at the end of *Moby-Dick*: "And I only am escaped alone to tell thee."

Nobody will ever know the devastation I experienced this summer.

We never heard anything more about the convoy of 27 March, 1942 (the one that took Mme Schwartz's husband away). There was talk of the Eastern Front, with deportees being made to walk ahead of the front lines to detonate the Russian mines.

There was also talk of asphyxiating gas being administered to the convoys at the Polish border. There must be some truth behind these rumours.

And to think that every extra person arrested yesterday, today, this very minute, is probably destined to suffer this terrible fate. To think that it is *not over yet*, that it continues with diabolical regularity. To think that if I am arrested this evening (which I have been expecting for ages now), in a week's time I'll be in Upper Silesia, maybe dead, and my whole life, with the infinity I sense within me, will be snuffed out abruptly.

The same thing awaits every individual who has been through this trial, and who is also an entire world.

Do you understand why Antoine Thibault's diary moved me so deeply?

I am not afraid of death at the minute, because I think that when I face it *I will have stopped thinking.* I will be able to remove from my mind all thought of what I am losing, just as I find it so easy to forget what I *want*.

And then so many other people sacrifice their lives every day. Men have suddenly brought Death much closer to us; they have broadened its scope, enhanced its strength.

I do not want to think of Death as a personification, like Death in Dürer's engravings or the Middle Ages, or in Axel Munthe. I must think of it not as a separate entity but as a manifestation of God's will.

Only it's hard to do that when I see so many deaths inflicted by men. Everything makes it seem as if there are two Deaths! – death meted out by God, or "natural" death, and death created by men.

Only the former should exist. A person does not have the right to take another person's life.

It is raining Death on earth. Those killed in war are said to be heroes. Why did they die? Men on the other side imagined they were dying for the same thing. Whereas each life has so much value in itself. The pity of it, Iago! O Iago, the pity of it, Iago!

What I am writing would shock many people. Yet if they thought for a moment, if they looked into the bottom of their hearts, what else would they find? I do not think I am a coward, so I allow myself to write such things. People who would throw up their hands in horror on hearing me, in the name of "valour", "courage" and "patriotism", are simply in the grip of false passions. They are wrong, they are blind.

Anyway, is it not the case that men who spent two years at the front during the last war experienced what they thought was "disillusionment" but which was simply the loss of these false passions? When they confessed that they did not even hate the Krauts any more, that they no longer knew what was happening. In Duhamel's *The New Book of Martyrs*, in the last part of *Les Thibault*, in Guy de Pourtalès' *Shadows Around the Lake*.

At that time, however, they assumed they had been overtaken, as it were, by a fate too mighty to permit protest. The fact is that men had set this "fate" in motion; it was the work of human beings.

I mentioned *The New Book of Martyrs*, which I received as a name-day present from Mme Schwartz. My name-day celebration was necessarily incomplete without Jean, but there was sweetness in it all the same, from my friends, and from Jean's letters too. Now I feel as if I have been stripped of everything, to the skin, and stand naked to the awaited stroke.

Yes, *The New Book of Martyrs* is a book that made me desperate, because it rises to that level of impartiality that I prize above all else, but from that great height all there is to see is desolation. What's the solution? Maybe people who take sides are happier because they find a solution, however erroneous it may be, and they have a goal: having something to hate *is much less stressful than feeling no hate at all.*

I now believe that the highest degree of perfection to which humanity can aspire is that kind of impartiality. Afterwards . . . I don't know; I can't see a solution: I can't talk about it, it's like life in the future. I simply have an intimation that once that level has been reached, *the* solution is to be found along the same road.

That's why, despite everything, despite its withholding an explicit judgement, *The New Book of Martyrs* remains a splendid lesson. Duhamel does not come down on one side or the other: he provides facts impartially, the results of that blind, crazy, furious thing called war, and he displays in its naked horror the horrible error that lies at its root.

I remember having been astonished, almost irritated, by the lack of passion. "What is he trying to say?" more or less sums up what I was thinking. I eventually understood what a huge lesson the book teaches by implication, and it finally became clear to me.

"Nothing ever becomes real till it is experienced; even a proverb is no proverb to you till your life has illustrated it" (Keats). I write this sentence, which has no connection to what precedes it, because it struck me this morning; it sums up the main problem facing me: that of human understanding and sympathy. It feels as if *everything* grows out of that.

This morning I studied Keats, I let myself get carried away, as I used to.

What vast worlds our minds can embrace in just a few hours!

———

Spent two hours with Nicole S.

Françoise Woog, always the same people. Pérez, Eliane Roux.

Tuesday, 2 November

This morning I took Maman to Neuilly.

They all wanted to come home with me. Grandpa Kahn was quite carried away – I can still see his imploring look, his black eyes, so black against his golden hair, about to sparkle with laughter – he said: "I want you to sleep by me!" It was the highest expression of his love.

Wednesday, 3 November

Another morning of such richness that it leaves me stupefied. I was free this morning. I've finally become accustomed to a life without a regular pattern: I allow myself to seize hours of freedom as they come, to stop doing things according to preset plans. Without this terrible upset in my life and the intractable events that have stopped me leading a normal life for the past year, I would never have managed to do this, to *give in* – yes, give in, because nobody ever resisted change more than I did. It went so far as to make me fear enjoyment and new experiences, however enticing they were (such as a trip away or an unexpected event), because of the disorder they would cause in my existence, and also because they *intimidated* me.

So, this morning, I worked in my old bedroom. Made notes on Keats's *Odes*.

Two hours later I realized the truth of Wolff's statement: the essence of Keats's art is its power of suggestion. The *Ode to Autumn*, for instance, lingered deliciously in my mind long after I reread it.

I want Jean to have my notebook too, especially the large one with the brown cardboard cover, because there is as much of me in it as there is in this diary. I haven't yet had time to say what I thought of Keats, but my selection of critics shows exactly what it is that I like and dislike in his work.

———

This morning was the first meeting of students taking Cazamian's course, and I was there.

The feeling I had before it started: this is the third time I am re-enrolling as an "amateur" without the right to a place among the students working for the *agrégation*. Will the start of this academic year retain the charm of novelty?

Will I be able to re-accustom myself to this normal part of my life after such a shock, after my lonely summer?

Will I fall prey to the memory of last year, when I went to the first lecture and suffered because Jean did not come (he was still in Paris)?

The feeling I have now: I am overflowing with plans and ideas, borne along by enthusiasm to work, to write essays and seminar papers. I didn't feel I was out of my element, a lot less, in any case, than I did last year. Perhaps the Sorbonne has now become too much part of my life?

The irony of it! I have so little time. How can I fit it in with Neuilly and all the other things that fill all my time? How will I manage?

I'm ignoring the obstacles for the moment. I put myself down for a third-term paper on Shelley. But now I can see I'm just chattering to myself, it makes me smile; but it entertains me, it's a step into an otherwise dark future.

———

Saw Savarit again. Memory of same time last year. I definitely do not like him.

Friday, 5 November
Mme Huchon's lecture course.

First lesson at Nadine's. A year gone by already. There's nothing better for measuring time than the regular recurrence of such things.

A year, and nothing has changed.

Saturday
Mme de la V. to dinner. Nadine Henriot, then music at the Jobs'.

British radio has apparently rebroadcast frightful details about life in the camps in Poland.

Sunday, 7 November
Charles and Simon.

On Sunday evening when we were alone together in the drawing room, Charles told me the details of his separation from his parents and their arrest: "I was so distraught that I didn't know how to cry any more."

He was saying that without emotion, matter-of-factly. But he didn't invent the memory; it is something that *truly was*.

Monday, 8 November
Library, a German came by looking for Anglo-Saxon books. If he had only known whom he was asking! Strange too that the only language we could communicate in was English. The situation was quite ironical.

Marie-Louise Reuge is back from Corrèze, where the Germans

apparently marched in with *machine-guns* to hunt down Jewish refugees. No *département* will be spared in the long run.

I took Anna to the Hôpital Rothschild and she told me about one of her cousins, a Polish immigrant who lost four of her sons in the war. Her husband had been gassed in the last war and died. Her life is ruined, and everything had been lost for France. Now she is in hiding, on the run, like a madwoman.

When I arrived at home, I found another postcard from that unfortunate PoW who asked me if I had made any progress in my inquiries about his twelve-year-old son, about whom he has heard nothing for more than a year. Can there be situations more atrocious than that of prisoners who will come home to find their wives and children gone?

Tuesday, 9 November
This morning I took a little girl of two and a half to the Enfants-Malades, she looks like a little Arab. At the hospital she cried the entire time and kept saying "Maman" instinctively, automatically. *Maman* is the word that always comes out of its own accord when you are in pain or unhappy. When I deciphered those two syllables in the midst of her sobbing, I shivered.

Her mother and father have been deported, the girl had been put out to a wet nurse, which was where they came to arrest her! She spent a month in the camp at Pithiviers.

The gendarmes obeyed orders commanding them to arrest a two-year-old baby in a nursery and intern her! What more lamentable proof could there be of the mindless stupidity, of the total collapse of moral awareness into which we have fallen? That's what is so dire.

Is it not dire that I, reacting to and rebelling against this, am an exception, whereas it ought to be the people who are *capable* of doing such things who are abnormal?

It's always the same story, as the inspector told Mme Cohen when on the night of 10 February he turned up to arrest thirteen children at the orphanage (the oldest was thirteen and the youngest five – these were children whose parents had been deported or who had disappeared, but they needed "some more" to make up the next day's trainload of a thousand Jews): "Sorry 'bout this, lady, I'm just doing my duty!"

Imagining that duty is unconnected to conscience and unrelated to justice, goodness and charity shows just how inane our supposed civilization is.

The Germans, for their part, have been subjected to a process of re-stupidification for a generation now (it's a recurrent phenomenon). They have no intelligence left at all. But we could have hoped it might be different among us.

———

The terrible thing in all this is that you see very few people actually *doing it*. Because the system has been so well designed that the men in charge are few and far between. It's a great pity, because otherwise revolt would be much broader.

Or is it because I see things from the outside? Organizing and carrying out these persecutions could not be done without a certain number of men, that's for sure.

———

The other day, in the street, a thought: "No, the Germans are not an artistic nation if they can ban people like Menuhin and Bruno

Walter, if they refuse to listen to a violinist because he is of another faith or even, as they maintain, another race. Refusing to read Heine . . . the two things cannot be reconciled."

Wednesday, 10 November

I am horribly worried about the others. I was coming back from my appointment with Mme Morawiecki, worn out from a long day but clasping to my heart the bar of soap Jean had sent to me via his network. It's lavender-scented, as were his hands on the day he left me, and inside the bar there was a piece of paper – a souvenir of another bar of soap (the one I sent to him last year). Nothing could have convinced me more directly that he was thinking of me despite the silence that separates us. And I've also got the last photograph taken of him.

Papa also read me Yvonne's sibylline letter. They say something about moving house. I got it straight away. The talk I had with Marie-Louise Reuge has left me too clear-headed not to understand the reference immediately. They must be applying their methods to each *département* in turn. I am frightened; that kind of safety will soon be shattered too.

Those of us here who have become accustomed to it want to protect the others; they must feel so vulnerable all of a sudden. What can be done if all the protective barriers collapse in sequence?

The tiny haven in which Jean's parcel and photo might have sheltered me for however brief an instant is not to be. I am too worried for the others. I am not complaining; I am not sorry. This trial is probably all the better for being harsher.

What a day! I went to Annie Digeon's wedding at Saint-Germain-des-Prés, then to the reception. The Pineaus were there (and lots of classmates). As always, seeing the Pineaus makes me feel sad. And weddings are always depressing and tiring events.

Friday, 12 November
After lunch Mme Agache came rushing in because she had just heard that young Mme Bokanowski, who had been sent to the Hôpital Rothschild with her two infants when her husband was in Drancy, had been taken back to Drancy. She asked Maman: "You mean to say they are deporting children?" She was horrified.

It's impossible to express the pain that I felt on seeing that she had taken all this time to *understand*, and that she had only understood because it concerned someone she knew. Maman presumably felt the same thing I did and replied: "We have been telling you so for a whole year, but you would not believe us."

Not knowing, not understanding even when you do know, because you have a closed door inside you, and you only can *realize* what you merely know if you open it. That is the enormous drama of our age. Everyone is blind to those being tortured.

And this was going through my mind: can those people speak of Christian charity when precisely what they do not know is the meaning of fraternity and human sympathy? Do they have the right to claim to be the heirs of Christ, of that Christ who was the greatest socialist the world has known, and whose doctrine was founded on equality and brotherhood? They don't have any idea what brotherhood is. Their pity, sure, they give us that, like Pharisees, because pity almost always presupposes superiority, condescension. It's not pity they should be giving, it's *understanding*, the understanding that will allow them to feel the profound, irreducible suffering of others to its full extent, to feel and be revolted by the monstrously unjust way people are being treated.

What I wanted to say to Mme Agache, what was going through my head, was this: "Now do you understand why we are in such pain, why we feel such sorrow? We experience the pain of others, we hurt for all humanity, but all you feel is pity when you hear about it."

But has she ever seen inside my heart? I appear normal to her, just a busy person doing lots of things. It's my fault too. My appearance is deceptive. I ought to let myself show what it is like inside, I should give up the modesty or the pride that forces me to carry on behaving like other people, and also refuse their pity. I should show my anguish the better to serve my goal: to unmask human suffering in all its forms.

Often I feel that I am play-acting, and that my duty ought to be to appear not normal, to reveal it, to display the real gulf separating us from other people instead of trying to ignore it or even avert my gaze, which I often do, out of respect, so others are not aware of my reproach.

If only people knew what ruins are in my heart!

———

At the hospital yesterday they took away forty-four patients, including one with terminal TB, two women who had abdominal drains still attached, one woman with a paralyzed tongue, a young woman at the onset of labour and Mme Bokanowski.

Why? Why deport them at all? It makes no sense. Are they going to put these invalids to work? They will die on the journey.

God, God, what a monstrosity! All is so dark tonight, I can't see any way out. I am alert to all the horror stories, I gather up all the miseries, but I can no longer see any solution, it is all too much.

———

Helène Berr with unknown children, c.1943

I've lost the feeling I had because I repressed it as unworthy of existence. But before dinner I thought: is it bad to wish for a haven of affection and love at long last? To be caressed and cherished, to melt the hard shell that has grown out of facing the tempest alone. No, nothing needs melting, but vast depths need to be awakened. Will I ever have the chance to be not alone and captain of my soul; will I be granted the maternal affection I would like to have from Jean, paradoxical though that may seem? I want to be cradled like a baby. Me, who looks after other babies. When it's over, I want lots and lots of love. Because for the minute I am sure I do not have any right to it.

I cannot ask Maman for it because her soul is as much a bed of coals as mine is. I can see my own torture and anguish in her, so that she is more my equal than my mother; suffering is a leveller. When she lets me sit on her lap and kisses me gently, it just makes me cry. But it does not comfort me; I feel she can no longer give me consolation.

One week ago I was brimming with enthusiasm for work. But it was just a passing phase. I actually knew it was an illusion. It was dissipated by a minor detail, in itself unimportant but which crystallized a lot of other things. Having returned last night at 7.15 from Saint-Denis, I missed the beginning of Delattre's lecture. And he allocated the paper I wanted to do to someone else. When I went to apologize after the lecture and ask him if he could reassign the topic to me (which he could have done, even if he hadn't been kind enough to give it to me in my absence, as M. Cazamian did that morning), he refused, saying: "When you're not there, other people step into your shoes." Disappointment, indignation, also the hurt I always feel when I am dealt with a bit harshly, brought tears to my eyes, and I didn't stop feeling indignant for an hour. I thought about all the effort I was making to cling on to this academic world which was so essential to me; I thought he really ought to know that the life of the mind mattered to me, and that I was more suited to it than many other people; and I thought about what I had given up of my own free will. And that the essay topic could have been some small consolation.

And then, without much difficulty in fact, because I can easily give a thing up, and even forget it, and *make of myself whatever I decide* (I never managed to explain that expression to Mme Schwartz – and yet it contains the essence of my character), I simply gave up trying to work for the *agrégation*.

Saturday, 13 November

Yesterday evening I read *Winnie-the-Pooh*, which Jeanine Guillaume brought me. I smiled with all my heart and even laughed out loud. It's so completely that English children's world that I love; it reminds me so much of Miss Child. And the perfection of its verbal inventions, its benign and serious tone, respecting and laughing at children at one and the same time, understanding that children are infinitely superior to us. I was entranced.

This morning after my German lesson I walked up the steps of rue Rodier as far as Lamarck beneath a torrential downpour that created splashing rivers down the steps of Sacré Coeur.

Denise, François and Mlle Detraux came to lunch. I just had to tell someone about *Winnie-the-Pooh*. As I began, I could see nobody was interested. But I persevered, aware I was imposing myself on others, aware I was boring them. I overcame my repugnance at being boring. But I would not accept other people not knowing about *Winnie-the-Pooh*. It's always the same: sharing my passions with other people, my only joys are those I can communicate to someone else. I am bereft of all those with whom I used to be able to do it, Jean above all.

Mlle Detraux listened nonetheless and admired *Winnie*'s charming drawings; kneeling beside her armchair, I explained the story. I didn't do it very well, I didn't convey the delight of the book very well, because it is untranslatable into French, and Mlle Detraux is much further removed from that world than Maman or Denise. But I continued talking, and my cheeks were burning. The others were chatting over us; it isolated me, it isolated us. I lost sight of everything except my effort to share the magic of A. A. Milne.

Afterwards Maman was a little sleepy and asked me, smiling: "So what happens to Winnie in the end?" But I knew she was asking me more because she had been struck by my excitement than out of interest in *Winnie-the-Pooh*. It wasn't the book, it was me she was interested in. She also wanted to please me, that's certain. And it was entertaining. But she didn't understand this book the way I wanted her to.

I went to Galignani's. I didn't find *Winnie-the-Pooh* but did find *Through the Looking-Glass*, the sequel to *Alice*, and a book of children's poems by the same author as *Winnie*, which was also beautifully illustrated.

Then I went to tea with Mme Crémieux. She had just come in when I arrived.

The desolation of a life like Mme Crémieux's can never be understood. I realize that I can only guess at it. Nobody can know. At one point she said: "You can't imagine, Hélène, there are times when I think I am dreaming. I open the door and I think: 'My husband's on his way', I tell myself it's impossible for him not to be here." My God, how much sorrow I felt!

The telephone rang several times; one of the calls was a warning that there would be a deportation on Monday. We could not pick up the thread after each call; something stopped me resuming the conversation. And yet it was a duty, it really was not worth making her think about that kind of thing.

She looked something up in her notebook, the notebook that had been in Mme Schwartz's desk drawer. So that whole piece of life is dead and gone. The office, Mme Schwartz with her grey eyes always sparkling with affection when she looked at me with her hesitant smile. Françoise laughing, coming and going with papers in her hand. Mme Robert Lévy, always her tall, pretty, well-turned-out self, with her good cheer and her optimism. Mme Cahen always whinging amidst her squabbles with the delivery men; Jacques Goetschel, who dropped in to check the card index; Mme Horwilleur, who was already hugely upset and overwhelmed by sad events – all that comes back to me but like a thing that has lost its voice, like a dumb show, troubling because the voices cannot be heard, there are only images.

Yet that catastrophe was not a punishment; all we were doing was trying to relieve other people's misfortunes. We knew what was happening; every extra regulation, every deportation squeezed greater pain out of us. People called us collaborators, because those who came to see us had just had a relative arrested, and it was natural that they should react that way when they saw us sitting behind desks. Department for the exploitation of other people's misfortunes. Yes, I can see why other people thought that's what we were. From the outside it must have looked a bit like that.

Going into work every morning as to an office, but where the callers were people coming to ask if so-and-so had been arrested or deported, where the cards and letters we filed were the names of wives, children, old folk, men whose fate was so agonizing. An office! It had a sinister side.

I remember that once or twice, simply because I walked the same way every morning at the same time, I even came to think of that life as "office life", as a regular, ordinary sort of thing, and looked forward to seeing my friends. But even if that was reprehensible (and who would not have felt the same, seeing that to all appearances the life I led was entirely an office life), I swear that as soon as I climbed the first step up to the building, it vanished; I swear I was fully conscious that the business at hand was human suffering, and I knew it was not ordinary pen-pushing and that people were wrong to reproach us for what we were doing. I fully accept that from the outside it must have aroused disgust. Because I remember the horrible feeling I had the first time I went to rue de Téhéran when Papa was arrested. Seeing men working in an office where their business was suffering wilfully and rationally inflicted on other people by the Germans.

Why did I accept the job? To be able to do something, to come as close as I could to misfortune. We did all we could to assist the internees. People who knew us well understood and judged us fairly.

As for people on the outside who thought we had got into the U.G.I.F. in order to be protected by that notorious "legimate" status and the I.D. card that went with it, well, if I had ever even thought of it that way, I would have refused to accept the job. When we started work in July 1942, just after the round-up of 16 July, all our friends were escaping from Paris in a frenzy. M. Katz had told Maman that if we insisted on staying, and God knows how many people were urging us to leave, then we had to have an occupation; there were rumours that young people without jobs were being picked up at random. When he gave us our U.G.I.F. cards, it was something extra, additional, and he told us: "If someone from the Gestapo stops you in the street, just show them that." At that time the card wasn't worth what it came to be worth later on (a value it has lost since then). We hardly thought about it. All we thought about was the sacrifice we were making by getting involved with that type of association. I've changed since then, I've cleaned myself up inside, at huge cost and with enormous losses. People who believed we were in it merely to protect ourselves have been proved massively wrong by the round-up of 30 July [1943].

Anyway, nobody knew better than we did how unstable and unsafe our situation was. I remember what Mme Schwartz used to say.

Why did I stir up all these memories? As I think back on it now, the past yet again turns into a dumb show. It's all dead.

But I see why I was all at sea and out of sorts when thinking about it, why it all seemed dead to me. I am forgetting that I am leading a posthumous life, that I should have died with them. If I had gone away with them, then the new life would have felt like a continuation of what had gone before, and I would not have felt like this.

I left Mme Crémieux's at 7.00 in the pouring rain; we first waited for the 92 but ended up taking the métro. When I got off at Trocadéro we ran home in the dark, stepping in unseen puddles, battered by the wind and the rain.

In rue Fourcroy, when she took my arm and ducked under my umbrella, a big, old umbrella of Grandma's, Mme Crémieux said: "Hélène, what do you think *they* are doing in weather like this?" What could I say?

It's awful not to be able to be consoling.

Sunday, 14 November

I went out very early to see Mlle Ch. for Charles. More worries on that front, and Maman has left it all to me. It's surely a token of esteem, but it makes me feel so alone. Before leaving, I went to say hello to Charles; he threw himself at me, then left his arms on my shoulders as he talked to me. I was astounded by these expressions of affection, I could hardly believe they were intended for me.

From there I went on to Neuilly to fetch little Odette and bring her home. She's a girl of three, with cornflower eyes and golden hair like an English doll. She didn't speak at all. There was only one thing she obviously liked – being cuddled.

I took her back at 4.00 and then went to see Denise; I was exhausted when I got there. Fortunately she played the piano. But it suddenly brought back the time, still so recent, when she practised piano and I would hear her as I came up the stairs, and all the affection she showed me. I understood one of the reasons for my loneliness: her being away from home. I had not really come to terms with her being married.

In the morning I was held up by a telephone call from Denise Mantoux, back in Paris for a short stay; I'll see her next time. But she told me that her brother Gérard was also here and would be very pleased to see us again. The Mantoux belong to such a distant past returning to the surface, I don't know if I would like that.

Last night after dinner I was reading Goldsmith's *The Good-Natured Man* when the doorbell rang. It was a young man sent to us by Mlle Detraux, to ask our advice about two children he had taken in after the arrest of their father (a medical doctor), their mother and the two youngest children, aged twelve months and two years. When the father was stopped in the street for an identity check, he made as if to run away, so then they came to arrest the family, who were in the midst of packing their bags – too late, alas! Apparently the German who came to arrest the wife said: "Why won't you say where the other two children are? Families are supposed to stay together . . ." Of course! When you separate husbands and wives as soon as the train arrives in Metz!

Because what they are doing now is deporting whole families; what do they think they will achieve? Set up a Jewish slave state in Poland? Do they believe for one minute that these unfortunate families who have long been settled here, in some cases for five hundred years, will ever think about anything except coming back?

After that, I could not carry on reading. I had to go to bed. The problem of evil loomed before me once again as something so huge and so desperate!

Tuesday, 16 November

On boulevard de la Gare, where they've opened a branch of Lévitan (a holding centre where "spouses of Aryans" among the "privileged" internees at Drancy[17] sort objects the Germans have

17 Jews who married non-Jews ("spouses of Aryans") were – in theory – not to be deported. Other "privileged categories" included French widows of French soldiers and decorated veterans. But none of the rules were actually applied.

stolen from Jewish homes and pack them up for dispatch to Germany), there are currently two hundred people, men and women living together in one room, with one sink between them. There is no privacy at all; men and women are being stripped of their modesty with exquisite refinement.

That's where M. Kohn is, and Edouard Bloch, who is severely disabled; how does he manage? Mme Verne, the banker's wife, as well. Anyway, what difference does social class make? They are all suffering, it's just that for people who are intensely sensitive and delicate like M. Kohn it must be even worse.

Went to Neuilly, waste of time.

To Saint-Denis at 11.30.

Wept after dinner.

Wednesday, 17 November

I'm just back from the Enfants-Malades, where I'd been summoned by a ward nurse because of a child. A kind-hearted woman wanted to save Doudou; I explained to her that there was nothing we could do because he was "blocked";[18] I realized that she was hesitant about the U.G.I.F., and that hurt. I understand her perfectly; it's so difficult to explain the situation to anyone. Officially, because it is not a secret organization, it is a monstrosity. But who would have looked after the internees and their families without the U.G.I.F.? And who can speak of all the good that many of its members have done?

She told me she had a ward orderly who had just returned from Poland, and who had observed the following scene with his own

---

18 "Blocked" children were those whose parents had been deported and who were then entrusted to an orphanage run by the U.G.I.F.; they could not be released. Most blocked children were eventually deported.

eyes: French workers over there aren't allowed to go out beyond a specified perimeter. The young man had left his hut one night and had wandered beyond the perimeter, found himself at the edge of a lake and suddenly heard noises. Taking cover, he witnessed an unspeakable event: he saw Germans pushing a group of men, women and children in front of them. There was a kind of springboard on which these people were forced to step. And then splosh! into the water; those are the words she used. The marrow froze in my bones. Those people were Polish Jews.

So I do not know everything, but each new story makes my mind feel even more like an open wound.

She added that it's very likely that as they retreat before the Russian advance the Germans will return to those places, find the corpses and proclaim that they were murdered by Bolsheviks in order to strike fear into the hearts of the French bourgeoisie. Who knows if Katyń wasn't also their doing?

This orderly was in a camp with some Russians. It was the same camp where there was that terrible typhus epidemic for which Lemière was sent to Germany (without being able to do anything, she told me). Fourteen thousand Russians died in that camp. Each evening the Germans harnessed four Russians to a tumbrel and piled naked bodies in the back, men who were not yet dead together with the others, higgledy-piggledy.

As for the Russian women, when French prisoners tried to give them something to eat, they were thrown into a dungeon. In the afternoon they were brought out and made to parade stark naked in front of the French workers, who yelled at the Germans so loudly that they crammed the women back into the dungeon.

Am I, who know all that, supposed to be normal and work

regularly? Yes, this morning I had decided to work on my disserta-tion; I knew deep down that it wasn't going to work and that some new shock would stop me. First there was the news that Yvonne and the others had scattered to avoid danger. Then there was that. How can you maintain your equilibrium, which depends above all on singleness of mind, when as soon as you turn your eyes away from the evil rampaging through the world it manifests itself again?

The only people who can be happy must be those who do not know.

Wednesday, 24 November

There's a wave of pessimism at the moment. Is it because of the winter, the third long winter without hope? Is it really because we have no strength left? Human beings have an unbelievable capacity for resistance. You would never have believed that we could put up with what we put up with. How is it, for example, that Mme Weill, the mother of Mme Schwartz, remains sane? How does Granny Schwartz, with two deported sons, a deported daughter-in-law, a son-in-law who is a PoW, an interned daughter and a senile husband, keep her senses?

Apparently in Germany the Party is still so powerful that the war could go on for a long time yet. Men are being forced to remain in the bombed-out cities; women are being sent to other factories; and children from age six are being sent to Nazi schools. Children! Why should we believe that the Germans see the situation as we do, that they can see both sides of the question, that they can see the pointlessness of the war? We should not try to compare the state of mind of a German today with our own. They are poisoned;

they have stopped thinking; they have lost their critical faculties: "The Führer thinks for us." I would be afraid to be with a German, because I am sure there would be a total breakdown in communication. Their courage is now scarcely more than an animal instinct, the instinct of a beast. Those among them who fight not simply to follow orders and behave like sheep are behaving like fanatical hotheads.

There is nothing I can admire in them, for they have lost all human nobility. That is why the war could go on, that is why the future is so dark.

This morning I was reading Shelley and his *Defence of Poetry*, yesterday evening, one of the dialogues of Plato that he translated. How desperate to think that all this, all these magnificent fruits of refinement and humanism, all that intelligence and breadth of mind, are dead. To live in times like these and be drawn to all these works is absurd, it's almost incompatible. What would Plato have said? What would Shelley say? They'd tell me I was a useless dreamer. But surely what is false and wrong are other people and the tide of rabid evil sweeping through the world. Had I been born in another time, it would all have been able to blossom.

Jean left a year ago today. A year ago I returned home and found the bouquet of carnations. Since the anniversary of the last time he was here, on Saturday, when beginning in the morning I relived the details of that last day, I have as it were crossed a line. I have overcome the obsessive remembering that each anniversary used to prompt in me.

Friday, 26 November
Bad night; I thought I was about to get an ear infection, it hurt as

much as it did two years ago, around that sinister 12 December. I must have had a fever. I felt odd all day. All the same I went to see Nadine. The Adagio from Beethoven's Trio No. 5 ["Ghost"]. What beauty!

Sunday, 28 November, noon
On Friday evening, just after Maman left her, Grandma died suddenly.

I am so tired I can't think. What's more, I haven't taken it in yet. I'll understand when it is all over. What's happening at the minute, sitting in her bedroom with the body, the sight of her laid out on the bed, is a trial inseparable from everything else, not horrible in itself; it hasn't made its mark by prompting revulsion, or tension, or fear (though it is the first time I have seen a corpse). It is all utterly simple, her face has barely changed; she looks as if she is asleep; her complexion has begun to resemble old ivory. When I went in yesterday morning for the first time, what struck me most was her immobility, like a block of marble. For three days now she has been sleeping, sleeping uninterruptedly; nothing can wake her.

But I'm aware *that*'s not what will make me grieve for Grandma. I can't manage to connect *that* with the living memory of her. It's that memory and the thousand associations that will flow from it which will finally make me grasp the reality of her passing.

For now, all I feel is that we have lost the last mooring that held us in place and in time, between past and future.

I prefer to be awake. Last night I had such nightmares that I made myself stay awake.

Affection overwhelms me as I sit beside this ivory body that appears to be sleeping. It is a blessing that she has changed so little.

Yesterday morning Nicole S. said: "It is like a light going out, she ran out of life." It's true, and there's no sense in protesting. Moreover, it's gentler and more peaceful than the reality outside.

Tante Marianne looks like she's been nailed to a cross. She is the last one left of that generation, and that's a huge issue for her. Oncle Emile, Grandma, Tante Laure, all gone. She sat by the bed for hours, saying nothing, her head to one side, buried in her furs, her face as pale and drawn as Grandma's. None of us can possibly feel as much grief as she does.

I was born in the bed in which Grandma died, and so was Maman. Maman told me that this afternoon. I found it comforting to know that life and death were thus entangled.

This evening I found Jean's letter of 27 June, in which he wrote about Grandma when she was so poorly. Everything has changed in the six months since then; a great emptiness has formed all around me.

I would so much have liked Grandma to know him; I feel as though I will always be one blessing short. If she had met him, her having smiled at him and spoken to him would have connected him at a single stroke to my inner life and to my past. It hurts me so much not to be able to do it, this long, drawn-out absence coming on top of such incomplete acquaintance.

Monday, 29 November, evening
Just back from Tante Marianne's. How sad it is. There was Denise, talking with unfocused eyes, walking with difficulty, asking the same questions over and over again. And what a sight it was for Tante Marianne, who has been laid so low by Grandma's death, to see Denise suddenly burst out singing at the top of her voice and

prance about, chanting refrains from music-hall songs off the recordings she has. And that's the only time she talks properly and makes sense.

Tante Marianne was so happy to see me.

I can't make sense of it; I can't manage to put the two things together, Grandma as she was before and as we have had her these last few days. It's the former one who will live on and whose memory, as I gradually become aware of it, will be painful. I have felt no fear of the latter, but she seemed like a stranger. I didn't go into the room when they were putting her in the coffin, not because I was frightened (I could have overcome the fear, and anyway, she hadn't changed), but because for me *that wasn't Grandma*. I spent part of the afternoon beside the coffin; this morning I bought carnations, yesterday I brought violets, to put in the coffin; none of that upset me. I arranged the flowers on the lid.

When I returned home this evening, I found two exquisite letters of condolence from Nadine Henriot and Mme Crémieux. Receiving the affection of others makes me cry. I suddenly realized that they were both friends I owed to Françoise [Bernheim]. The thought of Françoise made my heart miss a beat.

Tomorrow I shall have to get off the métro at Père-Lachaise. That was where I first had a proper conversation with Mme Schwartz, about a year ago, around 5.00 p.m., with trains passing by all the time; we sat on the platform bench and talked. I told her about Jean, because I could not hide it from people to whom I had given my heart. Now I don't have to make that effort or that confession, since all the people I loved have vanished. I can still hear her, her eyes shining with affection (her eyes were always so bright with love): "A girl like you is such a lovely thing!"

Mme Duchemin said something very true in her letter to Maman when she spoke of the peace in which Grandma had now taken shelter. They'll never be able to get her. I'm thinking of the hospice, which we feared for her like the plague; it's a house of squalor overflowing with people in pain. And isn't her peace much finer, vastly superior to our lives of perpetual anguish and torment? We never stop being afraid for our loved ones; we can never plan for the future, not even for tomorrow. This isn't just rhetoric – the beauty of these lines of *Adonais* struck me deeply, and I was tempted to memorize them:

> He has outsoar'd the shadow of our night;
> Envy and calumny and hate and pain,
> And that unrest which men miscall delight,
> Can touch him not and torture not again;
> From the contagion of the world's slow stain
> He is secure, and now can never mourn
> A heart grown cold, a head grown grey in vain . . .

At one point today I really did make those lines my own.

———

Beginning of true awareness of the loss.

Apart from being a tradition and a celebration of a very gentle religion of the past, calling on Grandma had become a refuge from our lives of anxiety; I didn't talk to Grandma about reality; it was still a green island of the good old days, an outcrop of peace.

I drew succour for myself from the feeling that I was giving her gentleness and affection. What will become of me without her?

———

Poor Mme Basch yesterday! When she said that Grandma was the only lucky one among us; she was collapsing from anxiety about her husband, from worrying about her eighty-five-year-old parents, and from the effort involved in pretending to them that things are all right. She has marvellous courage, for she knows about everything and yet maintains the appearance of calm and normality. Only yesterday, she went to pieces and sobbed on the stairs.

We put the bouquet of violets I bought on Sunday, a sprig of lemon balm that had been in my linen cupboard at Aubergenville (the only remaining souvenir from Bayonne) and the carnations I bought on behalf of Yvonne and Jacques into the bier (not into Grandma's bier; the two things do not go together).

Tuesday, 30 November

I wrote to Yvonne this morning and to Jacques last night. It's strange how Grandma's death has resuscitated the grandchildren we used to be, just as it has made the bonds that tied us tighter still.

Is the wish she described in her last letter, that all her grand-children should remain close, coming true? It seems a wonderful idea.

The only immortality of which we can have certain knowledge is the immortality that consists in the continuing memory of the dead among the living.

No-one can say anything about the other kind of immortality since no-one knows anything about it. For many people the belief in an afterlife is merely an illusion to mask the fear of death; unfortunately Catholicism has played on those feelings and fostered them. Maybe there are people who *know*, who have been illuminated. But most people believe in heaven and hell because they have been told to since childhood, just as Germans today believe that Jews are crooks. In truth it is an unfathomable mystery, and on that issue I put myself in God's hands. The only human being who was ever right about it was Hamlet, in his soliloquy "To be or not to be".

The memory of Grandma is a happy one, first because she died simply because her life had come to an end, and there is great beauty in the ineluctable. Human beings ought to treat life and death as ineluctable. What you understand you can accept. What we do not accept is the criminal lunacy of people who spread death by artificial means, who slaughter each other. Death belongs to God.

The second reason is that her memory consists of unalloyed sweetness, there's no other way of seeing her. She leaves only memories of happiness which make the heart swell with affection whenever they come to mind.

30 November, 1943

If only death could be as it is in *Prometheus Unbound*; that is what it would be if men were not evil:

> And death shall be the last embrace of her
> Who takes the life she gave, even as a mother
> Folding her child, says, "Leave me not again" . . .

Astonishingly, that's what I was trying to express just now. I've just found it, like a light in the darkness, as I was reading Shelley's *Prometheus*. It's about the resurrection of the world after the death of Prometheus. The Earth is speaking.

> Flattering the thing they feared, which fear was hate . . .

Why did God endow humanity with the power to do evil, as well as the capacity always to hope to be free?

> The loftiest star of unascended heaven,
> Pinnacled dim in the intense inane . . .

Like Keats:

> Bright star! would I were steadfast as thou art –
> Not in lone splendour hung aloft the night . . .
> As the billows leap in the morning beams . . .

Gaiety.

> Once the hungry Hours were hounds
> Which chased the day like a bleeding deer,
> And it limped and stumbled with many wounds
> Through the nightly dells of the desert year.

That's now.

For me. And how much more so for the deportees, the prisoners.

Shelley was not exaggerating when he said that poetry is the perfect and consummate bloom of all things. Of all that is, it is the closest to truth and to the soul. (Badly put but felt.)

Doesn't the magnificent dream of Act IV draw its value from what does not exist, from being only a hope locked in struggle with reality? That's the worrying question you can always ask about utopias.

Monday, 6 December, evening

I could dance, run, and skip. I don't know how to restrain my joy: we have news of Françoise and the others. Oof, that's it, I've said it. When I returned home I found a *pneu* from Mme Schwartz's mother telling me she had just got a postcard from her daughter, dated 25 October, from Birkenau. Françoise sends her love to her father; Mme Robert Lévy and Lisette Bloch are with them. The silence has been broken at last.

I'm stopping to think how I can get the news to Cécile, Nadine, Monique de Vigan. None of my friends have a phone, dammit! Can't go out, it's 7.30. I'll go to rue de Lille at first light. I rang the Canlorbes from the Ebrards' apartment. Nicole's husband took the call. Fortunately he'll be able to pass it on.

May God be praised! I prayed a lot.

Knowing where they are! Hearing from them after that horrendous departure. A mooring for a blindly drifting mind.

Tuesday, 7 December, evening

Jacques has just written two extremely affectionate letters to Maman. His professor, M. Collomp, was brutally gunned down at Clermont-Ferrand during the attack on Strasbourg University[19] that we have just about been able to piece together. We knew that the school had been surrounded, that a professor of Greek had been shot dead, and that the teachers and students from Alsace

---

19 Strasbourg University relocated to Clermont-Ferrand in 1939 and resumed operations in 1940 after the annexation of Alsace and Lorraine by the German Reich. It became an active centre of resistance. On 25 November, 1943, the Gestapo carried out a major raid. Paul Collomp, a papyrologist, was shot dead, 1,200 people were arrested, and 110 were kept in prison.

and Lorraine had been made to queue in the courtyard with their hands up for more than ten hours and then deported. The whole business had been led by a French student, the son of a French military officer, who revealed the identities of each of the people from Alsace and Lorraine to the Germans. So the murdered professor was M. Collomp.

I can see why Jacques is upset. At a stroke, in a single shock, he has seen all that has been tormenting me for months. He writes of human suffering. He wants to write a dissertation on suffering in ancient Greece. I am brimming over at the thought that he is experiencing exactly the same evolution as I did, that he will fully understand the letters I wrote to him, why *Hyperion* excited me so much. I'd like to tell him in writing. I would like him to understand what went on inside me, how alike we are. Also I'd like to help him, because I know what it's like.

———

I've just seen Mme Lehmann, and she's truly downcast by a nasty trick her partner played, selling the entire business without telling her. It has brought down the full weight of anxiety that her work surely helped to keep at bay. When she left she said: "We'll get some rest when we're dead."

That's a sentence I read somewhere a while ago, in a Russian novel – I think it was Kuprin's *The Duel* – and it's from Chekhov: "We shall rest . . . We shall rest!"

She said: "Of course those people tell me, your children are still young, they'll cope, they'll stand up to it. But I told them: 'They won't stand up to a bullet in the neck.'"

What will they do with the camps when events turn against

them? In Kiev they massacred twenty thousand Jews. In Feodosia, in the Crimea, twelve thousand in a single night.

———

A busy day. Took the métro five times this morning to give M. B. the joy of adding a line to Mme W.'s reply. When I read Mme Schwartz's postcard and saw her signature, her typical "Thérèse", my heart leapt, and at the bottom I added my own sentence in mangled German. What a feeling it is to have in my hand a letter that will be in hers in perhaps two months' time.

———

Jean C. S. has escaped. Amazing story. In solitary, beaten; shots through the skylight, sworn statement of those fourteen men.

———

Mme Morawiecki came to tea. She brought the rag dolls she has made.

She listens and takes an interest in everything she's told.

But I still can't quite pin her down, and I don't know if I like her or not. I think there's a lack of softness or even affection in her, which means I can only get so near to her. On the other hand the dolls were a touching idea. She is interested in us. But does she like me? Has she accepted me as I wish her to, or is she still in the same place?

Monday, 13 December, evening
I don't know why I have a sense of foreboding. For the last two weeks or so there have been rumours that we are all supposed

to be arrested before 1 January. Today, at the English Department, Lucie Morizet stayed behind on purpose to wait for me (I had gone downstairs with Denise to buy some books for Jacques), to tell me that one of her friends had told her to warn all her friends of our kind that they would be taken before 31 December. She was adamant I should do something. Do what? I'd have to lift a whole planet.

This is not the first time such rumours have made the rounds. It is not the first time people have given us that kind of advice. So why am I so worried?

Objectively there's good reason to be worried. Because it seems to me that we are the last shovelful, and we won't slip through the net. There are not many Jews left in Paris, and as arrests are now being made by the Germans, we don't have much prospect of keeping out of the way, because we won't be tipped off.

Subjectively, the night before last I dreamt, with my habitual precision, that the time had finally come for each of us to look for our places of safety, that we had to split up and go into hiding. I awoke in high anxiety. It was so much like reality.

Why am I worried? I am not afraid. And I've been expecting it since the beginning. But I've been expecting it for so long now that I've come to wonder if it isn't stupid to wait while knowing what lies in store. Whether it isn't a way of giving up. I don't think so, since I stay on in full awareness of what may happen; it is a conscious choice.

But why did I make that choice? Not because it is the courageous thing to do or because it represents my duty; such a position would be too much like pride, in the first place, and, in the second place, in reality, I don't feel there is a duty involved. If I were a medical doctor and the question was whether or not to abandon my patients, it would be different.

Yet if I suddenly abandoned my "official" life, it would feel like I was defecting. Not from other people but from myself. I would have become too accustomed to suffering, struggle and misery to be able to acclimatize to another life. Because the trial leads to greater purification.

There are immense practical obstacles to hiding, because it would mean hiding everyone – parents, Denise and the S.'s. But with determination we would manage. I'm well aware that nobody in the family if left behind here would have that kind of resolve in the face of danger, and it would perhaps be too late.

I said I was not afraid. But I wonder whether that is only out of ignorance, from not knowing the suffering to be endured, not knowing how far my resistance will go. Whether once I am over there I won't think we'd been mad and blind to stay on.

I know that if we are taken I will be deported separately from my parents and that the separation will be atrociously painful for all of us, above and beyond the fact of being deported.

So I'll ask myself how, since I knew that, could I have done nothing to avoid it?

If anyone reads these words after *it* has happened, he or she will be struck as by the hand of Keats and will ask: Yes, how? How could you have done nothing?

But my worries are not about me. I could cope with my side of things on my own. My real worry is for other people: Denise and François. Denise, in her condition, will be separated from François.[20] She'll have that moral suffering on top of the physical

---

20 Denise was pregnant with Nadine, Hélène's niece.

hardship of hunger, rough treatment and lack of medical care.

There'll be poor Tante Ger, who is so fragile and already so depressed (from the beginning she has moreover cultivated a kind of fatalism that often disgusts me); Oncle Jules, who won't be able to take it; and Nicole, Nicole especially; and Jean-Paul. When she talks about it with such detachment, she has no idea what it will be like. I've put it badly; I reckon I see things more clearly than they do.

Maybe it's all just more scaremongering. Should we abandon everything and take such a grave decision when it's quite possible that nothing will happen at all?

Even if it is just another rumour, that does not alter the fact that thousands of people have been and are being arrested every day, that the number of deportees has now reached almost a hundred thousand, and that with or without a "scare", reality exists, and we owe it to chance alone not to have experienced the same fate; the scares serve only to rend the veil in which we were shrouded, to make us aware of what we *should have been aware of* all the time, since it existed, and it was aimed at us.

———

Yesterday after lunch I let myself go and wept. It was set off by a trivial incident, one of those unending conversations about the British, which made me realize yet again that you can't discuss anything with Maman, because as soon as someone has put an idea forward, instead of accepting it in order to discuss it she aggressively asserts the opposite. For instance, when someone says that British foreign policy is selfish and often ungentlemanly (which can't be denied), she butts in with: "We have no right to object, we betrayed them", or "Do you think the Germans behave better?" (On both these points, we agree.) Isn't it still possible to have an independent mind? Especially if we recognize our own errors. I was so irritated at not being able to make Maman think impartially, at feeling myself rebelling against her, at feeling her anger at that moment, at not knowing if I ought to give up on seeking the truth and concentrate on accepting Maman as she is – it was one of those cases where my conviction that people must be accepted and understood completely, by seeing things from their point of view and granting them legitimacy to have their own point of view, comes into conflict with something else. All my latent unhappiness flowed into my irritation and dilated it, and I cried, or tried to cry, for half an hour.

———

22 December

I've not noted anything in this diary for at least a week. Last time I was prompted by Lucie Morizet's entreaties when she told me we were soon to be arrested. It went on all week, coming from all sides, ending with M. Rouchy on Saturday. But on Saturday something else came up to worry us a great deal more, probably mistakenly. I'm unable now to recreate the horrible atmosphere of that day, of that afternoon, which appeared to make one of my unceasing fears come true: in the morning a uniformed German went to Denise's apartment and asked to look round. Since then we've been told that it happens all the time. At that moment, however, what I saw, what we all saw, happening was Denise and François being forced into hiding, the apartment emptied, living on the streets, two more people living like that until the end of the war, and this time two of our own. Denise, in her condition! Over lunch, stunned by the inspection, she was visibly trying not to burst into tears. All afternoon I stayed here on guard duty, while Maman, Denise, Andrée and her husband were at the apartment, and François and Papa went to see Robert L. We had to put up with the Robert Wahls coming by.

I carried on dressing the dolls like an automaton. The morning after, I was as woozy as if I had spent the night at a dance.

———

Yesterday evening Maman told me that André Baur and his wife had been deported together with their four small children. It haunts me. It's just another story of the same kind. But we were so certain they would not be taken. And at Christmas, when I'm making trees for what is a children's holiday. That's what made me grieve so much.

Monday, 27 December
Yesterday we decorated the Christmas tree at home. That's right, but there has hardly been a break between these two days, since I slept for barely three hours because of my blocked nose.

I went to fetch Pierre and Danielle [Schwartz]. When I saw Danielle, and each of her expressions and her eyes reminded me of her mother with startling intensity, I was overcome by pain of a kind I'd not known before; it was something other than the pain I've felt up until now. My image of Mme Schwartz had grown hazy and my memory of her was no more than a feeling, sadness. Danielle brought her face back to me.

Today at 2.00 I was getting ready to go out for my German lesson when Odile arrived. I can't say I was amazed. I took the situation in straight away and accepted it without hesitation. Anyway it seems like it was only yesterday that she left me. Is that the result of loneliness? It feels as if we picked up our conversation where we had left off.

Friday, 31 December

I wanted to devote this morning to work; I am fully aware that work now cannot signify anything but my own wish to forget for a brief moment, nothing more. I am perfectly conscious that I have not resolved the conflict between academic work and reality, between self-fulfilment and the tyrannical demands of reality, and that the battle will resume at noon, as soon as I close my book. I wanted to work yesterday evening but was too tired. In those few free hours that are so precious to me because they have in a sense been stolen, I didn't do anything because Denise was at home when I came in, because I was overtired (I haven't taken a single day off), and I had another fit of crying as I did when Maman came home the other day; I can't help it, it's like a dam bursting.

So this morning I wanted to work, and I still sometimes think of a studious morning as a wonderful prospect; my mind turns to poetry and to all the joys I might take from it, to what I might be able to create. But how can I have failed to understand that it is not going to happen, that it cannot happen again? How can I have failed to abandon the idea, to acknowledge that it is impossible? Anyway, this morning I was supposed to get down to it but only until 11.00, because I have to go the hospital to see Michèle Varadi. (Yet another restriction imposed by the Germans: Jews no longer have the right to hospital care.) But Maman has just read the newspaper, and suddenly the glimmer of hope, the tiny supply of artificial happiness I had struggled to gather in, fell to pieces, because reality scored a victory. Two things: Darnand has just been appointed Commissioner for the Maintenance of Order. I don't know who he is, apart from being one of those gangsters protected by the Germans who are cropping up all over the place. But what that means is civil war for sure, with yet more arrests and deaths. There's death everywhere. And what is dying? Putting an end to lives full of sap and promise, among them inner lives as buzzing and intense as my own. And doing it in cold blood. It's killing a soul at the same time as a body, but the murderers see only the body. The more this continues, the more corpses there will be. Once blood-letting has begun, there is no end to it.

How quickly morality and the respect for humanity disappear once a certain boundary has been breached! In a single leap people revert to behaving like animals. The Nazis did that a long while back. They play with their revolvers; they toy with death as if it was a pocket handkerchief. They are the prime movers of this frightful machine which is now running faster and faster.

I think I shall go mad. At times I lose my equilibrium.

The second thing was the speech of Gauleiter Sauckel, anti-"Jew" from beginning to end. It makes me weary just to think about it: haven't they committed enough torture, murder and persecution these last four years? There are hardly any Jews left (and how much unspeakable suffering does that mean for human beings who surely had more of a right to life than a monster like Sauckel), and has that won the war for them? Has it got them anywhere?

I wonder what effect a speech of that kind can have on people who are not involved? Probably, in part the same impression it has on me: it must seem stupid and useless. But not the other part: a grieving awareness of all the suffering it implies.

The other evening I read a short story by Kuprin, *Gambrinus*. It's the story of a Jewish musician in Russia, written with the sweetness and impartiality of a Duhamel (of *The New Book of Martyrs*) or a Roger Martin du Gard. The pogroms are barely sketched. But for *me*, they were strikingly real. The cold logic and searing cruelty of the methods used are clearly signposted. To think that it has always been thus, and always without the slightest excuse.

———

When I write the word *Jew*, I am not saying exactly what I mean, because for me that distinction does not exist: I do not feel different from other people, I will never think of myself as a member of a separate human group, and perhaps that is why I suffer so much, because I do not understand it at all. I suffer from the spectacle of human beastliness. I suffer from the sight of evil falling upon humanity; but as I do not feel I belong to any particular racial, religious or human group (because such a feeling always implies pride), all I have to keep me going are my inner debates and reactions, my conscience. I remember a remark Lefschetz made when we were at rue Claude-Bernard and his speeches in support of Zionism disgusted me: "You have forgotten *why* you are being persecuted." That's true.

But the Zionist ideal seems too narrow. Any exclusive grouping, whether Zionism, or the hideous fanatical Germanism we are witnessing, or even chauvinism, always contains an excess of pride. I can't help it; I shall never be at ease in any such group.

———

1944

Sunday, 10 January, 1944, evening

Will I make it through? It's an ever more harrowing question. Will we come out of this alive?

Two main paths lie before us now, and both lead to danger and perhaps to annihilation: deportation, which hangs over us still, and what will happen here until the war ends – the events that will bring it to an end and which, as I now see more clearly since Gérard [Mantoux] talked to us about them, will be frightfully dangerous.

I fear for Jean, because his life will be in danger. If we do get back together after all this, if I avoid the risk we have been running for two years now, and if he comes out of this hurricane of fire safe and sound, then we will have paid a high price for our happiness. What extraordinary value it will have acquired.

How different his return will be from what I imagined. The doorbell won't ring. I won't have to wonder which would be the right room for welcoming him home. Will I even be here? Even assuming that nothing happens to me, where will we be in the great upheaval that will shake France from top to bottom?

In three months' time, perhaps? Three months is a very long time for people who live through them expecting the landings to happen every day for no reason other than hope and misleading rumour. But once you look on it as something that will definitely happen, once you suddenly see it as a done deal, it becomes very short.

Yes, long, terribly so for those who are suffering, for people who as Mme Poncey told us are in a concentration camp near Vienna and are so weak that they topple over when hit by the crusts of bread thrown to them by French prisoners nearby. For the deportees, for those who are dying of hunger, for those under torture in prison.

Today, at Breynaert's, François told the following story which he heard from one of his colleagues, a railway engineer at Châlons-sur-Marne. A train carrying deportees (objectors to S.T.O.) stopped at Châlons. Prisoners in one of the carriages unbolted the floor and lay down between the rails, hoping they would get away. The train left. But the Germans had anticipated the prisoners' trick: all the carriages are locked and sealed except the last one, which is open and full of German soldiers. As the train left the station, they could see the deportees lying on the sleepers, and they opened fire with everything they had, using explosive bullets which tear people to shreds. Two or three men got up and tried to run for it, but they were shot down. They carried on shooting until everyone was hit. Then they got off the train, prodded the wounded with their rifle butts to make them get up, then shot them again, and finally they piled all the bodies, including dying and wounded men, into the guard's van, and the train moved off. With twelve dead men we shall never know about.

It is atrocious. Death is raining down on every side, copiously and blindly disbursed by that exasperated race for the sole reason that not everyone has accepted its claim to be the master race.

I couldn't play any music because I suddenly had an acute foreboding of the evil that may befall us. For instance, Denise in a cattle truck; the idea was unbearable.

I felt almost angry with her because I thought: She doesn't realize, she is unaware of the danger, and that's criminal. She should go into hiding this minute. If we wait to be alerted, it could be too late. How can we stay here and take such a risk?

On Friday the issue was discussed at Mme Milhaud's. She was saying: Later on, if misfortune should befall us, we will not understand why we stayed on, and if we had had the possibility of getting out, we will think that we must have been mad. Lack of awareness probably does play a role. But for my part, I am aware, and that is why I am so tormented.

Tuesday, 11 January, 1944, evening
This afternoon I experienced afresh, in every detail, what it means to be re-immersed in atrocious reality.

Yesterday I thought I had grabbed a lifebuoy: André Boutelleau came into the library, chatted with me for two hours and offered me a contract to translate *A Defence of Poetry*, something I had mentioned to him vaguely earlier on. All of a sudden it gave me a goal that was more accessible and more tangible than my dissertation. It really was a lifeline, because for a while now I have been drowning, literally. The conversation gave me back some of my confidence, I went back a little to being what I was three years ago, when I felt so excited about the awakening of literary sensibility, and everything seemed new and magical, the time that came to an end when Jean left, it was the time when I sat my English literature exam, when I worked and passed my diploma.

Now I can see that there was something rather forced about the pleasure I felt yesterday, because it can never be what it was. Then, it was a spontaneous gush, a permanent fizz. Now, I feel I am going against reality; I struggle to retain the sense of pleasure, because it is surely something indispensable if I am not to become completely unhinged. The tangible form in which this state of mind manifests itself is, for example, being certain that I live in two worlds and that I cannot integrate the one with the other, that André Boutelleau cannot and will not enter into the world of misery and suffering that I have discovered, and that I would be obliged to give only a part of myself to what he's asked me to do. But the essential me is unity of purpose, single-mindedness.

So I had retrieved a little of my balance, but it was like a sick man trying to cure himself. The proof that it was an artificial, imposed and fragile equilibrium was the fact that it took just one jolt to dislodge it. When I got to Neuilly, Jeanine told me that Mme Schouker had just had a telephone call informing her that her son (age eleven), whom she thought safe in Bordeaux, had been arrested.

That was all it took to re-immerse me in reality. I was haunted by a feeling of moral disquiet.

I spent the later part of the evening at the home of Mme Schwartz's mother. Among other things I learned about the following:

the arrest of a young woman I had met at her home, a Mme Carcassonne, together with her husband and her eleven-year-old son. A fragile child (I think he was even abnormal). The doorbell rang at 1.30 a.m., the boy tried to escape down the servants' stairs, he was beaten up. Down in the street, she went on her knees to beg them *not to take* her child (you have to have a fairly clear idea of what to expect to beg to be allowed to *abandon* a child). Request refused. The Carcassonnes had to wait for an hour in a car in the street while they went back up to wreck the apartment and loot it. Supplies for boulevard de la Gare. All three have been deported.

the sister of another lady I had also visited (who was also arrested subsequently), who was taken with her eight-month-old baby and another child of four. Mme Schwartz's mother said: "What can you do with an eight-month-old baby? Here she took it for walks and put it to bed . . ." Words like that make you see it all clearly, with nightmarish precision.

at boulevard de la Gare *there are aisles for every sort of thing*, furniture, sewing kits, haberdashery, jewellery. Entirely comprised of things stolen from the dwellings of people who have been taken and deported, which are packed and crated by the interneesthemselves. The crates are sent to Germany straight away.

Thursday, 13 January
I returned home this evening crushed by the full awareness of what is occurring. There are moments when I see it all, and I feel as if I am flailing in the ocean in the pitch dark, without a glimmer

of light. I've felt like that quite often (I remember, last February, when they rounded up children). But now it comes back all the time, I think that's what the normal, real state is, that's to say reality as it really is, the state I would be in all the time if I was always fully conscious.

And what set off this new crisis? Just assembling a few facts, facts like thousands of others, that happened to be in my mind. This morning, for instance, I went out to the Sorbonne; I wanted to talk to Josette about my translation. (To say that I was moved and excited by reading Shelley yesterday evening – that self also exists, it is as true and deep as the other self, but does it have a right to exist?) The concierge at the English Department came up to me and asked if "there were any problems"; it's always the same story, "someone" had told him to warn students in my category to be very careful. What could I say? I know all about it; I believe it's perfectly possible I will be arrested; and I completely under-stand why he's tipping me off. But after two years it has become so wearing.

Then the conversation turned to current events. He told me that the other day an Italian student had come up to him and said: "Concierge, I've seen something horrible!" "I'm not surprised, everything is horrible nowadays," A. replied. "I saw a German lorry piled high with corpses that weren't even covered."

Probably men who had been executed; no-one will ever know anything about them.

After that I sat in for an hour on Cazamian's course on Walter Scott. A little respite. Then I went to the Enfants-Malades to see my three wards. Mme P. spoke to me about her plans to take revenge on the disgusting cowards who denounce other people and pillage their homes when they are arrested (she knows a concierge who does exactly that).

After lunch I went to Neuilly to fetch two children to take them to Julien-Lacroix.

The little Schouker boy was arrested in Bordeaux during a general round-up: all the Jews of Bordeaux were arrested at 1.30 in the morning. When they get to Drancy we'll try to have him released. Eleven years old, all alone, arrested at 1.30! That little fellow really must have been a threat to the security of the Reich!

Two weeks ago they tried to arrest the Chief Rabbi of Bordeaux. But as he was not at home, they arrested, by way of reprisal, all the old folk and sick people at the hospice. The local U.G.I.F. director, Mlle Ferraya (I always used to see her name when I was working in the Internee Department) committed suicide.

A four-year-old boy turned up at Neuilly, we know nothing about him except his name, and yesterday we slipped him into the arms of a Turkish couple who had been "liberated" to go into the hospice. He's very cute, he skips all the time, but he can't tell us anything about Drancy.

Met Mme Bayer, who told me that they'd come to arrest Algerian families in her street, and that the French gendarmes *went to fetch the children at school*, keeping the mothers and parents back while they went to get the children from their schools.

Dr Seidengart and his family come to mind: his parents, his wife and a daughter age four living next door to each other while he is in a PoW camp. One day they came to arrest the family. The wife disappeared, nobody knows what happened to her, and her father-in-law has been deported. Then his mother and his daughter went. When he comes back, won't he be driven mad by what he finds?

Deloncle is dead, they say he was murdered by the Gestapo; at the moment they are settling scores with everybody who was too close to their doings at the start.

17 January, 1944

At Neuilly we've got a boy who arrived there who knows how; he was foisted on to a Turkish couple as they were being released from Drancy. He's adorable, he kisses people all the time. He's four years old and seems to know how to look after himself. He is very well brought up; the other day he went up to one of the nursing staff and said: "Please, miss, if it's not too much bother, could you make up my room?" Apparently he cries when he goes to bed at night and calls for his mother. Where is she? In the camp? Deported? No-one knows.

How many little children are there like that who are calling out for their mothers and don't even have a Neuilly to go to?

Nicole S. turned up at the English Department in a state of great distress. Jean-Paul has written saying he's going to leave again, and she is going to have a horrible time. I feel that he was her world, and that is probably what made her a little blind, or at any rate what made me wonder, when I was in one of my moods of dismay, whether I was mad, since everybody else seemed to be remaining calm, or whether I was not a Cassandra, exaggerating the coming doom. She said: "This is the worst catastrophe for him and for me." I've been there too but not in the same way: I didn't realize it until I had been without news for a long time. What could I do for them?

Gérard says it's wrong to get out.

Saw André Bay, a nice man; was introduced to M. Catin and Marie-Louise Reuge.

Tuesday, 18 January

I had only one free morning this week. I didn't even dare make use of it, it was such a gift. At 9.00 the post brought an S.O.S. from the Bordeaux people. I rushed round all day to no great effect. Parents don't want me to go out. Rochefort, Denis, Lamarck etc.

Odile Varlot was arrested two months ago when she was on her way to a convent with clothes for the children she had hidden there. She had been denounced and was deported in her sandals and summer frock (in Nice).

Saturday, 22 January

More rumours about round-ups; there were some last night. Mme Pesson alerted Maman.

Papa says we have to think about when we should leave. I'm still afraid it is too late. If they ring the bell, what do we do? If we don't open the door, they'll knock it down.

Open up and show our I.D.: the chances are a hundred to one against getting away with it.

Make a run for it: what if they are at the servants' entrance? Quickly remake the beds so they can't see we've just left. Up on the roof there'll be the cold, the reaction and the knowledge that come the dawn we would be living like hunted animals. I've still never left home. Open the door, the warrant, dress in a hurry, no rucksack allowed, what should we take? Consciousness of the looming catastrophe, of total change, no time to think. All we're leaving behind, the car waiting for us in the street, the camp, meeting all the others, unrecognizable.

Will it be or will it not?

———

Wednesday, 24 January, 1944

An avalanche of new things, things to do, and a harsh descent into the depths.

Yesterday morning I took little Gérard to Mme Carp. He didn't want me to leave him: "Will you stay? Will you have a meal with me?" he said in his pleading, affectionate voice. Fortunately he took to Mme C. straight away. (The C.'s really know the meaning of charity and simplicity. When I said that to them this morning, her husband answered: "Poppycock! The only problem is that there aren't a few more of us.") What a shame that one half of humanity is *manufacturing* evil and a tiny minority is trying to put it right!

Miraculously my afternoon, all of it, was free. I wanted to play some music with Denise. (But it would have been impossible because we'd discussed the risk she was taking, and that I was choosing to take, and I knew that she would be angry with me, or perhaps offended by my calling on her, but there was something that pushed me to override my feelings – but the atmosphere was quite spoiled). As a joke I told myself: "Something is sure to turn up."

At 2.00 the eldest of the Biéder girls came by; her whole family is in a panic, obviously, a single mother with eight children, and to have a little space she wanted at least four of them taken off her, that gave me something to do. I went back with the daughter, who is dim, to their place, and then to Marie M.'s, ever ready (yet another member of that small élite), then to Mme B.'s, where I failed to find Mme Milhaud.

Robert Neveux and his wife came to dinner. They talked about Jean, Robert's brother, who was home on leave in his spanking German uniform, with both the French *Croix de Guerre* and the German Iron Cross in his buttonhole! What a problem of conscience! It's driving me mad, because I just can't imagine how free men, endowed with souls, consciences and the faculty of judgement, can be turned into fanatics and machines. What's been done to Jean Neveux is the same thing on a smaller scale as what Nazism has done to the Germans.

This morning when I got up there was a *pneu* from Danielle's grandmother. It's kept me busy all morning. I must jot down some details of the kind that must never be forgotten. Mme W. told me this: Near where she lives they arrested an old lady with an amputated leg; the wound hasn't healed because she has diabetes. The first time they came, the inspector saw the condition she was in and left her alone. Two days later, they came back with a stretcher to get her and interned her at the Hôpital Rothschild.

But the Rothschild is packed to the rafters, and since other hospitals are not allowed to admit invalids of our kind . . . A few days ago the Hôpital Saint-Joseph had to discharge a paralyzed woman, and "Jews" no longer have the right to be taken by ambulance, nor do they have the right to be seated in a German office any more. An old lady in failing health was summoned the other day and went with her nurse to the *Kommandantur* to be greeted this way: "Sit down, you (said to the nurse) – Jew woman, stay standing!" (for two hours).

Who has the right to treat human beings like animals? This is what we have come to two thousand years since the coming of Christ.

Even *private* clinics are now obliged to turn Jews away. Denise had booked a room at the maternity clinic in rue Narcisse-Diaz for the birth of her baby. Yesterday the lady came (in tears) to give her back the deposit. What is to be done? And who knows about these things? I have to tell them. But people who have not had direct experience, even my friends, even the Léautés, who will hear about it from me, will never grasp it. They will feel sorry for *us*, as individuals, but they won't realize the true import of this detail and what it means.

Another story: this morning Mme Biéder told me that her daughter had lost a printed cotton scarf, she was fond of it because it was a present from her father. The other day she saw it being worn by someone who lives in her area (Porte Saint-Denis). She asked the stranger if she had found the scarf by chance. The woman replied: "No, your concierge gave it to me, it belonged to her sister-in-law who has just passed away, and as she can't wear it because she is in mourning, she gave it to me." In fact the concierge picked it up on the staircase (and she has never worn mourning). Is it possible to be so base as to steal from a family of eight children with a deported father that can barely scrape by? Just to think of it nearly made me vomit with indignation. Poor Mme Biéder is constantly obliged to give the concierge something (wine, potatoes – but she and her children have only had boiled potatoes to eat for a month) to ward off the risk of denunciation. She is in the concierge's hands.

———

Monday, 31 January, 1944
Georges came to lunch yesterday as usual. I had brought Raphaël and Dédé from Neuilly. While they were playing in the drawing room I suddenly intuited (such intuitions have become so familiar) that Georges was giving the parents bad news. I crept closer. I wasn't wrong.

Suzanne is all alone, completely dispossessed (she hasn't even got her handbag); Marianne, Edith (François' wife) and Mme Horace Weill senior have been taken; fortunately Emmeline wasn't in, nor was Jean-Paul; young Bernard was saved as well.

I felt a pain in my heart; there is no other kind of news these days. But when close friends and relatives are involved, the pain is of a different kind. The wheels of horror are turning and turning and grinding away without stopping. Some turns of the wheel crush strangers, others crush your own folk, leaving nothing behind but an inextricable mess of suffering and cares.

The W. R. family is a case like a thousand others. We can all tell stories like this: François, killed in June 1940, an officer in a tank battalion, fatally wounded in his lung by shrapnel as he was giving the order to scuttle his own tanks so they would not fall into enemy hands. I never managed to understand that, and the injury that his death dealt to his family has never healed. He left a two-year-old baby, Bernard, and a wife, a Litwak nobody knew very well. François' grandmother has been almost solely responsible for looking after the child.

August 1941: Maurice, François' father, is arrested in the first round-up of lawyers. He spends a year at Drancy before being deported in such pitiful health that it is virtually certain he won't come back.

December 1941: Georges and Robert, Suzanne's two brothers, are arrested. Released after a hundred days at Compiègne. Robert died three months ago, probably from the effects of Compiègne.

After Maurice's deportation, Suzanne goes to be with her children in the Free Zone. And now . . . Marianne, her daughter, her mother-in-law and her sister-in-law have been deported.

———

Not long ago I quoted a sentence I appreciated from a Russian play that I came across in *The Duel*: "We shall rest . . . We shall rest!" The sleep of the dead is what is meant. I am more and more inclined to tell myself that only the dead can escape from this oppressive persecution; when I hear of the death of a Jew, I think in spite of myself: "Now he's out of the Germans' reach". Isn't that horrible? We have almost stopped grieving for the dead.

The life we lead is so oppressing and a man's life is worth so little that you are obliged to wonder if there isn't anything more than this life. No doctrine or dogma will ever make me believe in the hereafter; but the spectacle of the life we lead may succeed in doing so.

I don't want it to do so because it would mean that I no longer have any taste for living. There surely is a good life, there surely is happiness in some other part of the world, being kept in waiting, for me if I survive, and most certainly for other people. But what will never be erased from my mind is the awareness of how little a human life is worth, or of the evil that is in humanity, or of the enormous strength that evil can acquire once it has been awakened.

31 January, 1944

Françoise came yesterday to bring me the response about Danielle. She told me that one of their friends who works opposite the Gestapo H.Q. (place des Saussaies) has been obliged to move offices, because he couldn't bear hearing the screams all day long. Prisoners have things shoved under their fingernails to make them confess, they're interrogated for eleven hours at a stretch, then they are sent to "rest" under the guard of an enormous police dog that will tear you limb from limb at the slightest move, such as taking a handkerchief out of your pocket.

What is going on in our prisons? Those people too will have tales to tell.

Tuesday, 1 February

Yesterday morning I went to get Doudou out of hospital. His nurses and the other children in the ward didn't want to let him go.

Then I called on Mme Weill. She's in a desperate state of nerves. Concerned about the children. Worried about coping.

Must not forget this. Pierre, at boarding school, has an old teacher who has to be humoured with gifts. In class, in front of all the others, after some kind of reprimand, he said directly to Pierre: "As for you, you would do better to stay with folk of your own faith in Le Bourget!"

It makes your heart bleed. When you know just how atrocious the implications of that remark are, when you know what Drancy actually means.

Of course Pierre's classmates immediately quizzed him about his faith. Can you force a child to lie? How could he ever get out of such a tangle? One to one, "swearing not to tell", he admitted what he was.

Nowadays, and this is new, when I see a German man or woman, I notice, with amazement, that a wave of anger rises up inside me, I want to strike them. For me they have become the people perpetrating the evil I come up against every minute. I used not to see them that way. I saw them as blind, dumb and brutal zombies but as people who were not responsible for what they were doing, and maybe I was right? But now I see them through the eyes of a simple person, and I have an instinctive, primitive reaction – have I learned to hate?

Why should I reject this primitive attitude? Why do I try to argue, to elucidate the causes and origins of who and what is to blame, when they don't do so themselves? A question worth asking? Does the conscious effort to suppress hatred in any way mitigate the evil that has been done? Will they ever understand anything other than an eye for an eye? This is a harrowing question.

Yesterday was the eleventh anniversary of Hitler's accession! Eleven years, we now know, of a regime whose mainstays are concentration camps and the Gestapo. Who can admire that?

I hardly slept last night; yesterday evening, when I arrived at home, Papa announced his decision not to spend the night here any more. I am torn between Papa, now committed to a decision that has been gestating for quite a while, and Maman, who is too worn out to accept it. Who will turn out to be right? Papa, who can see the facts, or Maman, who has her feelings? Is Maman blind and Papa clear-sighted? The truth is that all the care and fatigue of the life we lead will be borne by Maman; it's always the woman. Before dinner, Maman wept as if she had suddenly broken down. It's true, for months on end she has been putting up with everything on behalf of everybody and hasn't let herself go. She is overstretched. My God! What will come of all this?

We will have to give up even the little bit of family life we had left. Our evenings together. On the other hand, should that carry any weight in the face of danger, if the danger is real? Papa has already seen what the risk is; I understand his decision. But I also understand Maman's extreme weariness.

Friday, 4 February, evening

This time, the storm will break soon. The abscess has been
swelling since the beginning of the week. At noon we had a visit
that left us "bewildered" – some woman sent to alert us by Mme D.
There was talk about a marriage which confused us, made us
think it was all a red herring. We scratched our heads, and I was
sorry not to have a detective's mind.

But it was genuine. When I returned home, I encountered Papa
coming down the stairs. N. had called on him to say: "Alert for
the next three days."

I had been at Nadine's. Lessons have been suspended yet again.
The pianist who played with us was arrested on Monday evening
with his sister and has surely been deported. Denounced. Mme
Jourdan and Nadine played a Beethoven sonata. Suddenly, during
the Adagio, the cruelty and lunatic injustice of this new arrest –
after a thousand, ten thousand others – seared my heart. A boy of
such talent, a boy able to offer the world such pure joy through an
art oblivious to human malice – up against brutality, matter devoid
of spirit. How many souls of infinite worth, repositories of gifts
others should have treated with humility and respect, have been
similarly crushed and broken by Germanic brutality? Just as a
precious violin, full of dormant capacities to awaken the deepest
and purest emotions, may be broken by brutal, sacrilegious force.
All these people the Krauts have arrested, deported or shot were
worth a thousand times more than they are! What a waste! What
a triumph of evil over good, of the ugly over the beautiful,
of strength over harmony, of matter over mind! Souls like
Françoise's, entire worlds of purity filled with marvellous abilities,
have also been swallowed up by this machinery of evil.

Let's close our eyes. Let's forget what is, and ask: "Can you imagine that in some other place, evil men are able to slaughter some other multitude of innocent people in their millions, as has happened here to the Jews?" Because when you strip it down to the essentials, in the mind of any decent human being, that is the question, that is what has been done, what the Germans have done.

Yet I still believe that good is superior to evil. In the present moment everything contradicts my belief. Everything is trying to prove to me that true superiority, real and concrete superiority, is on the side of might. But the mind denies the facts. What is the source of this ineradicable belief? It certainly does not derive from tradition.

Poor Jean Marx. How is he going to bear it all? Although I can't say why, I feel that artists suffer a hundred times more than men of action. Because it wrenches them completely out of the ideal world in which they live. And then, they are hypersensitive to the slightest scratch.

And Jean-Paul came back today!

Another phase comes to an end. I'm going to live like a tramp and a down-and-out. Here endeth my "official existence".

Monday, 14 February, 1944
Schwab, Marianne, Gilbert.

More than a week ago I stopped writing this diary, wondering if I had reached a turning point in my external life. Nothing has happened yet. I carry on sleeping at Andrée's, and the parents sleep at the L[oiselet]s'. Every evening as we are on the point of leaving, a question hangs in the air; uselessly, because we have already gone over things and are past reopening the discussion. We know that no-one can aspire to being absolutely right, and we have no right to go against Papa, who has already been through it.[21] It's just fatigue, the temptation to spend the evening at home, to sleep in our own beds, which reawakens an opposition that has already been considered and consciously rejected.

This week we received a message from Marianne asking for warm clothing. They are at Drancy. We made a parcel of our own clothes; I made her a little sewing kit, which I would like to have myself. There are many details in the life of a deportee which I can imagine. A trainload of fifteen hundred people left on Thursday. Maybe they were on that train.

Gilbert's mother has been arrested in Grenoble. That brings a life of suffering full circle: they lost all their money, then her husband died, and a year later her son Yves passed away suddenly at the age of eighteen. She had stayed in Grenoble only for the sake of her aged mother-in-law, who was not taken.

Yesterday Georges told us the story of a woman of eighty who was arrested together with her husband in the round-up at Troyes. Her son was concerned not to have had news of her. He inquired at the hospice, then at the hospital. In the end they told him she was at the morgue. She died at Drancy, and they took her to the morgue, without a nightdress or even a sheet to cover her, which means they removed the clothing she was wearing when she was taken in. Maman cried: "Things like that must be recorded, to be remembered afterwards!" Does she know what I am doing, and that I'm trying to forget as little as I can?

During the alert the other day, thirty people with stars were

21 I.e., been through detention at Drancy.

arrested, sent to Drancy and deported, just because they were out and about (simply to amuse themselves, obviously!) – Rabbi Sachs was returning from a funeral. Another man was turned out of the métro station at Cité (presumably not an official "Air Raid Shelter") on his way back from a church service in memory of his son, who had died in the war, and was taken by the German police. "Aryans" who break the curfew get fined 1,500 francs, others are deported.

Tuesday, 15 February, 1944

This morning at Neuilly I saw Mme Kahn, who has just had a week at Drancy. She was arrested at Orly and, as a member of [the U.G.I.F.] staff, was released the day before the last convoy departed. From her I learned details we will only ever know from people coming back from deportation. She went so to speak to the very brink. From that point on lies the unknown, secrets only known by deportees.

Life is bearable inside Drancy itself. She wasn't hungry during her week there. What I wanted were details about the departures. I know the camp at Drancy, I went there every day for two separate fortnights last year; I can imagine the life people lead inside. I can still see the big windows of the buildings and faces at those windows, faces of people shut in, condemned to idleness, or else scrabbling about for whatever food they could find and eating on their bunks at any time. Just opposite the P.Q.J. was the Klotz family, father, mother, a son and two daughters, the mother a beautiful, distinguished woman with white hair. I would like to tell about that, but who am I to tell the story in the place of people who were inside, and who suffered?

I asked for precise details. A day or two before the convoy is scheduled, they sort them into rooms which correspond to a wagon-load, sixty people, men and women together (families are not separated, presumably as far as Metz). For sixty people they put *sixteen* straw beds on the floor of a sealed cattle-wagon, one slop pail (maybe three); when are they emptied? For food, each deportee gets a parcel before departure containing four large boiled potatoes, half a kilo of boiled beef, 250 grams of margarine, a few dry biscuits, a piece of Gruyère, a loaf and a quarter. Rations for a six-day journey.

Do they starve? In what must be a stifling atmosphere, in the smell of slops, the smell of bodies. No ventilation? I don't expect so. And what about cramps; not all of them can lie down, or even sit, when there are sixty to a wagon.

Invalids and old folk in with them. It might be manageable if you were with respectable people. But you have to reckon on all types being unpleasantly close.

Washing, in the camp, is done by men and women together. Mme Kahn said: "You can manage washing without being seen, if people are decent, and then when a woman is not well, when she goes to the bathroom, another woman stands to shield her." Mme Kahn is very brave, and she is a nurse. She said: "For people who become embarrassed about these things, it is obviously a huge bother." But there are such people.

I asked: "Who empties the slop pails in the cattle cars?" (The question bothers me.) She doesn't know. I asked her if she saw arrestees coming into the camp (I was wondering if she had seen Marianne and her grandmother, but she was released before they were jailed). She said: "In my room, for instance, there was a family of thirteen people, parents and children, who had been arrested in the Ardennes; the father was wounded in the war and had a medal, with eleven children from fifteen months to twenty years old. When Fuidine (another Orly staff member) saw I had taken them into the room, he said: 'Well that's a great find you've made!' But I can assure you they were clean and well brought up, all of them. And the mother was so dignified! Never said a word." My heart wept as I listened to her tale.

Eleven children! Whatever are they going to do with the younger ones? If they deport them to put them to work, what use are the children? Is it trué they are put in German workhouses? They don't send wives and children with the non-Jewish workers who go to Germany. The monstrous incomprehensibility and illogical horror of the whole thing boggle the mind. But there's probably nothing to work out, because the Germans aren't even trying to give a reason or a purpose. They have one aim, which is extermination.

So why do German soldiers I pass in the street not slap or insult me? Why do they quite often hold the métro door open for me and say: "Excuse me, miss" when they pass in front? Why? Because those people do not know, or rather, they have stopped *thinking*; they just want to obey orders. So they do not even see the incomprehensible illogicality of opening a door for me one day and perhaps deporting me the next day: yet I would still be the same person. They have forgotten the principle of causality.

There's also the probability that they do not know everything. The atrocious characteristic of this regime is its hypocrisy. They do not know all the horrible details of these persecutions, because there is only a small group of torturers involved, alongside the Gestapo.

If they knew, would they have feelings? Would they feel the suffering of all these people torn from their homes, of women severed from their own blood and flesh? They've become too stupid for that.

And they have stopped thinking, I keep coming back to that, I think it's the root of the evil; it's the solidest prop of this regime. The destruction of personal thought and of the response of individual consciences is Nazism's first step.

Mme Kahn said: "I saw people coming in from Bordeaux, from Nice, from Grenoble (Mme Bloch?), from the coastal towns." I reckon the suffering of people like that must be even worse because the change was so abrupt. Here we, I for instance, know it all, we know better. But for them, the people who were living almost normally at the other end of France, what a wrench! How hard it must be for them to adapt!

"Going into Drancy was nothing really; the shock came when they told me I was getting out." I also know the "landscape" of Drancy. But, what will it be like when I feel I am locked up right and proper, that an entire portion of my life has ended and, who knows, maybe my entire life, though I do want to go on living, even in the camp.

Isn't all the above just like a newspaper article? "I saw X, who has just come back from . . . He agreed to answer these questions." But what newspaper would publish articles about these things nowadays? "A Visit to Drancy". Who will talk about that?

Is it not an insult to the unspeakable suffering of all these individual souls, each person with his or hers, to speak of them as if for a news article? Who can ever say what each person's suffering has been? The only truthful report worthy of being written down would be one that included the full stories of every individual deportee.

All the time at the back of my mind are passages from *Resurrection*, from Volume Two, where the journey of the deportees is described. It almost comforts me (strange comfort) to know that someone else, Tolstoy as it happened, saw and wrote things of the same kind. Because we are so isolated, our special suffering creates a barrier between us and everyone else, and as a result our experience has become incommunicable, without precedent and without connection to any other experience of the world. Afterwards this impression will fade and vanish, because people will know. But it must never be forgotten that while it was happening, the human beings who suffered all these tortures were completely separated from people who did not know about them, that the great law of Christ saying that all men are brothers and all should share and relieve the suffering of their fellow-men was ignored. Because there is not just class inequality, there is also inequality in pain (which sometimes, especially in peacetime, corresponds to class inequality).

This time last year I wrote to Jean about *Resurrection* in oddly exalted terms. I even copied a page out for him, the passage in which Tolstoy tries to account for all that evil. Now I can't even mention it to him. The other day at Andrée's I came across my diary, begun in a year that turned out to be both tragic and wonderful, the year I met Jean, and when we picnicked at Aubergenville.

Now tragedy has become unrelievedly dark, and tension is a permanent condition. Everything is shrouded in grey; there is nothing but unending, monotonous worry, all the more dreadful for being the monotony of anguish.

. . . It was two years ago. It makes me dizzy to think that two years have gone by, and it is still going on. I sort the months into years and they turn into history; and that's when my shoulders feel as though they are going to collapse.

When we were in the sickroom undressing two four-year-old twins who had just come in, Mme Loewe asked me: "Well, then, how are things going for you?" I answered: "Not good." So she tried to boost my morale and said: "Come on, now, don't let it get you down. They'll pick us up at the same time and we'll make the journey together. *Nous serons de la même fournée.*"

She thought I said what I said because I was frightened for myself. But she was wrong. It's for everybody else, for the people who are being arrested day after day, for all those who have already been through it. It pains me to think of others in pain. If I was the only one, it would all be so easy. I've never thought about myself, and I'm not going to start now. The thing itself hurts me, the monstrosity of organized persecution, deportation in itself. How wrong she was!

7.15 p.m.

I've just seen a former prisoner from the camp where young Paul is, who had written to ask what I could do for him.

His eyes were hollow and he was as thin as only released prisoners can be. I was happy to see him because he is a man who has suffered, who has seen and understood. He didn't know the Germans were attacking women and children. But he didn't try to stop me getting him to accept that fact.

He told me that on a farm near Hamburg, he saw twenty or so Jewish women of all social classes, including the better kind, coming in from Vienna. I asked him how they had been treated. "With unimaginable brutality. Awakened at 5.00 a.m. with lashes of a whip, out in the field all day long, back at nightfall, sleeping in two tiny rooms, tiered bunks. The farmer beat them, but his wife had a little pity and fed them, more or less."

Who gave that farmer the right to treat human beings like animals? – human beings whose spiritual value was surely superior to his?

He also told me, about the pits at Katyń, that he had *witnessed* identical scenes. In 1941, thousands of frightfully deprived and starving Russian prisoners came into his PoW camp. Typhus took hold and hundreds dropped dead each day. Each morning the Germans went round with guns finishing off those who were no longer able to stand up. So the sick, trying to avoid this fate, used to get themselves propped up by their healthy comrades. The Germans used their rifle butts to smash the hands of the men holding their comrades upright. The sick fell to the ground, they piled them onto carts, stripped them of their boots and clothing, hauled them to a pit, unloaded them *with pitchforks* and threw them into the pit alongside the corpses. A sprinkling of quicklime, and that was that.

More or less the same story as what the young man at the Enfants-Malades told me. *Horror! Horror! Horror!*

A Letter from Hélène Berr to her Sister Denise, Written on the Day she was Arrested

8 MARCH, 1944, 10.20 A.M.

This morning at 7.30, ding! I thought it was a *pneu*!! You know what happened next. Personal measure. Henri[1] was the target, allegedly because of too many involvements eighteen months ago. Short trip in a private car to Gaston Bébert[2] over the road. Long wait in the car. And once we got here, we're in the eighth-*arrondissement* police cell underneath the Raincy circus! Marcel[3] was unpleasant this morning, in my view. Here, they are nice. We are waiting. There's a cat called Negus! Haven't brought much with us. Would like ski trousers and boots (for Maman) and rucksack for me. Small case for Maman.

Hope that Denden [Denise] will look after her health; little Jito[4] would be comfortable staying with my cousin Paul.[5] Henri has only one child with him, Hélène, he's very attached to her. But if Denise came into the world,[6] do everything to help.

Nickie must go see her mother-in-law and tell her. I had time to save the books from the Sorbonne. What a tidy girl I am! Please try to find *supponéryl*[7] for Minnie.[8] Maybe Andrée[9] has some? U.G.[10] will probably try its hardest. In any case, whatever happens, we certainly intend to come back. I was so looking forward to it! I haven't yet paid a visit to the *gospodje*.[11] Papa says it's all right.

Denden ought not go see Elisée.[12] Minnie is firmly against it.

Philippe D. will cope with Aubergenville, as he knows. And speak to Charles [13] and Lucie,[14] we are thinking of them with all our heart. They think I've still got a sense of humour (the proof being my *gospodje* story). All is well, darling. See you soon. Love and kisses.

Linlin

NOTES

1 Code for: Raymond Berr.
2 Code for: police station.
3 Code for: French police.
4 Code for: Denise's unborn baby.
5 Code for: the midwife in the village of Hargeville.
6 Code for: gives birth.
7 Sleeping pills.
8 Code for: Antoinette Berr, Hélène's mother.
9 Andrée Bardiau, the family cook.
10 Short for "U.G.I.F."
11 Serbo-Croatian for "Gents"; a family joke deriving from a holiday in Yugoslavia.
12 Short for Elisée-Reclus, meaning that Denise should avoid going back to her parents' apartment.
13 Code for: Jacques Berr.
14 Code for: Yvonne Schwartz.

45 - 20

ce matin à 11h30 pardieu! Je voyais
que c'était un peu— !! Vous savez la suite—
Mesure individuelle— Henri visé, soi-disant,
à cause de trop nombreuses interventions, il y a
18 mois— Petit voyage en auto particulière
29. en place chez Gaston Bébert— Station
de l'auto— Et arrivée ici déjà des types
sous le cirque Raro (Marcel ce matin était
désagréable (à mon avis)— Ici, ils sont gentils—
No attendons— Il y a un chat nommé Negus! Nous
N'avons pas empêté beja d'affaires— Voudrais intout
teste et bottines (m pour maman)— et mksai"
pour moi— petite valise pour Ramáa—

Espère que Dendea fera attention à sa santé ; le petit
Tito serait bien chez mon cousin Paul— Henri n'a
qu'un enfant, Hélène, il y tient. Mais si Denise venait
au monde, faites tout pour elle—
que Nickie aille voir sa tante— pour même pour lui
raconter—
J'ai eu le temps de mettre de côté le livre de la Sorbonne—
avons voyez si je suis soigneuse! Qu'on tâche de trouver
Supponeryl pour Dinnie— Andre on a peut-être?
Probable que U.S. fera son possible— En tous cas,
quoiqu'il arrive, nous avons bien l'intention de
revenir— Je n'y attendais tellement!
Je n'ai pas encore écrit le gossedge d'ici— Papa
dit qu'il est pas convenable—

A Stolen Life

MARIETTE JOB

To my parents, Denise and François Job, at the heart of the storm, who agreed to answer all my questions and to pass on to me what they had experienced, with all my affection.

MARIETTE JOB

———

Nadine, Didier, Maxime, Yves and Irène, the sister, brother and cousins of Mariette Job, who were all born during or just after the war and have always been marked by the story and the tragic end of their aunt Hélène, together with their children, warmly thank Mariette for her invaluable labour in handing on Hélène's journal with passion and respect.

A Stolen Life

MARIETTE JOB

It makes me happy to think that if I am taken, Andrée will have kept these pages, which are a piece of me, the most precious part, because no other material thing matters to me any more; what must be rescued is the soul and the memory it contains.

The only immortality of which we can have certain knowledge is the immortality that consists in the continuing memory of the dead among the living.

Hélène Berr, *Journal*, 27 October and 30 November, 1943

Hélène Berr was born on 27 March, 1921, in Paris. Her parents, Antoinette, née Rodrigues-Ely, and Raymond Berr, were both Jewish and came from families that had been French for many generations.

Hélène was one of five children: Jacqueline, born in 1915, died at the age of six; Yvonne, born in 1917; Denise, born in 1919; Hélène herself, born in 1921; and Jacques, born in 1922. Hélène received her secondary education at a private school, the Cours Boutet de Monvel, graduating two times, in Latin and Modern Languages (1937) and in Philosophy (1938), obtaining the highest marks on both occasions.

In 1940–41 Hélène also got top marks in her first degree in English language and literature at the Sorbonne, and in 1942 she was awarded a *Diplôme d'Etudes Supérieures* for a well-regarded thesis, "Shakespeare's Interpretation of Roman History", for which she was awarded the exceptional mark of 18 out of 20. In October 1942, since she was prevented by the anti-Semitic legislation of the Vichy regime from enrolling in the courses leading to the *agrégation*, she registered for a doctoral thesis on "Keats's Hellenism".

From 1941, Hélène became involved in *L'Entraide Temporaire*, a clandestine network established by Denise and Fred Milhaud to save Jewish children from deportation.[1] Alongside her sister Denise and her cousin Nicole S., Hélène helped to place children with families prepared to look after them, particularly in the department of Saône-et-Loire.[2] Hélène's mother, Antoinette, also assisted the rescue organization by raising money from individuals and businesses. Hélène came into her own in support of Jewish children. She refused to abandon them and was prepared to give her own life in order to bear witness to their plight.

On 7 April, 1942, Hélène began to keep a diary in which she recorded the events of her daily life. She stopped writing on 28 November, 1942, and resumed her entries on 25 August, 1943.

Her sister Yvonne, who had married Daniel Schwartz in 1939 and had a son, Maxime, left Paris for the Free Zone, as did her younger brother Jacques. On 12 August, 1943, her sister Denise married François Job. From this point on, Hélène lived alone with her parents in the family home at 5, avenue Elisée-Reclus.

She gave the pages of her diary at regular intervals to Andrée Bardiau, who had been in the family's employ for fifty years, with instructions to pass them on to her fiancé, Jean Morawiecki, if she should be arrested. Hélène had met Jean in November 1941 in the main lecture room at the Sorbonne. On 26 November, 1942, Jean left Paris and made his way via Spain to North Africa, where he joined the Free French. He took part in the landings in Provence in August 1944, and in 1945 he was in Germany serving with the Allied forces.

From the summer of 1942, the Berr family was the victim of persecution. On 23 June, Raymond Berr was arrested at the head office of Etablissements Kuhlmann, of which he was managing director. (He had played a key role in the development of the French chemical industry in the inter-war period.) He was interned at the camp at Drancy. The German authorities released him on 22 September, 1942, against a ransom paid by Kuhlmann but required him to carry out his job from home, without coming into contact with the public. The noose was tightening nonetheless, and the family was more and more frequently obliged to leave their apartment to avoid arrest. On 14 February, 1944, Hélène Berr wrote: "I carry on sleeping at Andrée's, and the parents sleep at the L[oiselet]s'. Every evening as we are on the point of leaving, a question hangs in the air . . . It's just fatigue, the temptation to spend the evening at home, to sleep in our own beds, which reawakens an opposition that has already been considered and consciously rejected." Various people offered them refuge at that time. On 7 March, 1944, the Berrs decided to spend the night in their own home. They were arrested at 7.30 a.m. on 8 March and then transferred to Drancy. Hélène and her parents were deported on 27 March, 1944, Hélène's twenty-third birthday.

Raymond was sent to Auschwitz-Monowitz III and was

murdered at the end of September 1944. David Rousset, another inmate, wrote this about him in 1947:

> The memory of Raymond Berr helped Bernard [another inmate] to survive. Berr had been admitted to the infirmary for a boil on his leg, and was well cared for by the *Blockältester* of Hut 16, a Communist German Jew, and by Manelli, the young Polish orderly, but he could not escape the Polish head doctor, a crazed anti-Semite who, after operating on the patient, and probably acting on orders from above, had had to poison him.
>
> Bernard remembered with astonishment how well Raymond Berr talked about mathematics – clearly and entertainingly, even for an unsophisticated listener. And he used the same unique detachment of mind to examine with and for his fellow-prisoners his experience of the camps. Such willpower, such unflagging determination to maintain his self-control, inspired Bernard to fervent emulation. He was still so energetically young as to be capable of such enthusiasm.
>
> Bernard created ideal figures to admire in the way some people carry on believing in legendary heroes to their dying day. He wanted to end up like Raymond Berr.[3]

Antoinette Berr was gassed on 30 April, 1944.

Hélène survived deportation for over a year. In early November 1944, she was transferred from Auschwitz to Bergen-Belsen.[4] One morning, five days before the camp was liberated by the British army, Hélène, sick with typhus, could not get up from her bunk for reveille. When her fellow inmates returned to the hut, they found her lying on the floor. She had been brutally beaten. The last spark of life she had clung to had gone out.[5]

When news of Hélène's death was confirmed, her brother Jacques informed Jean Morawiecki and sent him the manuscript that Andrée Bardiau had given him. On 20 June, 1946, Jean Morawiecki wrote to Denise Job:

Beings like Hélène – and I'm not sure there are any like her – are not only strong and beautiful in themselves. They spread a sense of beauty and give strength to others who are able to understand them. For me, Helène was the symbol of strength – a radiant strength composed of attraction, beauty, harmony, persuasion, confidence and loyalty. It has all vanished. Her death takes away the woman I loved and, even more, a soul that was so close to my own (reading her diary completes her disappearance in a poignant way). She has taken with her all that I could give her – my confidence, my love, my energy. I can't even say she has taken it to the grave: that's truly awful. She has also removed that wonderful reservoir of strength that I knew I would be able to draw on in later life; and that I had already drawn on a little. But what are six months? Yes, six months were enough to forge a bond between our two lives that only death could undo, that only death has undone. Despite our being apart, Hélène occupied an ever-expanding place in my soul. Everything was being stored up for her. How could I have left her without knowing she was in a place of safety?

What is left of those six months that my memories turn into a century and which seemed to last no more than an hour? An indefinable perfume hanging in the air around us, a touch of lavender, I think . . .

In addition, an employee of Etablissements Kuhlmann typed up Hélène's *Journal*, and a copy was read by members of the family.

On 9 November, 1992, I decided to track down the manuscript. I thought of Jean straight away, because the *Journal* is dedicated to him. As I knew he had been in the diplomatic service, I wrote to him at the Foreign Office. He telephoned me as soon as he got my letter and offered to meet me at his home. Thus began a series of extraordinary encounters during which he told me his story and the story of Hélène's presence among us. On 18 April, 1994, he entrusted the manuscript to me and gave me full ownership of it.

What I had in my hands was a brown envelope containing a set of undamaged sheets from a student notepad. This long diary, whose form also speaks of its author's personality, is hand-written in paragraphs, with almost no crossings out, without any revisions. The text is astonishingly clear; it flows without any retractions, in a single sweep, maintaining a perfect balance between thought and feeling.

In 2002, with my family's agreement, I donated the manuscript to the Mémorial de la Shoah in Paris. I was fortunate to encounter Karen Taïeb, the director of the Mémorial's archives, to whom I also gave our family's records. Her keen ear and remarkable editorial work have allowed this document to live once more.

The *Journal* was published in France in January 2008, in a few weeks becoming a huge success. Readers of all ages wrote to me to express how moved they were by reading a person they all now call Hélène. From older readers I received memories and additional information which has been incorporated, where relevant, into this English edition.

On 1 May, 2008, Jean Morawiecki wrote to me:

The *Journal* of Hélène Berr has always been part of my life in both its forms – as a manuscript, and as one of the typescript copies. It was the latter that I reread from time to time. The original was too charged with emotion. Hélène's writing, her "hand", wiped out the years that had passed, and if it made her more present, it only emphasized the cruelty of her irremediable absence: a pale and frozen hand stretched out towards me so I could bring it back to life . . .

The terrible sorrow of 1945 persisted, but as time dulled its sharpness it also made me more aware of the suffering that Hélène expresses, and more conscious of my having been the absence that she laments. That filled me with a kind of remorse. The frozen hand stretched towards me was holding something out for me.

When I met you, Mariette, on a fine day in November 1992, you seemed to me to have a vocation to pass things on to others. You enabled me to experience the joy of talking heart to heart about my lost love. I supported your plan to publish the *Journal* without reservation, and I gave you the manuscript for that purpose. After years of persistent effort you have overcome the difficulties that stood in your way. The *Journal* has appeared, and we both know the impact it has had.

At long last I can look at the frozen hand that has now come back to life in people's memory, and think: *And thou be conscience-calm'd – see, here it is –*

In that "sink of iniquity", Hélène never gave up on the future. She never lost the strength to struggle against the abjection all around her. She preserved her soul and helped her comrades keep theirs, by singing her favourite melodies to ward off her own and others' distress: the Brandenburg Concertos and César Franck's Sonata for Violin and Piano.

May this *Journal* survive down the ages so as to nurture the memory of all those whose words were annihilated.

NOTES

1   About five hundred children were rescued by *L'Entraide Temporaire*. In all, eleven thousand Jewish children were deported from France, two thousand of them under the age of six.
2   In Burgundy, around the city of Mâcon, in the so-called Free Zone.
3   David Rousset, *Les Jours de notre mort* (1947; Paris, 2005), p. 512. This is the companion volume to Rousset's better-known *L'Univers concentrationnaire*, translated as *A World Apart* (London, 1951).
4   Information from Mylène Weil, January 2008.
5   Information given to Denise Job at the end of the war.

France and the Jews

DAVID BELLOS

Jews have been resident within the territory of France since Roman times, and some played prominent roles under the first French emperor, Charlemagne (*r*. A.D. 800–814). In the medieval period, Jewish communities flourished in Troyes, Rouen, Avignon and elsewhere, but recurrent waves of anti-Judaic sentiment led to repeated expulsions. From the end of the fifteenth century until the Revolution of 1789, there were no Jews living legally within the kingdom of France. However, uninterrupted Jewish settlements in the four cities under Papal jurisdiction (Avignon, Cavaillon, L'Isle-sur-la-Sorgue and Carpentras), in Alsace and Lorraine (which only became part of France in the seventeenth and eighteenth centuries), and especially in Bordeaux (where Sephardic Jews of formerly Spanish extraction were known as "the Portuguese") meant that on the establishment of the Republic and its modern boundaries (1789–99), France was already home to a varied set of sizeable Jewish communities. The Republic took the truly revolutionary step of emancipating them. On 23 December, 1789, before the Constituent Assembly, in a debate primarily concerned with the rights of the Protestant community, the Comte de Clermont-Tonnerre thundered: "We must disallow everything to the Jews as a Nation, in the sense of a constituted body, and allow everything to Jews as individuals . . . They must not become a political entity or order within the State, they must be individual citizens."[1] This was the fundamental doctrine on which the mostly good fortunes of French Jewry were based for the following 150 years, and it is the ideal by which Hélène Berr continued to define her own identity and position (in fact she alludes to these very words on p. 111). Jews would be French citizens first, and Jews – or rather, Israelites, as they came to call themselves – only in their private lives.

Fifteen years after their emancipation, Napoleon summoned the first Grand Sanhedrin since Biblical times to work out a way in which the Jewish community could be fully integrated into his new Empire. The out-turn was a bureaucratic structure putting Judaism on the same administrative level as the Catholic and Protestant churches, as one of the three recognized "cults" of France. A Central Consistory was established as an appointed body reporting to the Minister of the Interior and overseeing a network of departmental consistories, responsible for the upkeep of synagogues, Jewish education and charitable work. (To this day the French Ministry of the Interior [whose task is the maintenance of law and order] is called the "Ministry of the Interior *and of Cults*".)

As the first European country to give full rights to Jews, France became a magnet for Jewish immigration, and the community grew and thrived throughout the nineteenth century. After 1870, when France lost the eastern provinces of Alsace and Lorraine to Germany, many of the numerous Jewish families in those regions chose to move to France. French "Israelites" entered all the professions and rose to eminence in the military as well as in medicine, journalism, law and business; service in World War I firmly

cemented Jewish integration into the French nation. The Berrs
were stalwart members of this "Franco-Jewish" community, "*les
fous de la République*", as Pierre Birnbaum calls them[2] – prosperous
professional people more attached to the Republican tradition
which set their ancestors free than to a specifically Jewish way
of life. Raymond Berr, Hélène's father, was an Ashkenazi with
roots in Alsace, the son of an army officer and a decorated veteran
of World War I. Her mother, Antoinette, was a Sephardi whose
family (part of which had converted to Catholicism) derived
from the ancient "Portuguese nation" of Bordeaux. They attended
synagogue for weddings and funerals, and observed the High
Holy Days (Rosh Hashanah and Yom Kippur, see p. 129), but
attendance at other services is not recorded in Hélène's diary.
The ideological weight of the French model of integration may
have made it difficult for the Berrs to grasp that for others, and
for the Nazis in particular, "Jewishness" was a quality that over-
rode Frenchness and made it irrelevant.

In addition, Raymond Berr was a prominent figure in French
science and business. A graduate of the prestigious Ecole
Polytechnique, he was a leading researcher in the burgeoning field
of industrial chemistry and the author of a widely used chemistry
textbook. During World War I he was recruited by the long-
established Protestant-owned firm of Kuhlmann to help it rede-
velop. Berr became a key player in the technical development of
the dyestuffs and explosives industry, and was soon the firm's
managing director, working alongside his colleague René-Paul
Duchemin, who had been trained at the B.A.S.F. plant in Germany.
Duchemin, who figures in Hélène's diary as a solicitous and
powerful friend of the Berr family, was also a chairman of the

Raymond Berr

French Employers' Federation, as well as the man responsible for negotiating on behalf of the French chemical industry with the German authorities in 1940–41. With friends of that kind, Raymond Berr and his family felt they were unassailable.

France was also the country where modern anti-Semitism first arose. Edouard Drumont's *La France juive* (1885) denounced Jews on racial and cultural grounds as the prime cause of the decline of France that had set in with the Revolution. A turgid concoction of pseudo-scientific polemic and reactionary politics, Drumont's book sparked a long association of right-wing, anti-Republican thinking with hatred of the French Jewish community. The Dreyfus case, which dragged on from the 1890s into the twentieth century, divided France on the issue: could a person be both

French and Jewish? The skies darkened even more in the 1930s with outbursts of anti-Semitic propaganda in many fringe newspapers, as well as the emergence of political parties with anti-Semitic attitudes and policies, but in the respectable milieu of the Berrs it must have been easy not to take much notice of noisy ruffians. Hélène's conviction as late as 1942 that the Sorbonne and the Latin Quarter and its intellectual life constituted her birthright reflects a view based on what was by then a long history of successful Jewish integration in French society.

In September 1939, Germany invaded Poland, and Britain and France declared war on Germany. Nothing happened for several months on the Western Front, but in May 1940 German forces smashed through undefended sections of the borders of France and Belgium, encircled a huge part of the French army, and forced France into a humiliating armistice on 22 June. The atmosphere of the days of this "strange defeat" remains a strong memory in Hélène's mind (see pp. 50, 73).[3] The terms of the armistice divided France in two. The northern part of the country, from the Channel to the Loire, together with a narrow strip along the Atlantic coast as far as the border with neutral Spain, was put under direct German military administration (the "Occupied Zone"); the largely rural remainder of the country was left as the "Unoccupied Zone". A new French state was established under Marshal Philippe Pétain, with its capital at Vichy. The laws passed at Vichy held good for all of France, but their application in the Occupied Zone required the approval of the German military command.

Much of the French Empire accepted the Vichy regime. However, a French general, Charles de Gaulle, escaped to England after fighting a rearguard action and appealed to all Frenchmen to join him in London. Few actually heard the "Appeal of 18 June, 1940", and for the first two years of the war the merest trickle of patriots joined the Free French. It is noteworthy that both of the young men who sought Hélène's affections, Gérard and Jean, crossed the line and made their way via Spain and North Africa to join the F.F.L.

Inside France, resistance to the German Occupation was sporadic and ineffective until in the summer of 1941 Nazi Germany invaded the Soviet Union. From then on, the French Communist Party became involved in the internal resistance. Terror attacks on German soldiers prompted massive reprisals (see pp. 132, 169). Numbers in the Resistance and the movement's visibility grew dramatically from the spring of 1943: the defeat of Paulus at Stalingrad gave hope that the Allies might yet win the war; and the imposition in France of forced labour for French males of military age in German farms and factories (the S.T.O.) prompted many young men to join the *maquis* so as to escape a fate that was not then clearly distinct from deportation.

America entered the war in December 1941, and in November 1942 U.S. troops landed in North Africa. This caused Germany to abandon the terms of its armistice with France. The demarcation line was suppressed on 22 November, 1942; German forces moved to the south of the country to prepare defences against the Allied armies gathering in North Africa. Shortly thereafter, Algiers, previously loyal to the Vichy regime, fell to de Gaulle and became the new main base of the Free French administration (this is the news Hélène alludes to on p. 149).

In Italy, Mussolini was overthrown in the summer of 1943, and his successor, Badoglio, signed a separate armistice. By now,

American and other Allied troops were in control of Morocco, Tunisia, Algeria, Corsica, Sicily and the southernmost parts of Italy proper, and the Red Army was slowly rolling back German forces towards Ukraine. Hopes for further landings abounded, and by early 1944 an Allied invasion of northern Europe seemed imminent. Hélène knew that the war would eventually be won; what she could not know was whether it would be won in time (see pp. 237–38).

Operation Overlord took place on 6 June, 1944. After fighting in Normandy, Allied forces surrounded Paris, whose population at last rose up against the German occupiers. The Free French Second Armoured Division under General Leclerc entered the capital on 25 August, 1944. Gérard Lyon-Caen was among the soldiers liberating Paris; Jean Morawiecki was among those who had landed a little earlier on the south coast of France. Both of them took part in the remaining months of struggle until the fall of Berlin on 8 May, 1945.

The first legislative acts of the French state that emerged from the defeat of May–June 1940 had been measures setting draconian limits on what Jews were allowed to do in civil life. In its brief reign the Vichy government actually passed four hundred separate pieces of legislation affecting Jews, and it did not always take care to make sure that the persons concerned even knew what these regulations obliged them to do.[4] These harshly discriminatory laws are known collectively as "*le statut des Juifs*", the "Jewish statute", but their ultimate purpose was not known even to many of those who set them up or applied them.

The problem faced by the German administration of the Occupied Zone was that it had no means of applying Vichy's anti-Semitic legislation without knowing who was Jewish. Religious and ethnic identity had never been considered recordable facts about citizens by the French state. Consequently, a census of Jews was organized in the autumn of 1940. Nearly all Jews in Paris reported for registration; they thought it wiser to abide by the new laws, for nobody – not even the Gestapo – yet knew where they were leading. Once registered, Jews were required to carry identity papers marking them as Jews.

The earlier pieces of anti-Jewish legislation barred Jews from many professions, including teaching. That is why Hélène, who obtained her first degree in English literature (her *licence*) in 1941, took the classes for the *agrégation* out of interest but could not sit the exam, since this competitive qualification entitled successful candidates to a teaching job for life. She therefore submitted a short thesis to obtain a *Diplôme d'Etudes Supérieures* in June 1942, and registered the following year for a doctorate in English literature.

The *statut des Juifs* also expropriated Jewish-owned businesses. Raymond Berr had to abandon his share in Etablissements Kuhlmann to "Aryan" administrators (see p. 22). However, Article 8 of the law of 3 October, 1940 (the first major piece of anti-Semitic legislation) allowed "Jews who have given exceptional service to the French state in the literary, scientific, or artistic field" to be exempted. Berr was one of only three business leaders to win exemption from the *statut des Juifs* under Article 8 (the others were Gaston Gradis and Pierre Lyon), and he continued to work for Kuhlmann until the summer of 1942. He was arrested none-theless – to everyone's stupefaction – for a trivial reason. His eventual release from Drancy – again, a quite exceptional event – was negotiated with the Vichy authorities at the highest level. A ransom was paid by Kuhlmann and there were probably other conditions, but from then on, Raymond Berr was obliged to work as a consultant to the chemical industry from his home.

Persecution of the Jews in Occupied France proceeded by incremental steps of which the true import was hard to see in advance. There were restrictions on employment, on the use of shops (p. 102), on travel outside of Paris (p. 130), on travel on the métro (p. 55), then simply on being out on the streets (p. 153). To begin with, anti-Jewish legislation made a sharp distinction between citizens and non-citizens, deepening a significant and retrospectively painful division in the Jewish community itself. In truth, established French Jews did not see themselves as belonging to a "community" that included recent Jewish immigrants – mostly poor Jews from Eastern Europe. Non-citizens among the Jews resident in France became more numerous when, in October 1940, Vichy rescinded the liberal naturalization law of 1927 and then, in October 1941, gave its abrogation retroactive effect. Many thousands of people who held French nationality suddenly found themselves stateless, which turned them into pariahs without legal identity and with no means of support. It was these people – foreigners and denaturalized Jews – who appeared to be the main target of the measures; French Israelites like the Berrs were able to carry on thinking that they were not the essential objects of persecution but merely caught up in it. Until the spring and summer of 1942, in fact, not even the German leadership had a clear idea of what would be done about the Jews of France.

After the adoption of the plan for a "Final Solution to the Jewish Question" by the Nazi leadership some time between November

1941 and January 1942, however, a secret decision was taken to make France *Judenrein*. New and harsher measures were introduced by Vichy at German prompting, notably the obligation on Jews to wear the yellow star (29 May, 1942) and the dispatch of specified numbers of Jews to "the East". Prior to that time, substantial numbers of mostly foreign Jews had been rounded up and confined to what were then called concentration camps at Pithiviers, Beaune-la-Rolande and elsewhere. There had also been mass arrests of groups of prominent Jews – forty distinguished French lawyers on 21 August, 1941 (among them Pierre Masse, mentioned on p. 133), and of leaders of industry and finance – but deportation of camp inmates to the east had not yet begun. As the *Journal* opens in the spring of 1942, Hélène Berr is still able to see life as almost normal and full of promise. In this, she was not alone.

The internment camp at Drancy, a northern working-class suburb of Paris close to Le Bourget airport, was located in a not-quite-finished workers' housing block. Its usefulness was its proximity to the railway lines leading north and east towards the German border, and, once deportations began in earnest, Drancy became the hub of anti-Semitic operations secretly intended to exterminate the entire Jewish population of France. The first convoy left Compiègne for Auschwitz-Birkenau on 27 March, 1942; the last cattle-truck train (convoy 77) did not leave with its load from Drancy until 31 July, 1944, less than a month before the Liberation of Paris.

The Vichy authorities, although with initial reluctance, set up a representative council of Jewish organizations intended by the Germans to fill the role of the *Judenrat*, the "Jewish Governments" they had established in the ghettoes of Eastern Europe – that is to say, to control the Jewish communities prior to their extermination. The *Union Générale des Israélites de France*, or U.G.I.F., brought together representatives from the Central Consistory and several Jewish charities and community organizations, and was given the task of supporting the entire community, French and foreign alike. It ran homes for orphans, supplied welfare to internees, kept records, reunited families and was associated with the Jewish Scout movement, the *Eclaireurs Israélites de France* (E.I.F.). Those who accepted employment at the U.G.I.F. became "official" Jews, with special identity papers which in theory protected them from arrest and deportation. Some of the U.G.I.F.'s activities were supported by the American Jewish Joint Distribution Committee, which continued to have representation in Vichy France prior to America entering the war. Thereafter its agents acted clandestinely, devoting substantial funds to the rescue of Jewish children.

Hélène Berr was deeply shocked by the requirement to wear the yellow star. Her reactions to it are among the most interesting pages of the *Journal* from a historical point of view, for they record indirectly how the star was seen by different kinds and classes of non-Jewish French people. Hélène was even more horrified by the mass arrests of 16–17 July, 1942, when the French police seized 12,884 Jews, three-quarters of them women and children (the "*rafle du Vél d'Hiv*", the round-up of the Vélodrome d'Hiver; see pp. 100–105), and immediately applied to work in a voluntary capacity for the U.G.I.F., as did her cousin Nicole S. and her sister Denise. Hélène worked part-time as an office support but became increasingly concerned with saving Jewish children. Beneath its official cover, the U.G.I.F. had a "sixth section" that operated entirely illegal networks which smuggled Jewish children from orphanages and homes to farms, villages and other places of safety. The E.I.F. was the backbone of the rescue operation, and that is why Hélène mentions Scouting terminology so often. But she was also in touch with members of other rings: the *Entraide Française Israélite* (E.F.I.), led by Raymond Geissman; the *Entraide Temporaire*, run by Fred and Denise Milhaud; the Amelot Committee (so named after the street in which it met); and the *Oeuvre de Secours aux Enfants* (O.S.E.), itself linked to the (non-Jewish) *Service Social d'Aide aux Emigrés* ("Social Service for Assistance to Emigrés"), run by a senior social worker, Lucie Chevalley, honoured after the war by the Yad Vashem Memorial as Righteous Among Nations. In caring for separated and orphaned Jewish children, Hélène came into direct contact not only with profound human suffering but also with those parts of the Jewish community that had previously been completely alien to her – the poor, the foreign and the dispossessed. It was her second education.

The U.G.I.F. was of course a trap. Its offices were by definition a place where many Jews could be found, and on July 30, 1943, French police went to rue de la Bienfaisance ("Street of Benevolence!") and arrested all forty-six employees on the premises. All were deported to Auschwitz. Yet Hélène, who merely happened not to be there at the time, continued to work for the truncated organization and served twice, for two weeks each time, at Drancy camp itself (see p. 256) once the German authorities had handed over the feeding and welfare of the internees to the "Jewish Community", including a squad of (Jewish) camp police.

Retrospectively Hélène came to wonder if she had been right to work in this way for an organization of the state. Did it count as collaboration with the enemy? Her conviction that it was right

to help save the children is not special pleading. The networks
associated with the sixth section of the U.G.I.F. achieved spectacular results. About one third of all Jews resident in France were
deported and murdered. Of French Jews (those with non-
abrogated French nationality) the proportion was much smaller –
about one in six were killed, whereas about 60 per cent of the
foreign Jews lost their lives to Nazi barbarism. But *only one Jewish
child in ten* perished in the years of German occupation, and that
was very largely because of the courage and skill of people like
Hélène Berr, and the kindness and generosity of a vast network of
French well-wishers who took in Jewish children and hid them.

Hélène's journal contains almost no mention of politics, and it is
impossible to know whether this highly intellectual young woman,
who mixed in Latin Quarter circles which were highly political,
was hiding her views or really had no interest in Communism,
Gaullism or any other political creed of her day. She does say that
she has no taste for Zionism (in common with most French-born
Jews), and she sees more clearly than most that Nazi ideology is
not only abhorrent but leads on a steep path to disaster. It was
perhaps her apolitical mind (eloquently defended in one of the
long passages she copied out from Roger Martin du Gard; see
p. 192) that made her more than reluctant to cross the demarcation
line to the "safety" of the Free Zone while it lasted. By chance, her
sister and brother were in the south already; the two young men
she was attached to both left for the south (and to fight for de
Gaulle) in the course of 1942; but she determined that for her,
staying on was the more courageous course. In addition, her
apprehensions about life in the Free Zone were quite realistic.

Once the demarcation line was suppressed in November 1942, the south was no safer for Jews than the Occupied Zone. Indeed, in Hélène's work with the U.G.I.F. she dealt with children deported from Bordeaux and Marseille, far south of the Loire. There was no safety anywhere in France.

On the other hand, with her knowledge of English and her great love of English culture, why did she not try to flee to Britain? The idea does not seem to have occurred to her. The Berrs also seem to have harboured resentment at the way Britain was conducting the war. (It is not clear what event prompted the conversation on this subject recorded on p. 231.) Hélène decided that her place was with her parents and aged relatives, and also at the Sorbonne, her natural domain. Increasingly, her place was with the victims, whom she knew she would soon join.

*

The *Journal* is a precious and perhaps unique record of denial – of Hélène's initial unwillingness to see what was staring her in the face – and of the blindness of her family, her immediate milieu among the élite of Paris students and then, more broadly, of her neighbours, her colleagues at the U.G.I.F., her whole community, its policemen and officials. For that reason, it is also an historic document showing just how the Final Solution was imposed: by incremental stealth, by secrecy, in an atmosphere of utter confusion. It explains and demonstrates how so many people really did not know what was going on before their eyes.

It was just as impossible for Hélène Berr to know what Auschwitz meant as it is impossible for us not to know. Her *Journal* is overshadowed by dramatic irony worthy of Sophocles. We should resist the temptation of wishing that the young woman had understood sooner and drawn the conclusions that, with the hindsight we cannot now disown, we think *we* would have reached in time. Smugness is not a useful reaction to this searing work. We should rather pause and ask: Are we sure we know what is going on before *our* eyes?

NOTES

1   In the original: "*Il faut refuser tout aux Juifs comme Nation dans le sens de corps constitué et accorder tout aux Juifs comme individus . . . Il faut qu'ils ne fassent dans l'Etat ni un corps politique, ni un ordre, il faut qu'ils soient individuellement citoyens.*" Formal emancipation was not granted in the debate in which this speech was made, but rather two years later, by a vote of the Constituent Assembly on 27 September, 1791.

2   Pierre Birnbaum, *The Jews of the Republic: A Political History of State Jews in France from Gambetta to Vichy* (Stanford University Press, 1996) was originally titled "Les Fous de la République", meaning "The [French] Republic's Greatest Fans", and the term has stuck.

3   The phrase is from Marc Bloch's account of the fall of France, *Strange Defeat: A Statement of Evidence Written in 1940*. Trans. Gerard Hopkins. New York: Oxford University Press, 1949.

4   The order restricting Jews to the last carriage in the métro, for example, was issued by the *Préfet* of the Paris region with the rider that "no announcement [about it] was to be posted and no information given to the public".

Further Reading

Adler, Jacques, *The Jews of Paris and the Final Solution: Communal Response and Internal Conflicts, 1940–1944* (Oxford, 1987)

Bauer, Yehuda, *American Jewry and the Holocaust: The American Jewish Joint Distribution Committee, 1939–1945* (Detroit, 1981), chaps 6 and 10 ("The Jews of France"; "Under the Threat of Drancy")

Klarsfeld, Serge, *Vichy-Auschwitz: Le Rôle de Vichy dans la solution finale de la question juive en France* (Paris, 1983)

Marrus, Michael, and Paxton, Robert O. *Vichy France and the Jews* (New York, 1981)

Weisberg, Richard H., *Vichy Law and the Holocaust in France* (London and New York, 1996)

Acronyms and Special Terms

agrégation
: Competitive examination for entry to the highest echelons of teaching in secondary and higher education.

agrégée
: A holder of the *agrégation*, with a tenured post in education.

Amelot Committee
: Set up in June 1940 by delegates of various Jewish and Zionist organizations, it met at the "Colonie Scolaire" of rue Amelot; its members reluctantly accepted official association with the U.G.I.F. but maintained secret networks to save Jewish children from deportation.

Artisanat
: Probably a branch of the *Secours National*, a state-supported charity that gave help to children, among others.

C.G.Q.J.
: *Commissariat Général aux Questions Juives*, organ of the Vichy state charged with overseeing the implementation of the *statut des juifs*; run by the odious Darquier de Pellepoix.

Diamino
: A board game popular in the 1930s.

Diplôme d'Etudes Supérieures
: "Diploma of Higher Studies", equivalent to a master's degree.

Doriotistes
: Followers of Jacques Doriot, members of the anti-Semitic, pro-German P.P.F. (*Parti Populaire Français*).

E.F.I.
: *Entraide Française Israélite*, alternative name for the U.J.R.E., *Union des Juifs pour la Résistance et l'Entraide*, founded in 1943 from the remnants of Jewish Communist groups.

E.I.F.
  Eclaireurs Israélites de France, French Jewish Scout movement; functioned
  as the unacknowledged "sixth section" of the U.G.I.F.

Entraide Temporaire
  Clandestine child rescue network run by Fred and Denise Milhaud.

expropriation
  See "France and the Jews", p. 284.

F.F.L.
  Forces françaises libres, the armed forces of the Free French.

J.D.C.
  American Jewish Joint Distribution Committee.

O.S.E.
  Oeuvre de Secours aux Enfants, Jewish children's charity incorporated as the
  third section ("health") of the U.G.I.F.; also operated an illegal network
  to save Jewish children.

pneu
  From 1874 to 1966, Paris had a network of pneumatic tubes for distributing
  letters; a message sent by this means was called a *"pneu"*.

P.Q.J.
  Police aux Questions Juives, the enforcers of the C.G.Q.J.

S.T.O.
  Service du Travail Obligatoire, established 16 February, 1943; obliged
  Frenchmen born between 1920 and 1922 to work in German factories.
  In all, some 350,000 Frenchmen went to work in Germany under the
  S.T.O. or its less effective voluntary predecessors. However, about two
  hundred thousand evaded the call-up, and at least a quarter of these
  joined the internal Resistance.

U.G.I.F.
  Union Générale des Israélites de France; see "France and the Jews", p. 287.

Books Quoted by Hélène Berr

The Book of Job
The Gospel according to St Matthew
Beowulf
Baring, Maurice, *Daphne Adeane* (1927)
Bromfield, Louis, *The Rains Came* (1937)
Carroll, Lewis, *Alice's Adventures in Wonderland* (1865); *Through the Looking Glass* (1887)
Chekhov, Anton Pavlovich, *Uncle Vanya* (1899; quoted from Kuprin)
Conrad, Joseph, *Lord Jim* (1900)
De la Mare, Walter, *Poems* (1913); *Peacock Pie* (1913)
Dostoyevsky, Fyodor, *Crime and Punishment* (1866); *The Eternal Husband* (1870); *The Adolescent* (1875); *The Brothers Karamazov* (1880)
Duhamel, Georges, *The New Book of Martyrs* (1917)
Galsworthy, John, *The Freelands* (1915)
Gide, André, *The Immoralist* (1902); *Strait Is the Gate* (1909)
Goldsmith, Oliver, *The Good-Natured Man* (1768)
Goudge, Elizabeth, *Island Magic* (1934)
Grahame, Kenneth, *The Wind in the Willows* (1908)
Hardy, Thomas, *The Return of the Native* (1878); *Jude the Obscure* (1895)
Heine, Heinrich, *Gedichte*; "*Ich hab' in Traum geweinet*" (c.1826)
Hemingway, Ernest, *A Farewell to Arms* (1929)
Hofmannsthal, Hugo von, *Prose Writings* (French translation, 1927)
Huxley, Aldous, *Those Barren Leaves* (1925); *Point Counter Point* (1928); *Eyeless in Gaza* (1936)
Ibsen, Henrik, *Brand* (1865)
Keats, John, *Endymion* (1818); *Hyperion, A Fragment* (1819); *Odes* (1819); "*This Living Hand …*" (1819); Letters to Bailey
Kent, Rockwell, *Salamina* (1935)
Kipling, Rudyard, *The Jungle Book* (1894); "My Sunday at Home" (1898)
Kuprin, Aleksandr, *The Duel* (1904)
Martin du Gard, Roger, *Summer 1914* (1941)
Melville, Herman, *Moby Dick* (1851; illustrated by Rockwell Kent, 1930)
Milne, A. A., *Winnie-the-Pooh* (1926); *When We Were Very Young* (1924)
Morgan, Charles, *Sparkenbroke* (1936)

Munthe, Axel, *The Story of San Michele* (1929)

Pourtalès, Guy de, *Shadows Around the Lake* (1937)

Rilke, Rainer Maria, *The Tale of the Love and Death of the Cornet Christoph Rilke* (1904); *The Notebooks of Malte Laurids Brigge* (1910)

Shakespeare, William, *Macbeth*; *Julius Caesar*; *Anthony and Cleopatra*; *Sonnets*

Shelley, Percy Bysshe, *Prometheus Unbound* (1820); *Adonais* (1821); *A Defence of Poetry* (1821)

Sterne, Lawrence, *A Sentimental Journey* (1786)

Tennyson, Lord Alfred, *The Princess* (1847)

Tolstoy, Lev Nikolaevich, *Resurrection* (1900)

Valéry, Paul, *Tel Quel* (1941)

Webb, Mary, *Gone to Earth* (1917)

Streets and Places

Numbers refer to locations shown on maps 1 and 2 on pp. 8–11.

OUTSIDE PARIS

1/44   Aubergenville (Yvelines)
A pleasant country town on the Seine and on the railway line from
Gare Saint-Lazare to Rouen, where the Berrs had a country home.
After the war the huge Renault automobile factory at nearby Flins
completely altered the nature of the area.

La Baule
Seaside resort near Nantes, within the Occupied Zone (and also in a
security zone forbidden to Jews).

Bayonne (Pyrénées-Atlantiques)
Holiday resort in south-west France.

Bazemont (Yvelines)
Village near Aubergenville.

1/45   Beaune-la-Rolande (Loiret)
Internment camp built in 1939 for German PoWs but used by the
Germans to imprison Jews; closed 4 August, 1943.

Le Bourget
Industrial suburb north of Paris; rail terminal.

1/41   Clamart (Hauts-de-Seine)
Paris suburb, location of a Catholic orphanage that took in Jewish
children.

Compiègne (Oise)
Formerly a French military barracks and then a hospital, the Camp
de Royalleu at Compiègne became *Frontstalag 122* in June 1940, the
only internment camp in France to be run directly by the German
army. It was redesignated a "camp for Jews" in February 1942, and
the first convoy of French Jews left Compiègne for Auschwitz on 27
March, 1942.

1/40   Drancy
       See "France and the Jews", p. 286.

1/43   Enghien
       A spa town near Paris.

       Katyń
       Site of a massacre of about twenty-two thousand Poles, including
       eight thousand army officers, by the Soviet Union on 5 March, 1940.
       Discovery of the mass graves was announced by Nazi Germany in
       1943. The Soviet Union denied responsibility for several decades
       thereafter.

       Montmorency
       Jewish orphanage run by the O.S.E. where André Schwartz-Bart lived
       and worked for several years after the war.

1/38   Neuilly (Hauts-de-Seine)
       Refuge Israélite de Neuilly, in rue Edouard Nortier, a Jewish girls'
       orphanage, established in 1885 and part of the O.S.E. network
       from 1941.

       Nezel (Yvelines)
       A village near Aubergenville.

       Orly
       Suburb to the south of Paris (not yet an airfield); branch office of the
       U.G.I.F.

1/45   Pithiviers (Loiret)
       Internment camp a few kilometres from Beaune-la-Rolande.

1/42   Robinson
       Country town to the south of Paris.

1/39   Saint-Cloud
       Middle-class suburb of Paris, home of the Bernheims and the
       Morawieckis.

       Saint-Cucufa
       Wooded recreation area at Rueil-Malmaison (Hauts-de-Seine).

       Saint-Denis
       Working-class suburb north of Paris.

La Varenne (Val-de-Marne)
A holiday camp, then an orphanage for Jewish children, established
in 1934 and run by the O.S.E.

WITHIN PARIS

1/13   Faubourg Saint-Denis X
        Working-class area in central Paris.

1/14   Montmartre XVIII
        Central Paris neighbourhood with a significant Jewish population.

1/33   Tourelles XX
        Tourelles army barracks, boulevard Mortier, used as a holding centre
        for internees.

STREETS

2/20   Avenue Elisée-Reclus VII
        Home of the Berr family.

1/36   Avenue Foch XVI
        No. 72: head office of the Gestapo in Paris.

        Boulevard de la Gare XIII
        Expropriated furniture store used as a sorting station for movable
        property stolen from interned and deported Jews.

1/22   Place de la Concorde VIII

1/36   Place des Saussaies VIII
        Gestapo prison and interrogation centre.

1/28   Place du Carrousel I

1/5   Pont de l'Alma VIII~VII

1/26   Pont des Arts I~VI

2/5   Rue Claude-Bernard V
        A boys' hostel run by the U.G.I.F.
        (Centre 19).

Rue de la Banque II
Offices of the C.G.Q.J.

1/34 Rue de la Baume VIII
Head office of Etablissements Kuhlmann.

1/12 Rue de la Bienfaisance VIII
Offices of the U.G.I.F.

Rue de la Chaise VII
Surgery of Dr Redon, the Berrs' family doctor.

1/35 Rue de la Tour-d'Auvergne IX
Home of Mme Thérèse Schwartz.

2/10 Rue de l'Ecole-de-Médecine VI

Rue Julien-Lacroix XX
Heart of the Jewish quarter of Belleville.

Rue Lamarck XVIII
U.G.I.F. girls' hostel.

1/37 Rue Lamblardie XII
Rothschild Orphanage for Jewish Children.

Rue de Lisbonne VIII
French police station.

2/26 Rue de Longchamp XVI
Home of the Lyon-Caen family.

Rue Margueritte XVII
Home of Georges and Robert.

Rue de Montessuy VII
American Centre.

2/27 Rue Raynouard XVI
Home of Hélène Berr's grandmother and of her cousin Nicole S.

2/18 Rue de Sèvres VI
Hôpital des Enfants-Malades.

2/13 Rue Soufflot V
Student Centre.

1/11   **Rue de Téhéran** VIII
        Head office of the U.G.I.F.

1/17   **Rue Villjust** XVI
        Residence of Paul Valéry (now rue Paul-Valéry).

2/4   **Rue Vauquelin** V
        Girls' hostel run by the U.G.I.F.

INSTITUTIONS ETC.

2/24   A la Petite Marquise, 50, avenue de la Motte-Picquet
2/21   American Library
2/14   Budé bookshop
2/16   Ecole de Pharmacologie, 4, avenue de l'Observatoire
2/8   Ecole Normale Supérieure
1/25   Eglise de la Madeleine
1/9   Eglise Saint-Augustin
2/7   Faculté de Droit
1/18   Galignani bookshop
1/20   Gare Saint-Lazare
2/1   Gibert bookshop
1/2   Hôpital Rothschild, 11, rue Santerre
2/3   Klincksieck bookshop
1/29   Louvre
1/1   *Préfecture de Police*
1/31   Salle Gaveau, 45, rue de la Boétie
1/8   Synagogue, 44, rue de la Victoire
1/27   Tuileries

Index of Personal Names